MW00576420

Xi Jinping

Xi Jinping

The Most Powerful Man in the World

STEFAN AUST AND
ADRIAN GEIGES

Translated by Daniel Steuer

polity

Originally published in German as *Xi Jinping – der mächtigste Mann der Welt* © 2021
Piper Verlag GmbH, München/Berlin

This English edition © Polity Press, 2022

Polity Press
65 Bridge Street
Cambridge CB2 1UR, UK

Polity Press
111 River Street
Hoboken, NJ 07030, USA

ISBN-13: 978-1-5095-5514-7 (hardback)

A catalogue record for this book is available from the British Library.

Typeset in 11 on 14pt Warnock Pro
by Fakenham Prepress Solutions, Fakenham, Norfolk NR21 8NL
Printed and bound in the USA by King Printing Co., Inc. Lowell, Ma.

For further information on Polity, visit our website:
politybooks.com

Contents

'Seek Truth from Facts' …

… is a phrase from the *Han Shu*, a history of China dating to the first century. The phrase was deployed by Mao Zedong, the founder of the People's Republic, and later invoked by Deng Xiaoping in justifying his reform agenda – today it is therefore often ascribed to Deng.

'Seek truth from facts' was also our guiding principle in writing this book about today's Chinese leader, Xi Jinping. We have no political agenda. The book has not been influenced by the Chinese government's point of view, but nor do we engage in any sort of 'China-bashing' – that vague accusation often levelled at critical accounts of the Communist Party of China.

We are not interested in presenting a partisan perspective on Xi Jinping – whether for or against. As far as possible, we have sought to portray him as he is. Our account is based on his speeches, biographical sources, his political activities and our own interviews and reports. We leave it to our readers to form their own opinions about the most powerful man in the world.

Especially in the English-speaking world, we often came across people who doubted whether Xi Jinping was in fact the most powerful world leader. Our response was always the same: 'Who else could it be?'

For a long time, the US president was seen as the most powerful world leader. But the current president, Joe Biden, governs a deeply divided country. He is not even able to pass a law that would counteract restrictions on voting that disadvantage his Democratic Party, and the Supreme Court has a very clear conservative majority. It is true that the general secretary of the Communist Party of the Soviet Union was not subject to a separation of powers, but the Soviet Union was, in the words of Helmut Schmidt, West Germany's chancellor at the time, 'Upper Volta with nuclear missiles' – a huge military power, but an economically insignificant one. That is still true of today's Russia, and it rules out Vladimir Putin as a candidate for 'most powerful man on earth.' Russia's economic output is no more than twice that of Switzerland, despite having a population seventeen times larger.

In military terms, the US is still superior to China. But this does not mean much; in the age of nuclear weapons, the US is unlikely to make full use of its military capabilities. Wars are also unpopular in the US: even the poorly equipped Taliban fighters were able to force the Americans out of Afghanistan. What counts in today's world is economic power. In terms of purchasing power, China overtook the US in 2014. China's infrastructure is world-leading – that of the US and other Western countries often disastrous. The Covid-19 pandemic has weakened the US and Europe, but China has emerged from it more powerful than ever. Given its rates of growth, the question of China's GDP overtaking that of the US is a matter of 'when,' not 'if,' even though US politicians do not dare utter this simple truth. And Xi Jinping is making targeted use of his economic power, so that countries and global corporations will toe China's line in the future, as this book will demonstrate.

Developments since the German publication of this book have confirmed our claims. After Taiwan opened a representative office in Lithuania, Chinese customs authorities deleted the Baltic state from their database, blocking the import of products, from anywhere in the world, if they contain anything produced in Lithuania.

We have also found ourselves on the receiving end of Xi Jinping's power. For our previous books on China, we had held events at Germany's various Confucius Institutes – organizations that are jointly run by Chinese universities and universities in host countries. We had wanted to do the same with *Xi Jinping: The Most Powerful Man on Earth*. At the institutes in Leipzig and Freiburg, we encountered no problems at all. But a few days before an online event hosted by the

Confucius Institutes in Hanover and Duisburg-Essen, the managing directors rang us. They were clearly shocked: their Chinese partner universities had come under pressure from the very top, and they had to cancel the event. It apparently did not matter that the Chinese partner universities had explicitly approved the readings – their German counterparts had sent them key passages from the book and a translated summary. The head of the Chinese mission in Düsseldorf, Feng Haiyang, had intervened personally to prevent the event from taking place. The issue was not the content of our book, the managing director of one of the institutes told us. Rather, as she summarized the objections coming from the Chinese side: 'You can no longer talk about Xi Jinping the way you talk about any ordinary person. He is meant to be untouchable and non-negotiable from now on.'

It seems, then, that the personality cult around Xi Jinping will be enforced worldwide. Whether Xi himself is responsible for this, or whether it is a result of the anticipatory obedience of over-zealous officials, the result remains the same.

1

Who Cares If a Sack of Rice Falls over in China?

Since the emergence of Covid-19, we know that we all should

It is 30 December 2019. At the Central Hospital of Wuhan, the physician Ai Fen, director of the emergency department, opens a letter from the CapitalBio laboratory in Beijing. The letter contains an eagerly awaited report. In recent weeks, there have been several cases of patients with mysterious fevers and pulmonary problems that have not responded to the usual treatments. Now, Ai Fen has one patient's test results in front of her. Reading it, she shudders: 'SARS Coronavirus.' She circles the two words with a red pen, takes a photo of the page with her mobile phone, and sends the picture to the other doctors in the hospital. 'I broke out into a cold sweat,' she would later remember.[1] The SARS pandemic of 2002–4 had killed 774 people across the globe.[2] Might this be as bad? Ai Fen immediately calls on her colleagues to take precautionary measures, and informs the health authorities. In other words, she does what she considers her duty as a doctor.

Far from being thanked for this, however, she is summoned to appear before the hospital's disciplinary committee. 'How dare you ignore party discipline and spread rumour?' the chair of the committee shouts at her. Ai Fen is forced to agree to ask the 200 colleagues she texted to keep the information secret. She is supposed to meet each one individually, or contact them on the phone, but under no circumstances is she to write to them or use the online chat group, lest further traces of the event be created. 'You must not even tell your husband!'

She obeys. All she says to him that evening is: 'Should something happen to me, take care of our child.' Their child is only a year old. It will be weeks before her husband fully understands what Ai Fen was talking about.[3]

Today, Ai Fen asks herself how many lives could have been saved – in Wuhan, in China and all over the world – if she had not complied. And yet her actions did ensure that the news got out. One of the recipients of her warning was Li Wenliang, an ophthalmologist working on the third floor of the hospital. Li had kept in touch with seven of his former fellow students on WeChat, the Chinese equivalent of WhatsApp, and had passed on the information to the group. Seven people is not many, but it was enough to spur the Chinese government into action – not, however, action to combat the virus. Li Wenliang and his friends were summoned to the police station. Little in China escapes internet censorship.

The annual meeting of Hubei province's People's Congress is soon to take place in Wuhan, and the authorities want to make sure the high-profile event is not marred by bad news. The group of seven have to agree to a cease-and-desist declaration, with their fingerprints recorded in red ink at the bottom of the page. The policeman in charge of the interrogation tells them: 'We are warning you: if you do not let go of this, if you maintain this insolence and continue to take part in illegal activities, the law will punish you.'[4]

Dr Li Wenliang is anything but a dissident. His white doctor's coat sports the badge of the Communist Party – the hammer and sickle against a red background. On his blog, he rails against the protests in Hong Kong.[5]

In the following weeks, the new coronavirus spreads freely. Thanks to Li Wenliang, among others, the fact that an unusual illness is circulating in Wuhan has not been kept secret, but the line from official Chinese media organizations is that the virus is 'controllable and containable.' The official story is that bats are the likely source of the virus and that the virus is 'not transmissible from human to human.' China's ruling Communist Party does not want to spoil the mood ahead of the Chinese New Year; a banquet for 40,000 families is due to take place in Wuhan on 20 January 2020.[6] The banquet will turn out to be the super-spreader event that transforms a few isolated cases in a hospital into a pandemic. It goes ahead even though, on the very same day, 20 January, China's leading lung specialist, Zhong Nanshan, declares for the first time in public that the new virus is in fact transmissible from human to human – and fourteen medical staff in Wuhan are already infected.[7]

Three days later, in the early hours of 23 January, the Chinese government hermetically seals off Wuhan, a city with a population larger than those of Berlin, Hamburg, Munich and Cologne combined. The date of the Chinese New Year is based on the lunar calendar; in 2020, it fell on 25 January. But by that time, no one in Wuhan was in a mood to celebrate. 'Because the local hospitals couldn't cope with the surge of new patients, the entire system was brought to the brink of collapse', writes Fang Fang, the city's most famous writer:

> As it happens, that was precisely the period of the Chinese New Year when families normally come together for the holiday; it is a time of year that is usually filled with joy. But instead the world froze over; countless people became infected with the coronavirus, and they ended up traipsing all over the city in the wind and rain searching in vain for treatment.[8]

People had to walk; because of the lockdown, there was no public transport, and most people in Wuhan do not own cars.

'What did the president know, and when did he know it?' This is a question you often hear in the US. But it could also be asked of China's president, Xi Jinping. As Xi tells it, he presented a paper entitled 'Requirements for Prevention and Control of the New Coronavirus' to the Politburo Standing Committee as early as 7 January. But, while most of his speeches are published, this one was not. All we know from sources close to the party leadership is that Xi Jinping requested that the 'festive atmosphere' in the run up to the Chinese New Year should not be disturbed.[9]

As the 'core of the whole party' – his official epithet – Xi Jinping is untouchable in China.[10] It is therefore highly unlikely that the real answer to the 'how much did he know' question will be known until he is toppled or dies. There is all the more reason to find out now what makes the man who has been president of the People's Republic of

China since 2013 tick. Even more important than being president is the fact that since 2012 he has also been the general secretary of the Chinese Communist Party. He leads the party, and in China the party is above the state.

China's population of 1.4 billion is significantly larger than those of the European Union, the US and Russia taken together. In terms of gross domestic product and purchasing power, the country is already the largest national economy in the world, having overtaken the US in 2014. This is a major step forward – the US had been the world's leading economy since 1872.[11]

Our knowledge of China – and its president – has not kept pace with these developments. This is revealed by seemingly trivial details. For instance, on one of the two German state broadcasters, the ARD, the presenter of *Börse vor acht* [The stock markets today], Markus Gürne, who is also the economics editor of Hessischer Rundfunk responsible for stock market news, innocently referred on prime-time television to 'the Chinese president Jinping.' In Chinese (as, incidentally, in a number of other languages), the family name comes first. Thus, he is 'Xi,' just as 'Mao' is the family name of Mao Zedong. Calling the Chinese president 'Jinping' is therefore like referring to 'the American president Joe' or 'the German chancellor Angela.'

Xi Jinping's decisions have a direct effect on our lives, no matter whether the effects are positive or negative. Any lingering doubts about that fact have now been dispelled by the Covid-19 pandemic: it has cost the lives of several million people from virtually every country in the world, plunged the global economy into its deepest crisis since 1929 and destroyed the livelihoods and dreams of countless people. A German idiom, used as a retort to something one finds utterly insignificant, is: 'Who cares if a sack of rice falls over in China?' Today, if China sneezes, the whole world catches a cold.

The first people who caught Covid-19 in Wuhan were those working or shopping at the Huanan Seafood Market. As the Chinese say, this sort of market sells everything that can swim and is not a ship, everything that has four legs and is not a table, and everything that can fly and is not an aeroplane. In other words, it sells not just seafood, but crocodiles, dogs, bamboo rats ... and bats (though, because of Covid-19, the Chinese Ministry of Agriculture intends to take dogs and bats off the list of edible animals).[12] The Wuhan Centre for Disease Control and Prevention (WHCDC) is located only 300 metres away from the market. The fact that the centre's laboratories also carry out work on bats has led to the theory that infected animals may have found their way from the lab to the market, and that the virus might even have emerged from experiments carried out at the WHCDC. Alternatively, an employee might have become infected accidentally and then brought the virus to the market. 'I consider this very unlikely', says the virologist Christian Drosten, head of the Institute of Virology at the Charité in Berlin (and, since the outbreak of the pandemic, a German celebrity more famous than most popstars). 'Chinese laboratories work the same way as we do, with safety work benches where cell cultures are kept in certain areas. And from these work areas no air can escape. And even if some air did escape – let's assume that there is an accident – people are still wearing respirator hoods and only breathe in air from the laboratory that has been filtered and where no virus can get through.'[13] We should keep in mind, though, that Drosten is a virologist, not a sinologist, and therefore is not necessarily familiar with the sometimes relaxed attitude towards rules in China.

There is another laboratory, the Wuhan Institute of Virology, that carries out far more advanced research (and deals with more dangerous materials) than the WHCDC. But it is located far outside the city centre, 14 kilometres away from the Huanan Seafood Market. In 2017, the renowned scientific journal *Nature* wrote:

> A laboratory in Wuhan is on the cusp of being cleared to work with the world's most dangerous pathogens. ... Some scientists outside China worry about pathogens escaping, and the addition of a biological dimension to geopolitical tensions between China and other nations. But Chinese microbiologists are celebrating their entrance to the elite cadre empowered to wrestle with the world's greatest biological threats.[14]

The institute was the first laboratory in China to work at the highest biosafety level, BSL-4 (biosafety level 4), a fact that has further fuelled suspicions that something might have gone wrong. The *Nature* article quotes Tim Trevan, the founder of CHROME Biosafety and Biosecurity, a company based in the US state of Maryland, as saying that an open culture is important for keeping BSL-4 labs safe. Trevan wonders how such a culture could be achieved in China, a society that emphasizes hierarchy: "'Diversity of viewpoint, flat structures where everyone feels free to speak up and openness of information are important", he says.'[15] *Nature* later updated the article with an editor's note, first in January 2020 and then again in March 2020. The note now says:

> We are aware that this story is being used as the basis for unverified theories that the novel coronavirus causing COVID-19 was engineered. There is no evidence that this is true; scientists believe that an animal is the most likely source of the coronavirus.[16]

On Twitter, the spokesperson for the Chinese Ministry of Foreign Affairs, Zhao Lijian, suggested another theory: 'It might be US army who brought the epidemic to Wuhan.'[17] American soldiers had taken part in the Military World Games in Wuhan between 18 and 27 October 2019.[18]

On 17 April 2020, the Chinese government stated that there had been 3,896 deaths from Covid-19 in Wuhan.[19] One of the victims was Li Wenliang, the doctor who had been courageous enough to pass on the information about the new coronavirus. He was only thirty-three years old, and left behind a child and a pregnant wife. The Communist Party, of which he had been a member, posthumously declared him a 'martyr'.[20] Had the party learned from its mistakes? Just a few days before he died, Li Wenliang had said: 'A healthy society should accept more than one voice.'[21] Had the party taken Li's remarks on board?

In the interview from which we quoted above, Ai Fen, the director of the emergency department at the Central Hospital of Wuhan, describes how the coronavirus outbreak was covered up. In China, the interview was published online on 10 March 2020 by the journal *Renwu* ('Personality'), but within three hours it was taken down by the authorities. Being familiar with such suppression tactics, many Chinese internet users had taken screenshots of the article and posted them on social media. To throw off the detection technology used by the censors, they modified the images, for example by adding emojis.[22]

In her *Wuhan Diary*, Fang Fang says: 'Deeply engrained habitual behaviours, like reporting the good news while hiding the bad, preventing people from speaking the truth, forbidding the public from understanding the true nature of events, and expressing a disdain for individual lives, have led to massive reprisals against our society, untold injuries against our people.'[23] In China, Fang Fang's book has only been published online, and has been repeatedly censored: 'I'm not sure if I'll be able to send anything out through my Weibo account. It wasn't too long ago that I had my account shut down ... I tried to complain to Sina, the company that runs Weibo, yet there is really no way to get through to them, never mind file a complaint.'[24]

Fang Fang is not a dissident. She avoids any criticism of the all-powerful Xi Jinping. Her novels tell the stories of ordinary people, and that has made her a well-known figure in China. She was chairperson of the Hubei Provincial Writers' Association, which gave her a certain degree of protection. However, she has frequently been attacked on the internet by fanatical communists – she calls them 'left-wing extremists' – often using obscene or misogynist language. Even though the official mission of the censors is to 'keep the internet clean,' they delete her considered contributions but not the insults directed against her.

The censorship authorities are much tougher on ordinary Chinese citizens. For instance, following the outbreak of the virus, the Wuhan businessman Fang Bin (no relation) began to film the new reality of everyday life in his city and upload the videos to the internet from his mobile phone. They show overcrowded hospitals, with dozens of people surrounding reception desks desperately seeking help. With no more space on the wards, patients lie on gurneys in the corridors. People can be heard sobbing and screaming. Fang Bin asks a young woman who is staring at her mother how the mother is doing: 'She is already dead,' she says. In a minibus outside a hospital, he spots several of the deceased in body bags. His last video shows five policemen attempting to enter his flat. They want to ask him 'a few questions.' Since 9 February 2020, nothing has been seen or heard of Fang Bin. Others who posted videos, for example the lawyer Chen Qiushi, have also disappeared without a trace.[25]

CoroNation is a documentary by the artist Ai Weiwei, made using material recorded for him by residents of Wuhan. From loudspeakers in front of a crematorium, one hears the following announcement: 'Family members of the deceased with resident identity card numbers beginning 420111 and 420105, please come to Tianxiao Hall and queue up for the formalities.' Dozens of relatives sit in a long row on plastic chairs. 'If the leaders of Wuhan had closed down the city earlier, there would not be so many lost souls walking around', a young woman complains:

> If a father or mother dies, the life of the children is ruined. They are left behind and are alone. My father-in-law did not need to die. The government's mismanagement killed him. There are many cases like ours here. Some who died could not even be tested. They may not even have been counted as Covid victims. They simply died. That is the painful experience we have had. We were not allowed to say our goodbyes to our relatives. When we brought them to the entrance of the quarantine area, we did not know that this would be the last time we would see them. My father-in-law must have been very much in despair when he died. For our generation, those who lived through the pandemic, this will stay as a shadow darkening our hearts forever.[26]

With the relatives looking on, crematorium employees compress the bags containing the ashes of the dead, one bag for each, until they fit into the decorated wooden boxes which take the place of urns here. One employee wraps a red cloth around the box and hands it over to the relatives.

The film's first scene is a view of Wuhan's central train station from the air, shot by drone. High-speed trains, much more modern than German intercity trains, are parked, unable to operate out of the sealed-off city.

When we flew from Hamburg to London in September 2020 to visit Ai Weiwei, it was as though we were in a remake of his film. There were just one or two passengers in the front and rear rows of the Eurowings aircraft; the rows in the middle section were completely empty. After disembarking at Heathrow airport, we walked through silent corridors where there was hardly a soul to be seen.

In this last respect, the reality in Europe differs from that depicted in *CoroNation*. The film also contains a scene from an airport – Wuhan's, where, as in Heathrow, everyone is wearing a face mask. But in Wuhan there are plenty of people and there is a lot of noise. The scene resembles the opening ceremony of the Olympic Games: teams wearing identical jackets follow signs with the names of their province on them. But these are not athletes. They are nursing staff, flown in from outside Wuhan. Locals with red armbands line the sides, applauding and chanting: 'Welcome Hebei! Thank you, Hebei!' – 'Welcome Sichuan!' – 'Come on Wuhan!' The film also reveals how carefully choreographed the scene is: 'Just hold the sign – don't talk too much,' a young official instructs the members of the welcome committee. 'Do not spread any negative energy! You shouldn't even mention the situation with the virus. Simply say, "Thank you for coming." When you're on the bus, calm them down by pointing out some of the sights. Some of them are still attending nursing school. They are still children, so you need to cheer them up.'

At Heathrow, we hired a car and drove to Cambridge, where Ai Weiwei was now living after having spent some years in Berlin. The Gothic university buildings of Cambridge, which resemble cathedrals, were a surreal setting for our meeting. But we should not forget that among the alumni of Trinity College are the Cambridge Five – Kim Philby, Donald Maclean, Guy Burgess, Anthony Blunt and John Cairncross – a group of civil servants and MI6 agents who were recruited by the Soviet intelligence service (NKVD, later KGB) in the 1930s.

We stayed in the University Arms Hotel, which from the outside did not exactly look the part – it resembled an old theatre more than a hotel. We sat together in the hotel's library. 'It is a bizarre thing to say in these surroundings,' Ai Weiwei said, 'but in my youth we were taught Chairman Mao's phrase: the revolution needs only two instruments, the rifle and a pen – the latter meaning brainwashing. People will follow you because they have no other information.' What happened in Wuhan, he added, simply followed this principle. 'A piece of information becomes proper information only if the party decides to disclose it.'

Following the outbreak of the coronavirus epidemic, the Chinese leadership sacked some of the top officials in Hubei, the province in central China of which Wuhan is the capital. The writer Fang Fang saw this as scapegoating:

> But right now what I want to say is that what you saw from those government officials in Hubei is actually what you would expect from most government cadres in China: They are all basically on the same level. It's not that they are somehow worse than other Chinese officials; they simply got dealt a worse hand. Officials in China have always let written directives guide their work, so once you take away the script they are at a complete loss as to how to steer the ship. If this outbreak had happened in another Chinese province, I'm sure the performance of those officials wouldn't be much different than what we are seeing here. When the world of officialdom skips over the natural process of competition, it leads to disaster; empty talk about political correctness without seeking truth from facts also leads to disaster; prohibiting people from speaking the truth and the media from reporting the truth leads to disaster; and now we are tasting the fruits of these disasters.[27]

China provided the blueprint for lockdowns around the world. The model was more or less copied by almost all countries. In Beijing in the first months of 2020, wearing a face mask was mandatory, even outside in the streets. Residential buildings were cordoned off. Not only an army of policemen, but also security guards from housing management companies, activists from the neighbourhood committees and volunteers wearing red armbands were all on patrol. Together, they formed a public-health police force, controlling entry to buildings, inspecting permits, writing down the names of residents and visitors, and taking people's temperatures by holding thermometers to their foreheads.

In the following weeks, the system was perfected. Everyone had to install a phone app that gave the authorities access to identity card details and mobile phone numbers. These were used to create profiles of each person's movements. Every case of Covid-19 was recorded. A digital map on the mobile phone showed the location of infected individuals. Everyone entering a building had to scan his QR code. If the app produced a white tick inside a green circle, the person was allowed in. If someone was a confirmed case of Covid-19, the screen turned red. Anyone leaving the city had to self-isolate, which the app indicated by turning yellow. Red or yellow meant a person was not permitted to enter a supermarket – and in some cases not even their own flat.[28] Welcome to the brave new world of Covid.

The controls were not only aimed at containing the virus. A Chinese government document lists among possible crimes during the Covid outbreak not just stockpiling face masks and trading illegally in wild animals, but also the 'malicious fabrication of epidemic information, causing social panic, stirring up public sentiment, or disrupting social order, especially maliciously attacking the party and government, taking the opportunity to incite subversion of state power or overthrow of the socialist system.'[29]

Meanwhile, the virus spread across the world. The next hotspot was Italy. Initially it was suspected, plausibly enough, that the outbreak was connected to the large numbers of Chinese immigrants there. From the 1980s onwards they had come to places like Prato, in Tuscany, where they built what is almost a small-scale version of China. They set up textile factories that employed their compatriots. There are streets in which all the restaurants and shops are Chinese and the language spoken is almost exclusively Chinese. According to official figures, there are 25,768 Chinese people living in Prato today – at least a tenth of the population, and most likely the actual percentage is significantly higher, because many Chinese people live there illegally. Given their ongoing connections with family and friends in their native country, could it be that they brought the virus to Italy, perhaps on their return from a visit to China for the New Year celebrations? And did it then spread in the textile factories, with their poor ventilation and cramped working conditions? The figures do not support this theory. At just 0.07 per cent, the rate of infection in Prato was very low compared to other regions in Italy. By comparison, in Bergamo, which has only a very small Chinese population, the rate of infection reached 0.63 per cent.[30]

So who brought the virus to Italy? This question can't be answered: 'patient zero' is unknown. It is possible that the Covid measures themselves are responsible for this lack of knowledge. In early February 2020, Italy was the first European country to ban all direct flights to and from China. At that point, there had not yet been a single case of Covid-19 in Italy. To get round the ban, rich businesspeople in the economically strong north of Italy flew to China via third countries, and the authorities lost track.[31]

The Chinese stronghold of Prato nevertheless plays a role in the story of the coronavirus outbreak in Italy. When it began to spread there, Prato produced the most face masks. In addition, masks were sent from the People's Republic of China, while other EU countries prevented the export of masks to Italy in order to stockpile them for themselves. Around this time, a poll showed that a majority of Italians named China as Italy's best friend – and Germany and France as its worst enemies.[32]

Subsequently, in the course of 2020 and 2021, the number of Covid-19 cases continued to decline until there were hardly any cases in China, at least if the official statistics can be trusted. But in the US, where the president at the onset of the pandemic was a certain Donald Trump – whose suggested methods of treatment for Covid-19 included injecting patients with disinfectant – the figures were skyrocketing. By spring 2021, seventeen times more people had died in Germany than in China, despite the fact that China's population is many times that of Germany. And in Germany the numbers kept rising – not so in China. Even though the two countries' statistics cannot easily be compared because of the different ways in which they are compiled, and even if the People's Republic is not exactly a beacon of transparency, it cannot be denied that China's tough approach to fighting the coronavirus has been successful. The official news agency Xinhua is jubilant: 'Drawing on its institutional strength, China's decisive measures to control the outbreak are enlightening ... Under the leadership of the Communist Party of China, people from all walks of life have joined hands in fighting the epidemic with wisdom, action and morale. ... All these are vivid manifestations of China's system advantage.'[33]

These words express a feeling of superiority, a feeling that Xi Jinping also conveys to foreigners, including foreign entrepreneurs who come to China. Few know the country as well as Jörg Wuttke, president of the European Union Chamber of Commerce in China. Wuttke has lived in China for more than thirty years. When the coronavirus had practically disappeared there, but was still circulating in Germany, we had a Zoom meeting with him. From Beijing, he complained about unequal treatment: 'While 120,000 Chinese nationals with German residence permits can freely travel back and forth, foreigners who left the country over the Chinese New Year holidays have been stuck abroad for months now – globally there are about 120,000 of them – and they even dutifully continue to pay their taxes here.' Their visas were summarily declared invalid, and it is very difficult to get new ones.

When the pandemic broke out, there were racist attacks targeting Chinese and other Asian people in Europe and the US. Now, the situation is reversed: many Chinese people see foreigners in general as spreaders of the virus. The EU Chamber of Commerce in China reported on this discrimination in its *European Business in China Position Paper 2020/2021*. In spring 2020, some restaurants and bars were refusing entry to foreigners. Africans living in China are even worse off than the Europeans. In Guangzhou in particular, after some Covid-19 cases were detected in Nigerians, people were thrown out of their hotel rooms, and even flats, because of the colour of their skin.

The world watched as hospitals were built from scratch in Wuhan within a few days. After seventy-six days of quarantine, China's leadership opened the city to the outside world again. Even a critically minded writer like Fang Fang admits: 'The amount of energy the government later put into the quarantine and various other measures was indeed extremely effective.'[34]

Christian Drosten, Germany's celebrity virologist, agrees: 'No one in China asks whether someone feels that their freedom or civil rights are being infringed. Measures are simply taken. Without wanting to pass judgement on this, I can only say: from an epidemiological point of view, this certainly gives track-and-trace a resounding efficacy.'[35]

What should we believe? Did China's system contaminate the world with the coronavirus? Or is China saving the world? Some people have already made up their minds. When a Chinese plane with three million respirator masks and eighty-six ventilators landed in Hungary, the prime minister, Viktor Orbán, personally came to the airport and declared: 'This is impressive.'[36] On a similar occasion, Serbia's president, Aleksandar Vučić, kissed the Chinese flag and said: 'I believe my brother and friend Xi Jinping. The only country that can help us is China.'[37]

However, many people in the West take a different view – and not just Trump sympathizers, following his talk of the 'China virus.' Madeleine Albright, for instance – born in Prague to a Jewish family that had to flee the Nazis and then the communists – is one of them. She was the US's first female secretary of state, serving in Bill Clinton's government. When her memoir *Hell and Other Destinations* was published in 2020, we joined our colleague Martin Scholz of *Die Welt* to talk to her via Zoom. 'China has messed up,' she said, 'beginning with the way China communicated about the virus and how it treated its own population, for instance the doctor who was not allowed to speak about the threat posed by the coronavirus. I don't think China should get any recognition for that. Democracies are able to deal with this pandemic, provided their political leaders understand that the scientific facts need to be taken into account – for instance, the fact that a virus does not know any borders, that cooperation with other countries is necessary in order to get a grip on it. The question is not whether democracies or authoritarian regimes are better at finding a solution. It is a question of being competent or incompetent. I would find it fundamentally wrong to claim that dictatorships were more efficient in fighting this pandemic. Throughout history, we have seen too often what happens when countries turn into dictatorships.'

Doesn't the example of China show that dictatorships are better able to deal with a pandemic than democratic countries?

'But there are democracies that have dealt very well with this pandemic,' Albright replied, referring to New Zealand or Taiwan.

Ai Weiwei, by contrast, had something positive to say about the way the Chinese fought the virus. 'I admire this efficiency,' he told us. For him, his documentary was a case study. Despite knowing his country so well, he was unsure about how it would cope with this emergency. 'China is the only country which may come to a standstill or perform a U-turn at an instant. From the number one, Xi Jinping, down to the people living in the remotest village, everyone acts in unison. And they move like an acrobat who can quickly change his position without breaking a bone.'

Lenin, Ai Weiwei said, thought that the imperialists would inadvertently teach repressed peoples the skills they needed to defeat their oppressors. Now, that is what the West is confronting in China.

Intoxicated by the promise of China as a gigantic market, the West shared its technologies with the communists: 'Now China is laughing about the West, because China has the same technology but is better able to use it. The leadership takes simple, clear decisions, justifies them on the ground that "lives are at stake", and no one can say no.'

During the first months of the pandemic, Germans had to provide their personal details on small slips of paper when visiting bars. This itself was something of a health hazard, with many people using the same pen – and even then, some people gave false names. In China, by contrast, the process is contactless, using QR codes provided by the smartphone health app, the use of which, of course, is mandatory. Because the details of peoples' movements are recorded, chains of infection can be established immediately and automatically. In Germany, public health staff use phones to trace the contacts of infected individuals, and they can inform only those known to the infected person – they cannot trace chance encounters. At best, those at risk are contacted within a couple of days, but in most cases they are not reached at all. Compare this to the People's Republic, which makes use of every digital technology at its disposal to fight the pandemic, and at the same time to perfect its form of digital dictatorship. Ai Weiwei told us a story about an artist friend of his: 'The authorities were trying to reach him, but he had turned off his mobile, so they phoned a stranger who happened to be sitting next to him on the bus: "Pass your phone to the man sitting next to you."'

The coronavirus handed Xi Jinping an opportunity to carry out a unique experiment. It stabilized China – and set the rest of the world on a road to ruin. While the West stumbled from one lockdown to another, in China's nightclubs young people began to celebrate again without the need to keep a distance from each other. In early 2021, the number of cinema-goers in China reached an all-time high.[38]

Ai Weiwei emphasized that he very much likes living in Cambridge, where he is not threatened with eighteen years in prison – the sentence handed to Ren Zhiqiang, a long-standing member of the Communist Party, in 2020. (Ren, a real estate entrepreneur, a blogger and the son of China's former vice-minister for commerce, had called Xi Jinping a 'clown' for his early handling of the epidemic.) 'But,' Ai continued, 'I am very concerned about whether this democracy will be able to survive this. In the time that China builds ten airports, Berlin does not manage even one. And even when it is at long last completed, no one is flying any longer.' Is Covid-19 a wake-up call? 'Yes, but sometimes people go back to sleep after the alarm rings, or they smash the clock.'

Ai Weiwei knows the secret-police minders who were responsible for him in Beijing very well. When he was still living there, they stood outside his door day and night. They even brought his mother presents on festive days. There is a certain mutual respect here, which has partly to do with the fact that Ai Weiwei sees himself unambiguously as Chinese: 'China is my nation. I never changed my passport, although I could easily obtain citizenship in a Western country. I am not anti-Chinese.' When they heard about his Covid documentary, one of the officers texted him: 'This creates so much trouble for us you might as well have punched a hole in the sky.' The topic is very sensitive, the officer said, and the West will use it against China.

After Ai Weiwei sent the documentary to the officer, he received another message: 'Brother! I watched the film, it is pretty good. The normal people working and living through the pandemic reflect the true situation of ordinary people, how they react to the epidemic. At the same time, the film shows the ideological differences with regard to surveillance, stability, and care, which are unique in our country.'

Ai Weiwei's *CoroNation* is available on the video platform Vimeo – Amazon and Netflix turned it down. Nor did the film festivals in Venice, Toronto and New York want to screen it. Ai Weiwei regards these as acts of anticipatory obedience: the Chinese market is important, and the companies and festival organizers understand that promoting the film could have negative consequences. Ai's minder in Beijing has another theory. His text message read: 'I personally don't think the reasons are economic. Rather, they fear that the film shows the audience how successfully China fights against the epidemic. That is in sharp contrast to the way the West deals with Covid.'

Christopher Jahns is an economics professor and CEO of the Berlin-based XU Group. His main area of expertise is digitalization, and he has taught, among other places, at the renowned Tongji University in Shanghai. In October 2020, this fit and healthy fifty-one-year-old caught Covid-19, not in China but in Germany. 'An experience you can do without', he told us. 'There's no comparison with a flu. With a flu, you have a quick onset of symptoms, then they slowly ebb away. In the case of Covid, I had a few symptoms during the first couple of days, incredibly strong pain in the limbs, for instance – I mean really strong, and I am usually never ill. Then there was a progressive worsening. On the sixth or seventh day I woke up suffering from fairly extreme shortness of breath. I then had my lungs X-rayed at the hospital. They sent me back home, and did not have to put me on a ventilator. But after taking a few steps up the stairs, I had to stop and rest – and I am normally a sportsman. After exchanging a few words with someone, I needed to catch my breath. It makes you worry, when you see how the illness is getting worse. You think: today I am short of breath, and tomorrow I'll be in hospital because I need to be put on a ventilator. This is what makes this illness so unpredictable. I suffered for more than two weeks with this.'

According to Jahns, the fact that China came out of the Covid crisis so much quicker than Germany is '1,000%' down to the country's extensive digitalization. 'In Chinese cities, I stood in front of 18-metre-high screens, showing energy consumption, traffic flows, water used, and all in real time. With this kind of intelligence, it is easier to isolate parts and areas of a city, but you can also monitor the spread of infection. The major disadvantage from our point of view is the transparent citizen – but under such conditions, you have very different possibilities for controlling individuals. In China, you can detect and track a person who is Covid positive in real time and second by second. And those who fall ill can at every moment, wherever they may be in China, consult a doctor via WeChat and book an appointment with whatever kind of doctor they need.'

In Germany, Jahns's experience was very different. After he reported his infection, it took a full six days before the German coronavirus app informed his wife, who was with him at home during that time: the app showed about 200 contacts with a Covid-19 positive patient. 'The health authorities then rang me a week after the two-week [isolation] period had ended. I was in a telephone conference and asked them to ring again at 5pm. They replied that by then the office would be closed. And tomorrow all slots were booked. They never got in touch with me again.'

On our train to Berlin at the end of October 2020 – in fact, the day before the Chancellor Merkel and the prime ministers of the federal states agreed the second lockdown – there were only two other passengers in our Deutsche Bahn carriage. At least here it was probably impossible to catch Covid. We were on our way to talk to Sigmar Gabriel, the former vice-chancellor, foreign minister and minister of the environment. We met him in a town house whose architectural style is a mixture of early classicism and Baroque. The German physicist and chemist Heinrich Gustav Magnus once lived there. Today, it is the home of the Atlantik-Brücke, a non-profit association that promotes US–German relations, and whose members are decision-makers from the worlds of politics and economics. Sigmar Gabriel is the association's chairman. But more important with regard to the Communist Party of China (CPC) and its general secretary, Xi Jinping, is the fact that between 2009 and 2017 Gabriel was the chairman of the German Social Democratic Party.

'I gave my speech, was elected and wanted to leave the stage', Gabriel remembered about his first day as chairman. 'And there stood the Chinese ambassador, who handed me the written congratulations of the General Secretary of the Communist Party of China.' Back then, that was still Hu Jintao, but the message expresses a closeness that explains why Gabriel was later able to meet Hu's successor, Xi Jinping, on several occasions. The Communist Party of China and the German SPD had established ties in the 1970s, during the time of the Chinese reformer Deng Xiaoping and the peace-promoting German chancellor Willy Brandt. 'If you look at the respective numbers of party members, this is funny – I asked Xi Jinping if he could possibly send over a million members, as we were currently a bit short of numbers', the former SPD party chairman joked. In any case, the connection between the parties meant that, on his visits to China, Gabriel would meet not only his opposite number and the prime minister, as protocol required, but also Xi Jinping – a meeting of the party chairmen, so to speak.

We shall return to Sigmar Gabriel's impressions of China's paramount leader and his policies several times throughout the book. On Xi's response to the coronavirus, he said: 'In the beginning it was of course a disaster. A lot could have been avoided if the Chinese had begun to fulfil their commitments according to WHO rules earlier. The lack of transparency early on contributed to the fact that the world was pretty much helpless. Sure, later they tried to get a programme for international medical aid under way, to present themselves as the great saviour. China uses instruments that we, as a liberal democracy, cannot and also do not want to employ. But, of course, one must admit that they have in fact been able to get their economy going again in a relatively short span of time – that's true.'

Did China's lockdown succeed in eliminating the virus? 'I don't think so. You have to wonder: do we know everything? Probably not. But you can't get around acknowledging that they have brought it mostly under control; that, I think, needs to be said.'

What also needs to be said is that, at the beginning of 2021, European countries were struggling to get their own populations vaccinated, while China was supplying other countries, from Indonesia to Turkey and Chile, with its vaccines, Sinovac and Sinopharm. Xi Jinping was in this way making an important contribution to the global fight against the pandemic – and at the same time expanding his international power base. For instance, Brazil changed its mind about China's involvement in the expansion of the Brazilian 5G network after receiving Chinese medical aid. Now China is welcome to play a part in it.[39]

Spring 2022 marks a new episode in the ongoing Covid saga: most countries lift restrictions because large parts of the population are vaccinated and the Omicron variant in most cases produces only comparatively mild symptoms. China, however, continues its zero-Covid strategy in the face of a sudden new rise in cases. This rise is possibly a result of low infection rates in the past and the fact that China sealed itself off. Thus, the Chinese population did not develop sufficient immunity against Covid-19 and is left exposed to the more infectious Omicron variant. Megacities such as Shanghai are put under total lockdown. Millions of people are not allowed to leave their apartments and there are problems with the provision of food and medication. People who are suspected of being infected are detained in overcrowded quarantine centres. Infants who test positive are separated from their parents.

And again, all this is about Xi Jinping. He wants the 20th Party Congress of the Communist Party of China in the autumn of 2022 to confirm him in office for another period, in contravention of habitual practice. In order to achieve this, he needs to be able to present himself as the one who beat Covid. This is why victory over the virus is paramount, even if the negative effects of the measures are sometimes larger than the positive ones, as when, for instance, people suffering a heart attack cannot be brought to a hospital. The economic costs are also gigantic, not only to China itself but also – given that the country is at the centre of many international supply chains – all around the world. There are good reasons for being interested in Xi Jinping.

2

Xi Jinping's Family Background: The Formative Years

From Chinese nightmare to Chinese dream

Ai Weiwei has more in common with Xi Jinping than at first meets the eye. 'We belong to the same generation, have grown up with the ideology of Chairman Mao.' At sixty-four, Ai is only four years younger than Xi. But the commonalities go much further. To fully understand them, we need to go back to the end of the 1930s, to a remote place called Yan'an, situated 960 metres above sea level on the Loess Plateau. At the time, Yan'an was the final destination of the communist guerrillas' Long March. 'A small place, a little bit like Cambridge', says Ai, 'everyone knew each other.' And they all lived there: the chief of the guerrilla group, a certain Mao Zedong; the later prime minister Zhou Enlai; the later reformist politician Deng Xiaoping; Xi Jinping's father, Xi Zhongxun; and Ai Weiwei's father, the famous poet Ai Qing. Zhou Enlai had brought Ai Qing to Yan'an because he provided publicity for the communists – a role not unlike that of Bertolt Brecht in the German Democratic Republic (GDR). Even today, Chinese pupils learn Ai Qing's poems by heart. When he died in 1996, China's long-serving prime minister Wen Jiabao recited one of his poems at the funeral.

Despite all this veneration, Ai Qing was at one point sentenced as a 'right-wing dissenter' and exiled to the Xinjiang Uyghur Autonomous Region in the remotest part of north-west China. This is where Ai Weiwei grew up with his father. Ai Weiwei pulls his mobile out of his pocket and shows us an old black-and-white photograph he digitized and stored on the phone: 'Do you see this black hole here – every day we had to crawl into it. That is the cave in which we lived for five years.' But he also recalls a pleasant moment. At a bus station, they came across a member of the party leadership who was responsible for north-west China – none other than Xi Zhongxun, the father of the current president. When Xi Zhongxun saw Ai Qing, he asked how he was, and then turned to the local governor, who was standing behind him, to say: 'Ai Qing is my friend – treat him with decency.'

Xi Jinping was born on 15 June 1953 in Beijing, in privileged circumstances. Just four years earlier, the city had seen Mao Zedong proclaim the founding of the People's Republic of China. Xi Jinping's father, Xi Zhongxun, was a guerrilla leader fighting alongside Mao during the civil war between the communists and the nationalist Kuomintang. He was part of the Long March, the founding myth of socialist China. In 1934–5, 90,000 Red Army troops kept walking for 370 days, covering 12,000 kilometres. Only 8,000 survived.

Following the successful revolution, Xi Zhongxun became a top-ranking party official and deputy prime minister. His wife, Qi Xin, also played a part in the revolution. At just fifteen, she joined the Communist Party. During the Second Sino-Japanese War, she attended the Counter-Japanese Military and Political University and took part in combat missions. She then taught at the Central Party School of the Chinese Communist Party. Their son, Xi Jinping, can therefore be said to have been born a member of the 'red aristocracy'. He attended an elite school near the Zhongnanhai imperial gardens.[1]

Every tourist visiting Beijing will know about the Forbidden City – the old imperial palace. Tourist guides tell them that today, thanks to the revolution, even ordinary citizens can enter the complex. But what most guides do not mention is that only a few hundred metres away lies Zhongnanhai, meaning 'middle and southern lake', a part of the imperial complex that remains a forbidden city. Behind its high walls, today's red emperors do their work – some of it in rooms that the old emperors would have known, and some in newer, purpose-built buildings of grey and white. Here is where Xi Jinping spent his early childhood years.

What must it have meant for a little boy to grow up in such surroundings? Back then, he would have heard loudspeakers in the street blaring out the following song:

The east is red, the sun is rising.
China has made a Mao Zedong.
He strives for the people's happiness,
Hurrah, he is the people's great saviour!

The Russian writer Viktor Erofeyev, the son of a leading Soviet official, grew up during the Stalin era. The personal cult around Stalin was similar to that around Mao. In *Good Stalin*, Erofeyev remembers: 'So my papa now worked at the Kremlin. As for what he did there, I wasn't completely sure, but whenever my friends and I (in winter, wearing scarves pulled up to our eyes, in beaver-lamb coats, hats, and felt boots, and carrying small shovels so that we could dig in the snow in Gorky Park) went past the Kremlin, I would tell them in a voice that made it clear I knew what I was talking about: "This is where my papa and Comrade Stalin work." '[2]

In 1962, when Xi Jinping was nine years old, his father was arrested and imprisoned. According to the official 'profile' of the Chinese leader, 'his father was wronged and disgraced' by the justice system – as if it had all been down to a mistake made by some minor judge.[3] In reality, Xi's father was the victim of an ideological purge within the Communist Party. At the centre of the rift was something so trivial as to reveal the absurdity of Stalinist-type systems. It all began because of a novel. The book was to be published only with the permission of the deputy prime minister, Xi Zhongxun. There appeared to be no reason why he should not give his permission: the book was about Liu Zhidan, a hero of the revolution who was killed in 1936 while fighting against the Kuomintang. But Zhongnanhai was a hotbed of scheming and intrigue; in the tussle for power everyone distrusted everyone else – and the great Chairman Mao distrusted them all. Someone suggested to Mao that the book praised Liu Zhidan very highly – perhaps more highly than Mao himself. Further, this person suggested, Gao Gang came off rather well too – Gao was another 1930s revolutionary, but he was later accused of rebelling against the party leadership, in response to which he took his own life. For Mao, the case was open and shut: 'Using novels to be anti-Party is a new invention.'[4] In his view, the book implied nothing short of a conspiracy, and Xi Zhongxun was its leader. At first, Xi was not thrown into prison but 'only' placed under house arrest. Nevertheless, his treatment heralded a much larger power struggle.

To begin with, Xi's son, Jinping, was allowed to continue at the August 1st School, named after the day the People's Liberation Army was founded. The school had been set up during the civil war, in Yan'an, the final destination of the Long March, and was meant to educate the children of those fighting at the front. After the communist victory, it was moved to Beijing and became an elite institution for the children of high-ranking officials and army officers.

One might have thought that a nine-year-old who saw his father arrested would come to hate the state. Li Datong, almost the same age as Xi and a well-known Chinese journalist, explains why that was not the case for Xi Jinping:

> At nine years of age, he does not yet understand what is happening to him. When his father is sentenced as a counter-revolutionary, he must present himself as even more communist and even more revolutionary than the others if he wants to survive. In order to prove that he is a 'good child' of Mao, he redoubles his efforts to study Mao's works. He learns his speeches by heart, until Mao's heritage is deeply rooted in him. When he opens his mouth, it is Mao who speaks.[5]

Beijing, 18 August 1966. Hundreds of thousands wave Mao's Little Red Book, which every Chinese person is now obliged to carry at all times. Everyone wears a Mao badge – 4.8 billion of them have been produced. Students have come to the capital from all parts of China. They call themselves *hongweibing*, 'red guards'. Together they chant: 'Chairman Mao shall live 10,000 years!' Mao, now seventy-two years old, appears at the 'Gate of Heavenly Peace', Tiananmen, and tells the rally: 'Learn revolution by making revolution.' Girls scream and cry; many of them collapse. It is the first mass demonstration of the 'Great Proletarian Cultural Revolution'.

Two weeks before the event, pupils at a Beijing girls' school had beaten their headmistress, poured boiling water over her and kicked her to death. Now, one of the pupils is 'given the signal honour of putting a Red Guard armband on Mao'. The following day, their exchange was printed in every newspaper: 'Chairman Mao asked her: "What's your name?" She said: "Song Binbin." Chairman Mao asked: "Is it the 'Bin' as in 'Educated and Gentle'?" She said: "Yes." Chairman

Mao said: "Be violent!" Song Binbin changed her name to "Be Violent", and her school changed its name to "The Red Violent School."[6]

Song Binbin was not chosen at random. She was the daughter of Song Renqiong, one of the founders of the People's Republic of China, and one of the 'Eight Elders' of China's Communist Party. Later in the Cultural Revolution, he would himself be persecuted. But in this initial phase, the Red Guards movement was led by pupils from the elite schools, among them the August 1st School attended by Xi Jinping.

Xi was just thirteen years old, but he exploited the chaos to go travelling by himself. Mao had decreed that train journeys in China were free. His aim was not to improve the social situation, still less to protect the environment – there were no private cars in China in any case. Rather, Mao's decree enabled the Red Guards to travel to Beijing from all parts of the empire, so that they could demonstrate in support of him. Xi Jinping went in the opposite direction, travelling 2,000 kilometres to Guilin, an area in south China famous for its spectacular karst mountains and caverns.[7] As a result of Mao's decree, the trains became so overcrowded as to resemble those in India, and free travel was soon abolished.

When Xi Jinping returned to Beijing, the situation had changed. Mao's Cultural Revolution was supposed to be directed against 'capitalist roaders'. This was a strange claim, since genuine capitalists and big landowners had already been dispossessed in the revolution of 1949. Those who had not been able to flee to Taiwan were put in labour camps or shot.

The new enemies were communist politicians and intellectuals whom Mao took to be potential rivals and therefore accused of having capitalist leanings. Certainly, then, it would have looked incongruous had he continued to rely on the children of these enemies. Thus, new groups of Red Guards were formed, led by working-class children, to 'crush' the old Red Guards.

Xi Jinping's August 1st School was one of the targets. On 25 January 1967, 30,000 members of the new Red Guards encircled the school. They beat up the children of officials and put some of them in prison. The school was declared a 'counter-revolutionary institution' and dissolved.[8] Xi Jinping was arrested, accused of having criticized the Red Guards and thus of having opposed Chairman Mao. At the

Central Party School, where his mother worked, he was publicly humiliated. Attendees stood up, one after another, to criticize and condemn him for his 'mistakes'. His mother was in the crowd, forced to watch, unable to interfere without endangering herself. The Red Guards locked Xi up, and for days he had nothing to eat.[9] Xi Jinping rarely talks about this time, but in an interview for a Chinese journal in 2000 he said: 'The Red Guards told me a hundred times that they were going to shoot me. They threatened to execute me, and then I had to recite Mao quotations from dawn till dusk.'[10]

During the Cultural Revolution, Xi's mother, Qi Xin, was asked to distance herself from her son and husband, and also to inform on them. She refused. Soon after, there were messages on the walls of the Central Party School: 'Qi Xin, traitor'. She, too, was now dragged across the school grounds, with the Red Guards cheering and shouting.[11] Xi Jinping's official 'profile' does not give any details about these events, but confirms what happened in general terms: 'During the Cultural Revolution he suffered public humiliation and hunger, experienced homelessness and was even held in custody on one occasion.'[12]

The phrase 'public humiliation' refers to the so-called 'struggle sessions', mass events that took place during the Cultural Revolution in which the accused were publicly humiliated and tortured until they admitted their 'guilt' and engaged in 'self-criticism'. Xi Jinping's father, Xi Zhongxun, was repeatedly exposed to such treatment after he was expelled from Beijing, and he topped the list of 'rulers who are capitalist roaders'. Red Guards kept him in custody at the Northwest Agriculture and Forestry University, near the old Chinese capital city Xi'an, where the terracotta army would later be discovered. A photograph taken in 1967 shows Red Guards bringing him to one of the struggle sessions. A large sign around his neck reads: 'Party-hostile element Xi Zhongxun'.[13]

Xi Zhongxun was beaten so brutally that he almost died. News of this found its way to an old friend, Zhou Enlai, his former superior and at that point China's prime minister. During the Cultural Revolution, Zhou tried to protect Xi Zhongxun as best he could, but he had to tread carefully, lest he be stripped of his power, too. He arranged for Xi Zhongxun to be brought back to Beijing, and had him imprisoned for the next eight years. In that way, he saved his life: in prison, Xi was out of the clutches of the Red Guards and could receive medical treatment.[14]

After the closure of his elite school, Xi Jinping attended an ordinary school in Beijing: No. 25 Middle School. But by then, Mao had declared a new phase of the Cultural Revolution. All schools and universities were closed. The youth were taken from the cities and sent to the countryside, so that they could be 're-educated by the poor peasants'. That, at least, was the idea. Xi Jinping was forced to abandon school.

It is at this point that the heroic myth of Xi Jinping properly begins. At the age of fifteen, he went to Liangjiahe, in Yanchuan County in north-west China's Shaanxi Province, almost 900 kilometres from his hometown of Beijing. Like other city youth, he had been sent to rural China. The official 'profile' claims that he 'volunteered to live and work' there.[15] There is a kernel of truth in this. He did, indeed, choose this area in Shaanxi Province – he had distant relatives there. Nevertheless, it was a culture shock. There were no houses, and he moved into a cave of the kind that peasants in Shaanxi have used as their homes for centuries. He worked the fields, carried coal, built dykes. 'Life there was tough for an urban youth', the Chinese biographers write. 'In the beginning, fleas troubled him so badly he could hardly sleep. ... He was able to walk for 5 km on a mountainous path with two dangling baskets filled with almost one hundred kg of wheat on a shoulder-pole. Locals called him "a tough boy". ... Through gaining their trust, he was elected village Party chief.'[16]

Did Xi Jinping turn away from communism in the face of the suffering he and his family had to endure? One might have thought he would have, and many of his generation did. The official 'profile' contains just one mysterious hint, without further explanation: 'Back then, there was one moment when he wavered and had doubts.'[17] What happened? A couple of months after his arrival in the village, Xi was able to flee and make his way back to Beijing. There, he was captured, and locked up for half a year. The sixteen-year-old was desperate to return to his family. But by that point his mother and siblings had also been expelled from the capital. He was able to find only his aunt Qi Yun, the older sister of his mother, and her husband. Both were veterans of the People's Liberation Army. During the war, Qi Yun had introduced her sister to the communists. The aunt and uncle had gone to the countryside, too, to fight for the revolution. Now, they told their nephew that his behaviour was putting the whole family in danger. More importantly, they said, the young people of today had to live with the peasants and commit themselves to the fight against poverty, just as the aunt and uncle's generation had.[18] Xi Jinping heeded their advice. After his release from prison, he returned to the village.

This may have been the key moment. Xi Jinping decided to take a route different from that taken by many of a similar background. 'Because his father was treated with real cruelty during the Cultural Revolution, his son decides never to become like him,' suggests the Chinese writer Yu Jie in an interview. 'He takes Mao Zedong as his role model because he does not want to suffer the same fate as his father'[19] – or that of his older half-sister, Xi Heping, who took her own life after the humiliation she suffered during the Cultural Revolution. 'He chose to survive by becoming redder than red,' as a dossier compiled by the US embassy in Beijing has it.[20] He applied for Communist Party membership, but was rejected – probably because his father had been sentenced as a 'dissenter.' But he tried again and again – ten times, in total – until finally, in 1973, he was accepted.[21]

Xi took two suitcases of books with him to Liangjiahe. By the light of a kerosene lamp, he read Marx, Engels, Lenin, Stalin, Mao – but also the classics of world literature. Thanks to his upbringing, he had the intellectual ability to do so; in the village, where most were illiterate, he stood out early as someone who could read and write. He gained a reputation by reading out the newspaper at public meetings. Back then, the newspaper was not just a newspaper; it gave the party line, the opinion of the Great Chairman Mao Zedong, and Xi Jinping's voice brought it to the villagers.[22]

Xi, now twenty-one, took up the office of secretary of the Municipal Party Committee in his agricultural production brigade, becoming more or less the mayor of the village. And he shone in his new role: 'He led the farmers to reinforce the river bank in the slack season of winter in a bid to prevent erosion, organized a small cooperative of blacksmiths in the village to make farming tools, and built a methane tank for gathering cooking gas, the first in landlocked Shaanxi.'[23]

Xi's seven years in rural China had a decisive influence on his life. He would later tell an interviewer: 'When I went to the countryside as a fifteen-year-old, I was frightened and distraught. When I returned at twenty-two, I had a clear idea of what I wanted to achieve and was full of self-confidence.'[24] During his time in the village, the 'princeling' (as the children of top-ranking party officials are called in China) got to know a different world, one far away from the elite in Beijing. He experienced the poverty of the Chinese peasantry at first hand. His official 'profile' claims that, when he was named a 'model educated youth', and received a tricycle as a prize, he exchanged his reward 'for a walking tractor, a flour milling machine, a wheat winnowing machine and a water pump to benefit the villagers'.[25] What is certain is that he came to know the primitive conditions in which most Chinese people had to work. The village had no running water, no heating, no electricity and no radio – not to mention those things that even most people in the cities did not have, but to which a child of a party official was accustomed: bathtubs, toilets, toilet paper, telephones and televisions. Instead of motor cars, the peasants had carts pulled by donkeys. All this, Xi wanted to change.

Since becoming the Chinese leader, Xi Jinping has spoken about the 'Chinese dream'. In this context, he often refers to his experiences in the village of Liangjiahe: 'Like the locals, I lived in caves dug out from loess hills and slept on an earthen bed. The locals were very poor, and they could go for months without a bite of meat. I grew to understand what they needed most.'[26]

In 2015, he visited the village again. 'I went back to Liangjiahe, which now has asphalt roads, tile-roofed brick houses, and internet access. The elderly enjoy the basic old-age pension, the villagers are covered by medical insurance, and the children receive good education. Having meat for dinner is of course no longer a dream.'[27]

These achievements may sound trivial to the citizens of a rich nation, but in fact they signal a shift in the global balance of power. In Xi Jinping's own words:

> The Third Plenary Session of the 11th CPC Central Committee in 1978 started a new historical period of reform and opening up. Over a period of almost 40 years, China has maintained rapid economic growth for a period longer than any other country since the end of World War II. China's economy ranked 11th in the world at the beginning of reform

> and opening up; it came to the fifth in 2005, ahead of France; it was fourth in 2006, ahead of Britain; third in 2007, ahead of Germany; and second in 2009, ahead of Japan. In 2010, the scale of China's manufacturing surpassed that of the United States, ranking first in the world. It took us only a few decades to complete the development course that took developed countries several hundred years, a unique historic achievement.[28]

There can be no doubt that the new China is an unparalleled success story. 'Since China began to open up and reform its economy in 1978,' the World Bank says, 'GDP growth has averaged almost 10 percent a year.' Such a rate of growth has never been sustained over such a period of time by any other country. The result is that '800 million people have been lifted out of poverty.'[29]

Jörg Wuttke, the president of the EU Chamber of Commerce in China, puts a slightly different slant on the figures: 'When looking at the gross domestic product per head, you will see that China follows exactly the same path as Japan, South Korea, and Taiwan, and recently even lags behind them. China does not make full use of its potential. To the outside it appears to be so spectacularly successful because Taiwan has a population of only 24 million, Japan 126 million, but China boasts a whopping 1.4 billion. And so, if necessary, they can easily redistribute the money in such a way that Shanghai looks like the sunny uplands, while Qinghai, for example, remains comparatively poor.'

Nevertheless, what the West tried for several decades to achieve with development aid, the People's Republic actually has achieved. Today, the gap between rich and poor may in fact be increasing in China. We all have read the reports about the hardship faced by the country's migrant workers. But even they earn much more now than they did in their previous lives as peasants – that, after all, is why they have moved from the countryside to the cities. Only a few decades ago, most houses in China did not have electricity; there was no lighting or television. Today, Chinese cities look far more modern than European or American ones, and smartphones play a more integral part in everyday life compared to other parts of the world. Until 1978, it was inconceivable that an ordinary Chinese citizen would be able to take an overseas vacation. In 2003, 20 million of them travelled abroad, and by 2019 that figure had risen to 134 million.[30] Neuschwanstein Castle bustles with Chinese visitors, as does the Hermitage Museum in Saint Petersburg. The Chinese are better off today than they were – most of them significantly better off.

Xi Jinping is more focused than his predecessors were on those whose wealth has not increased: 'According to the 12th Five-year Plan (2011–15), the number of basic-need housing units built and houses in run-down areas rebuilt will be 36 million, and by 2015 the basic-need housing coverage will hit around 20 percent.'[31] In pursuit of such goals, Xi does not shy away from taking on the real estate tycoons who profited handsomely from the economic boom: 'houses are for living in, not for speculation', he told them.[32]

Xi Jinping concedes that there cannot be absolute equality, but he insists that no one should be left behind:

> Poverty alleviation of the impoverished rural population is our biggest area of weakness. Bringing about a moderately prosperous society in all respects does not mean that each and every individual is ensured the same level of prosperity, but if the living standards of the currently impoverished rural population of over 70 million do not improve noticeably, our realization of a moderately prosperous society in all respects will lack credibility.[33]

When it comes to the fight against poverty, the main goal is therefore to make sure that 'by 2020, the rural poor will be guaranteed food, clothing, compulsory education, basic medical care, and safe housing.'[34]

Education plays a key role in these plans: 'We will help children from poor families to access education in order to prevent poverty being passed down from generation to generation, and to give all children the confidence and hope they need to create a bright future.'[35]

Xi Jinping's talk of the 'Chinese dream' is, of course, intended as an allusion to the American dream. Like the American dream, the Chinese dream is about prosperity, but unlike the American version, it envisages that prosperity as being brought about not through ruthless competition but by everyone pulling together to create a stronger China. Where the American dream is individualistic, the Chinese dream is also about increasing the power of the country itself. As Xi

Jinping put it in 2012, when he first referred to the 'Chinese dream', during a visit to the exhibition 'The Road to Rejuvenation': 'History shows that the future and destiny of each and every one of us are closely linked to those of our country and nation. One can do well only when one's country and nation do well.'[36]

That comment has in mind the long stretches of history when China was the leading power in the world, periods to which Xi refers repeatedly:

> Ancient China thrived on agriculture and led the world in farming for a long time. It had a population of more than 60 million in the Han Dynasty (206 BC–AD 220), and an area of cultivated land of over 53 million hectares. The capital city of Chang'an in the Tang Dynasty (618–907) covered an area of more than 80 square kilometers, with a population of over one million. It had magnificent palaces, temples, and towering pagodas, as well as the prosperous east and west markets. A poem by Tang poet Cen Shen (c. 715–770) wrote: 'There are one million households in Chang'an City.' In the Northern Song Dynasty (960–1127), the maximum national tax revenue reached 160 million strings of coin [one string contained 1,000 coins], making China the richest country in the world at the time. None of the cities of London, Paris, Venice, or Florence had a population of 100,000, but China hosted nearly 50 cities each with a population of 100,000.[37]

As late as 1820 – a time when European colonial power had long been in the ascendant and China, the old global power, was in decline – the Chinese economy still accounted for a third of global gross domestic product. The Chinese printed books 800 years before Gutenberg. They produced steel 1,300 years before the Europeans. They invented paper, porcelain, gunpowder and the compass. 'Records show that China has 173 items among the world's most important 300 inventions and discoveries made before the 16th century', Xi reminds us, and was thus 'far surpassing Europe in the same historical period.'[38] These are the times of which Xi dreams. They are the reason he speaks of the 'great rejuvenation of the Chinese nation.'[39]

Throughout history, the West has on occasion been plagued by a trade deficit with China. The Chinese exported porcelain, silk and tea, but there was little the Europeans had to offer in return. Their clothes, for instance, met with scant interest because processed cotton was of a far better quality in China. The British therefore moved into drug dealing, and flooded China, the Middle Kingdom, with opium. The British East India Company, in particular, played a large part in the trade. Created by royal charter in 1600, it later assumed many characteristics of a state and behaved like a colonial power. The Daoguang Emperor wanted to put an end to the opium trade, to protect the health of the Chinese people. In 1839, he had 22,000 boxes of the narcotic burned. The British reacted by attacking China. This was the first of the two opium wars, and ended with the surrender of Hong Kong to the British.

In the second opium war (1856–60), the French supported the British in their campaign to secure free trade in drugs. The invaders reached the Old Summer Palace area at the north-western edge of Beijing, and set upon the place like vandals. They set fire to palaces and destroyed beautiful gardens that had been cultivated over centuries. They stole golden jewellery and porcelain vases, some of which were more than 3,600 years old. The French writer Victor Hugo described the events as 'Two robbers breaking into a museum. One has looted, the other has burnt. ... one of the two conquerors filled its pockets, seeing that, the other filled its safes; and they came back to Europe laughing hand-in-hand. ... Before history, one of the bandits will be called France and the other England.'[40]

To understand how the Chinese feel about these events, we need only imagine how Western Europeans would feel about the Chinese flattening Buckingham Palace or the gardens of Versailles.

Parts of Shanghai came under the control of the French, British and Americans. The invaders' flags flew from the tops of important buildings. The regulations of one of the city's parks barred Chinese and dogs from entering it. Europeans and Americans behaved like members of a master race, and were ferried around in sedan chairs carried by coolies. The Chinese were second-class citizens in their own country.

The Germans were also involved. Thirty-three years before Hitler came to power, Emperor Wilhelm II was calling for the mass murder of members of another ethnicity. On 27 July 1900, he delivered his famous

Hun speech to German troops departing for China: 'No quarter will be given! Prisoners will not be taken! Whoever falls into your hands is forfeited. Just as a thousand years ago the Huns under their King Attila made a name for themselves, one that even today makes them seem mighty in history and legend, may the name German be affirmed by you in such a way in China that no Chinese will ever again dare to look cross-eyed at a German.'[41] During the suppression of the so-called Boxer Rebellion, the Germans, together with the Japanese, British and other Western powers, conquered and looted Beijing.[42]

Who, today, still talks about Wilhelm II? These are events of a distant past, one might be tempted to think. But the Chinese do not agree. In China, you hear little about the 45 million who died during Mao's 'Great Leap Forward' (1958–61),[43] or the terror of the Cultural Revolution (1966–76), or the massacre in Tiananmen Square (1989), but a lot about the humiliation of China by the colonial powers. John Bolton has described a meeting between Xi Jinping and Donald Trump at the G20 summit in Osaka in 2019 – Bolton was US national security advisor at the time – at which they were to discuss the trade negotiations between the two countries: 'Out of nowhere, Xi answered by comparing the impact of an unequal deal with us to the "humiliation" of the Treaty of Versailles, which had taken Shandong province from Germany but given it to Japan. Xi said with a straight face that if China suffered the same humiliation in our trade negotiations, there would be an upsurge of patriotic feeling in China.' Hardly surprisingly, Bolton adds, 'Trump manifestly had no idea what Xi was referring to.'[44]

In China, the need to return the empire to its former glory is a common refrain. In 2016, Xi Jinping expressed it – in the slightly pompous language of the party – thus: 'At present, our main task is to complete the process of building a moderately prosperous society in all respects by 2020, as the centenary of the CPC approaches. This will lay a solid foundation for us to achieve our next goal in the middle of the century, which will see the 100th anniversary of the founding of the PRC – building China into a prosperous, democratic, culturally advanced, harmonious, modern socialist country.'[45]

This history of the Chinese dream, however, is blemished by one mistake: the fact that China's economic rise began not in 1949, with the victory of the communists and the foundation of the People's

Republic, but in 1978. That year was also an important turning point in Xi Jinping's life: his father, having previously fallen into disfavour, was rehabilitated and made a member of the party leadership again. He was put in charge of the important southern Chinese Guangdong Province (Canton). Even before his father's rehabilitation, Xi Jinping was allowed to return to Beijing and enrol at the renowned Tsinghua University.

Both China's economic rise and the rehabilitation of Xi's family are owed to Deng Xiaoping. Deng was another former deputy prime minister; he was also a victim of Mao, who, in 1966, forced Deng out of his leadership position and transferred him to work in a tractor factory. The same year, Red Guards locked Deng's son up in a radioactive laboratory. He could save himself only by jumping out of a window, with his injuries leaving him a paraplegic.

When Mao died in 1976, Deng was already seventy-two, but he would go on to change China more than Mao did. At the time, that possibility would have seemed inconceivable: Deng had just been stripped of all offices yet again. During the Cultural Revolution, a whole generation grew up with the chant: 'Down with Deng Xiaoping!' Perhaps this actually helped him. He was well known as a critic of the murders and the chaotic conflicts of that era. He also had more experience and talent than other members of the leadership. He prepared his comeback carefully, and in 1978 made the decisive move. At his insistence, the Communique of the Third Plenary Session of the Eleventh Central Committee of the Chinese Communist Party confirmed that what was required was to 'emancipate our minds, use our heads, seek truth from facts and unite as one in looking to the future.'[46] This was the Chinese way of saying that Mao was not right about everything, that the class struggle was over, and that the economy had to be modernized. This Central Committee meeting was the start of the 'reform and opening up of China' agenda that would be the leitmotif of Chinese politics to the present day.[47]

Xi Jinping's father played a central role in the reform and opening up process. The seasoned party official was sent to Guangdong Province to resolve a local crisis. In 1978–9, 120,000 people fled the province for Hong Kong – more people than came to West Germany from the GDR in 1989. As in the German case, in Guangdong Province there were concerns that the system would collapse. Xi Zhongxun asked people why they were seeking to flee. His conclusion was not that they were against China's political system as such, but that they were leaving for economic reasons – in Hong Kong they could earn a hundred times what they could in the People's Republic of China. Xi visited ordinary fishermen who had black-and-white televisions in their huts – a rare luxury at the time, bought, they told him, with the profits they made from smuggling vegetables to Hong Kong.[48] Xi's conclusion was that Communist Party rule would be secured only if China made it possible for these people to earn more money inside the People's Republic.

There were 30,000 people living in the rural area of Shenzhen, near the border with Hong Kong. Xi Zhongxun suggested to Deng Xiaoping that China should create a Special Economic Zone here.[49] In this zone – a kind of capitalist island in a sea of socialism – domestic and foreign enterprises would be allowed to invest and make profits. It was a daring project, and from the very beginning it was a fantastic success. People stopped fleeing to Hong Kong; instead, entrepreneurs from Hong Kong came to Shenzhen and built factories there. Two other Special Economic Zones, Zhuhai and Shantou, also in Guangdong, were similarly successful. This was the beginning of China's economic boom. Today, Shenzhen is one of the most modern cities in the world, and has grown to a total population of 12 million.

When the reforms began, Xi Jinping was studying chemistry and Marxism in Beijing. He later wrote his PhD in law, making him the first head of state of the People's Republic of China to hold a doctorate. His thesis was titled 'A Tentative Study on China's Rural Marketization'. It dealt with the new economic liberalization, and showed that food supplies improved after Mao's people's communities – comparable to the agricultural production cooperatives in the former GDR – were abolished.[50]

The standard of living in China began to improve only once the Communist Party interfered less in the economy, let the business-savvy and diligent Chinese people get on with it, and allowed the country to benefit from the know-how of the foreign companies that were now coming to China. Yet Xi Jinping still says that the Chinese people should thank Mao and the Communist Party. How does he square that circle? Here is his somewhat abstract explanation: 'The first generation of the central collective leadership with Mao Zedong as the core provided invaluable experience as well as the theoretical and material basis for the great initiative of building socialism with Chinese characteristics in the new historic period. The second generation with Deng Xiaoping as the core started the building of socialism with Chinese characteristics.'[51]

The British sinologist Kerry Brown, who lived in China for more than thirty years, puts it more simply: 'The main achievement under Mao, broadly speaking, was national reunification: he ended the era of division and fragmentation. ... Under Deng, the calculation was made that without economic and material strength, China's future would never truly be secure.'[52] But one thing remained constant: 'The overall vision has always been to use Marxism to fulfil the creation of a rich, strong, powerful Chinese nation.'[53] For Xi, it is also a family matter. This is the vision of China for which his parents fought as revolutionaries.

3

A Colourful Character in a Uniform Crowd

Xi Jinping, husband of a folk singer

The Chinese say that there are three ways to make a career: the yellow, the black and the red way. Yellow stands for gold, in other words making money, founding a company or rising to a managerial position in an already existing enterprise. Black signifies an academic career, because many believe academia is a black hole. Red means becoming a powerful part of officialdom, or a politician. Xi Jinping chose red.

In China, this path does not require one to go cap in hand to wealthy backers or to go on walkabouts to meet voters. Politicians are not elected by the population. There is not even the pretence of democracy, as there was in the days of the Soviet Union or the GDR, where candidates were elected with 99 per cent of the vote; nor are there rigged elections, as in Putin's Russia. Occasionally, though, Chinese propaganda claims that representatives are elected.

The second volume of Xi Jinping's collected speeches even contains a photograph of him casting a ballot, standing in front of an oversized red flag at his official residence in Zhongnanhai. There is no one else in the photo. Among our large circle of Chinese friends, colleagues and relatives, no one knows anything about when or where voting might have taken place – and no one has ever been invited to take part in it. Thus, politicians in China need to be liked not by their citizens but by their superiors – those who appoint them.

Career changes are rarely successful. If you want to get to the top, you need to work your way up from the bottom. This was also the case for Xi Jinping. After finishing university in 1979, he became personal secretary to Geng Biao, then a leading member of the Central Military Commission and who was soon to become minister of national defence.[1] Xi was able to establish useful contacts, and top-secret documents landed on his desk. But he was still only a personal secretary, and a young man approaching thirty. From a Chinese perspective, it was high time that he tied the knot.

Although arranged marriages are a thing of the past in China, it is still the case that parents and colleagues often feel the need to play matchmaker. In the case of Xi Jinping, it was his boss, Geng Biao, who introduced him to Ke Xiaoming, the daughter of the Chinese ambassador in London. They were soon married. But the two quarrelled continuously. Ke wanted to return to England, while Xi was eyeing a career in China, and in any case did not speak English. After about three years, the couple divorced.[2] Xi's first marriage is almost a state secret in China, and most people do not know about it. Today, divorce is common in China, but for party officials it is not the done thing.

Even at this early stage of his career, one can already detect a character trait that will carry Xi to the very top: every step in his life is calculated. His official 'profile' states that, in 1982, 'Xi gave up a comfortable office job in Beijing' and went to work as the deputy secretary of the party committee of Zhengding in north China's Hebei Province.[3] Even in Germany, it would be unusual for a ministerial civil servant to want to move from Berlin to some provincial district. And in China, at least back then, the differences between the big cities and rural areas were far more pronounced than in Germany. Everyone wanted to be in the capital, Beijing, where life was more comfortable. Xi Jinping, however, went in the other direction.

In Beijing, it was also the case that members of the 'red aristocracy' had a much better chance than ordinary citizens of having a successful career. Yet in Beijing Xi was only one of a number of 'princelings'. In the province, by contrast, he could make a name for himself. Or as the Chinese proverb has it: it is better to be the head of a chicken than the tail of a phoenix.

What the inhabitants of Zhengding remember most about Xi Jinping is that, unlike other officials, who went around in chauffeur-driven cars, he rode his bike: 'first it can train his body, second, it can bring him close to the masses, and third, it can save gasoline', he would later say in an interview.[4] Xi Jinping wanted to be an approachable, modest politician, and in this way to distinguish himself from colleagues who were aloof, or even corrupt.

Xi brought tangible benefits to the county. He created a park that resembled the garden in *The Dream of the Red Chamber*, one of China's four classic novels. Everyone in China knows this book, although it was briefly banned during the Cultural Revolution because Mao thought the novel's condemnation of nineteenth-century aristocracy insufficiently unequivocal. Through his Beijing connections, Xi Jinping knew that the Chinese broadcaster CCTV was planning a soap opera, running to thirty-six episodes, based on the novel, and he succeeded in getting the series shot in Zhengding. The county's reputation began to grow, and it started to draw in money and tourists – in the year after the series was broadcast, one million visitors came to Zhengding.[5]

In Chinese, one's network of personal connections is called one's *guanxi.* Of course, everywhere people rely on networking, but in China it is even more crucial. Take, for instance, the relationship between Xi Jinping's father and his old friend Xiang Nan, the party secretary of Fujian Province in south-east China. When Xi Zhongxun created the Special Economic Zone in Guangdong Province, he made sure that another one was introduced in Fujian Province: the coastal city of Xiamen. In 1985, Xiang Nan saw to it that Xi Jinping, his friend's son, became deputy mayor of the city, which is located across the water from Taiwan. Xiamen was flourishing, benefiting from economic relations with the seceded island, which at this point had become possible again. Giving his reasons for this next step in his career, Xi Jinping says he wanted to 'taste the reform and become open to the outside'.[6]

Xi was now deputy mayor of one of China's most important cities – but still only deputy. Beyond local politics, no one takes note of a deputy mayor – China is like any other country in that respect. It is time for us to bring someone else into the story, someone everyone in China knew even back then: Peng Liyuan.

Peng Liyuan was born a good nine years after Xi Jinping, on 20 November 1962, in the Yuncheng district of Shandong Province. Her father, Peng Longkun, was a party official in their village – comparable to a local government employee in other countries. Her mother was a singer, part of a group that travelled from village to village putting on outdoor concerts. As soon as Peng Liyuan was able to walk, she accompanied her mother on her tours, and eventually started to join in and sing, too. The other musicians told the mother that – who knows? – perhaps one day her daughter might have her job.[7] In hindsight, this was a phenomenal understatement.

When Peng Liyuan was four years old, the terror of the Cultural Revolution came to her village. As part of his job, Peng Longkun was responsible for traditional folk art, which was now deemed 'feudal.' As punishment, he was forced to clean the public toilets in the village. He was arrested, and for some time not allowed to see his family. The Red Guards stormed the family's house, shouting revolutionary slogans and accusing the mother of being a spy on the grounds that she had relatives in Taiwan, the enemy country, even though she had not had any contact with them for years. The Red Guards demanded that she 'confess', and they ransacked the house looking for 'evidence' of the Taiwan connection. Little Peng Liyuan watched all of this. With the parents no longer allowed to work, the family was plunged into poverty. They could afford to have a photograph of their daughter taken only once, when she turned seven. On the reverse it reads: 'This is the only photo from Peng Liyuan's childhood.'[8]

Peng Liyuan attended the village school, but in those years there was little real teaching. Instead, primary school kids learned quotations from Mao's Little Red Book by heart. Peng Liyuan was part of the school's propaganda group, singing revolutionary songs – and developing her talent.

In 1976, the Cultural Revolution ended. There was a lack of skilled workers in every field. At long last, there was training again, including in music. Peng Liyuan was highly talented, but she was also lucky. Her teacher presented her to the song and dance ensemble of Shandong. At the age of just fifteen, she was accepted by the Shandong Wuqi art school (from 1978 the Shandong Art College) in Jinan, the capital of the province, and studied traditional singing. At eighteen, she joined the organization that promised the most support for a young female singer: the People's Liberation Army.

The role of the military in China is unlike that in almost every other country. The military is under the control not of the state but of the Communist Party. As Mao said: 'Political power grows out of the barrel of a gun.'[9] The party came to power because the People's Liberation Army was victorious in the civil war. During the war, it had set up music, theatre and dance groups for the promotion of communism and the recruitment of combatants, and after the foundation of the People's Republic these groups continued.

Peng Liyuan served in the song and dance troupe of her home province, wearing the green uniform of the People's Liberation Army. Her soprano voice was striking, and at one performance she was noticed by the director of the Central Conservatory of Music in Beijing. She was given permission to study at the conservatory but remained a member of the People's Liberation Army. She cut her first record, and sang in films. Her repertoire comprised traditional folk songs as well as 'red songs' – the political songs of the new era. One of her first hits was 'On the Field of Great Prospects', a paean to rural China. But her real breakthrough came in 1982 with an appearance on the TV show celebrating Chinese New Year, watched by 800 million people. Since then, she has featured in the show almost every year, and has made many appearances on various other programmes.[10] Peng Liyuan is something like the Chinese version of the German singer Helene Fischer, except even more well known, and with a far larger audience.

Peng shied away from commercialism, and remained faithful to the army. She was invited to join the 'Central Military Commission Political Work Department Song and Dance Troupe', which of all of China's cultural groups, both civilian and military, is the one with the best artistic training. And she joined the Communist Party. Despite all these successes, many traditional Chinese people pitied her. For there was, as she herself admitted, one thing still missing from her life: a man.

Unsolicited matchmakers, probably from the Political Work Department of the Central Military Commission, took it upon themselves to help. As Peng Liyuan saw it, several facts spoke against the man they arranged for her to meet: he was divorced; he was more than nine years her senior; he was a bureaucrat in a distant province – 2,000 kilometres away from where she worked in Beijing. The only plus was that he was the son of Xi Zhongxun, who by this point had returned from Shenzhen to Beijing and risen to become a member of the all-powerful Central Political Bureau. She agreed to meet Xi Jinping.

Neither of them was particularly impressed with the other at first. Peng Liyuan would later say that he had been dressed in a simple, old-fashioned way, like a peasant. He knew little about her and her fame, and apologized, saying that he rarely watched television and had little knowledge of music. But she was more taken with him when he began to talk about himself: 'He is a good man. Many of his school friends went abroad or became rich. He had the chance to go abroad, but he chose the difficult path of helping the people.' Her parents, who worried that Xi might be a corrupt and decadent party official, were reassured.

About a year later, on 1 September 1987, the two married. As communists, and therefore atheists, it was not a church wedding. But even for Daoist or Buddhist Chinese people, weddings do not have much religious significance. Under Mao, large wedding parties had not been permitted, but by 1987 they were very much back in fashion. Xi Jinping and Peng Liyuan, however, kept it small, inviting a few friends and colleagues to a five-star hotel, the Xiamen Yeohwa, and its restaurant Red Madame Rouge, which serves French cuisine – on that evening, snails, among other things. But the real sensation of the night was something else. Xi Jinping had not actually told his colleagues who he was going to marry. As the guests arrived, they wondered: what is the famous singer Peng Liyuan doing here?[11]

As is customary in China, the bride retained her family name, Peng, and the two have a modern marriage as equal partners. Peng could have moved to Xiamen, but she stayed in Beijing, which had far more to offer a singer. Xi could have asked to be relocated to Beijing, but he continued to follow his career path as planned. That meant moving even further into the periphery, broadening his experience so as to be able to rise higher. In 1988, he became the party chief of the Ningde prefecture, which is also in Fujian Province. Ningde is not as elegant as Xiamen, but in Xiamen he was the deputy; in Ningde he was at the top.

Xi's short official 'profile' says: 'In 1988 he became Party secretary of Ningde Prefecture in southeast China's Fujian Province, one of the poorest parts of the country at that time. ... During his tenure at Ningde he often travelled for days on mountain roads to reach the furthest corners of the prefecture. The roads were so rough that he had to take breaks on the way to ease the pain in his back. He once walked for nearly five hours on a rugged mountain road to get to a village called Xiadang, which was not accessible by highway.' In Ningde, Xi began to practise the kind of democracy that he would later seek to implement in all of China: 'At one point he and other senior officials in Fuzhou met with more than 700 petitioners in two days, and solved many of their problems on the spot or set a time limit to find solutions.'[12]

Instead of competition between different political parties, Xi wants to appoint qualified officials from within the Communist Party to address the people's concerns. He explains the idea thus: 'Officials should love the people in the way they love their parents, work for their benefit and lead them to prosperity.'[13]

Back then, however, the 'parents' were rather dissatisfied with the way their self-appointed children were working for them. When the former party leader and reformer Hu Yaobang died in April 1989, thousands gathered on the Square of Heavenly Peace (Tiananmen). The spontaneous act of mourning turned into a protest. Students plastered the walls with posters reading: 'The wrong one died.' For them, although Deng Xiaoping had reformed the economy, he had clung on to the dictatorship of the party – a party of 'princelings' that functioned like a monarchy, with elders passing on power to their children. The accusation applied just as much to Xi Jinping. The rebellion grew. Workers and employees joined the students. There were demonstrations in more than 400 cities.

The popular movement for democracy occupied the Square of Heavenly Peace, the heart of the capital, for several weeks. Some protesters even constructed a nine-metre-tall replica of the Statue of Liberty from plaster and polystyrene. Despite all this, the party's general secretary, Zhao Ziyang, sympathized with the protesters. But in the background, Deng Xiaoping, as the Chairman of the Central Military Commission of the Communist Party, still pulled the strings. Until his death in 1997, he remained the de facto most powerful man in China. He ignored Zhao Ziyang and called on the veterans of the revolution to come together. 'We do not fear spilling blood,' he told them, 'and we do not fear the international reaction.' But one person opposed him: Xi Zhongxun, Xi Jinping's father. He wanted a peaceful resolution.[14]

In the early morning of 4 June 1989, tanks from the 27th and 38th armies advanced on Tiananmen Square. In the side streets, they opened fire. The People's Liberation Army was killing the people. A picture of a man confronting the tanks, plastic shopping bags in his hands, went around the world. In despair, he shouted: 'Why are you here? All you did was bring disaster over us. Because of you, my city is in chaos.' The tanks drove around him.

However, in other places in Beijing, the state acted with more brutality. A student from Beijing who was present at the events reported at the time: 'When the tanks had passed, there were only corpses, only dead people left, and immediately soldiers and policemen appeared who poured petrol on them and burnt the corpses there and then. This is how they wanted to destroy all traces so that no one can count and no one can know how many people were murdered. And then an ambulance appeared. In it were many wounded students. The drivers all had left because they had been afraid. Then, one student said: "I can drive, I'll drive you away." He climbed into the ambulance. When he was about to pull off, a policeman appeared, an "anti-violence policeman", that is a special unit, and shot the student behind the wheel. Then further policemen entered the vehicle and shot all the students in it. A fully occupied vehicle.' The Chinese Red Cross has analysed records from Beijing hospitals. According to its calculations, 2,600 people were killed and 7,000 wounded in the Tiananmen massacre.[15]

The Central Military Commission Political Work Department organized a concert for the soldiers who had been deployed in the massacre. The concert's theme: 'The army of the people loves the people.' Twenty especially ambitious soldiers were given the honorary title 'Guardian of the Capital' for their roles in the killing. A well-known artist was part of the programme: Peng Liyuan.[16]

At the time, the Tiananmen massacre divided the country, the party, and possibly even Xi Jinping's family. General Secretary Zhao Ziyang was in tears when he apologized to the students. He was forced to resign, and was kept under house arrest for the rest of his life. His successor was Jiang Zemin, an electrical engineer who wore thick horn-rimmed glasses. Xi Zhongxun was also quickly stripped of his posts, and he retired to Shenzhen. But he was at least given an honourable funeral in Beijing's Babaoshan Cemetery, where the greatest heroes of the revolution are buried. Xi Jinping's father was also posthumously awarded the titles of 'Outstanding Member of the Communist Party of China', 'Great Communist Soldier', 'Remarkable Revolutionary of the Proletariat', 'Great Political Leader of Our Party and Army' and 'Main Founder of the Shaanxi and Gansu Border Area Revolutionary Base'.[17]

When Zhao Ziyang, the former general secretary who had apologized to the students, died in 2005, only a handful of people were allowed to attend the funeral. One of the wreaths was laid by Qi Xin, Xi Jinping's mother.[18] Was this a silent protest against the massacre? Or was she simply paying her respects to an old friend and comrade, despite their differences of opinion?

There are no signs yet that Xi Jinping himself intends to rehabilitate the victims of the massacre. On the contrary, today commemoration of the event is suppressed more forcefully than ever. Many young Chinese people have no idea about the events of 4 June 1989. It would be like young Germans not knowing about the Berlin Wall.

On 25 July 1989, a few weeks after the massacre, all of China would come to know of Xi Jinping – but not because of what he had to say about the bloodshed. On that day, *Renmin Ribao* (*People's Daily*), the most important publication of the Communist Party – carried an article about a corruption scandal in Ningde, where Xi was the party chief. In Ningde, a poor area, 7,392 party officials had had their private villas built at the expense of the state, using resources that had been earmarked for education and disaster relief. Xi Jinping found out, and punished the guilty.[19] From now on, this would be the approach taken by the Communist Party, and in particular by Xi Jinping: corrupt party officials would be punished, albeit without calling into question the authority of the party itself.

Peng Liyuan communicated this message in her own way. As a young woman from a humble background, she seemed authentic. At a gala celebrating the seventieth birthday of the Communist Party of China, Peng was the main attraction.[20] But 1991 was no ordinary year for the party. The Soviet Union collapsed, and Chinese comrades feared that China might be next. They began to talk less about socialism, and instead sought to present themselves as a patriotic party of the people. Instead of class struggle, they preached harmony. The people were longing for stability. Peng Liyuan sang:

> On the road, full of sunshine
> in the air, the flags are flying.
> Development on a scientific basis
> and in harmony –
> this will lead China to brighter shores.

On 27 June 1992, Peng Liyuan and Xi Jinping's daughter, Xi Mingze, was born in Fujian Province. After three months of maternity leave, legally stipulated at the time, Peng Liyuan returned to Beijing – more concerts were coming up, among them a solo performance in Singapore. Their daughter stayed with the father and was brought up by Peng Liyuan's parents, a common arrangement in China.[21]

On 3 April 2002, we met China's then general secretary of the Communist Party and president of the People's Republic, Jiang Zemin. China's rulers rarely speak to the press. Even Chinese journalists find it hard to get close to them. The *Spiegel* interview with the president was supposed to follow a strict protocol: we would submit our questions in writing in advance, and at a joint photo opportunity receive the written answers. But the meeting, in the sealed-off government district of Zhongnanhai, took a very unexpected turn. Jiang Zemin greeted us in perfect German. During his studies, he told us, he often immersed himself in Goethe's *Faust*. 'Reading it a hundred times is not enough', he said with a flourish. He encouraged us to have a frank conversation with him.

The conversation took place in a large hall, the walls lined by heavy chairs with red upholstery, occupied by members of the party hierarchy keen to hear what the president had to say to a German magazine. Jiang Zemin looked at us expectantly, as if he did not know that his answers to our questions had already been given in writing. So we ran through our questions once again, this time face to face.

'In the course of my university studies, I have learnt German and read works by Kant, Goethe, Hegel, and Marx,' Jiang Zemin told us. 'I know Germany from several visits. I am particularly impressed by the German mentality, their logical way of thinking, intelligence, and discipline, as well as their diligence.'

We put it to him that, despite China's enormous economic upturn, many state-run enterprises were devastated and had huge debts.

Jiang responded modestly: 'You are right: we have successes that are acknowledged by all the world. At the same time, we soberly recognize that there are significant problems, which are a normal part of such a developing process. I am convinced that we shall get a grip on them.' His main concern, he said, remained reforming and opening up the economy. He wanted to improve living standards for all citizens.

Jiang was quite open about China's problems: 'Because of systemic deficiencies, but also because of the moral failure of some officials, there are indeed cases of bureaucratic abuse and abuse of power. We are facing these problems and decidedly fight these defects. We know no mercy in such cases. The masses support us in our fight against corruption, they are standing firmly with the party leadership.'

Jiang was also undogmatic about the interpretation of socialist teachings: 'Marx developed his theories over a hundred years ago in Europe – how should he have anticipated the situation we have here today?'

In hindsight, the most remarkable aspect of this conversation is that it took place at all. Today, a meeting of journalists with the leader of the Chinese state and Communist Party would be inconceivable. The reaction of the Chinese media shows how important the dialogue with foreign journalists still was back then: a report about the interview led the TV news bulletin – even topping a report on a meeting between Jiang and the EU commissioner for external relations, Chris Patten. The daily economics paper *Jingji Ribao* and the popular Chinese youth magazine *Zhongguo Qingnian Bao* both carried front-page articles, with photos, on the *Spiegel* visit.

That same year, 2002, Xi Jinping took a big step forward in his career. He became the party leader of Zhejiang Province, on the coast by the East China Sea. He moved, with his daughter and parents-in-law, to the province's capital, Hangzhou; Peng Liyuan stayed in Beijing. Hangzhou is 1,200 kilometres from Beijing and lies 180 kilometres to the south-west of Shanghai. The West Lake and its pagodas, a UNESCO world heritage site, make Hangzhou a popular destination for Chinese tourists. There is even a saying in China: 'In heaven there is paradise, on earth Hangzhou.' For Xi Jinping, however, even more important than its beauty was the fact that Zhejiang Province had a population of 50 million, more than Spain, Canada or Australia.

Here, too, Xi Jinping set out to be whiter than white. Under the pen name 'Zhexin', he published op eds in *Zhejiang Ribao*, the province's largest newspaper. One such contribution, which appeared under the slightly heavy-handed title 'Lifestyle is not a Trifling Matter', set out the future policy direction. The 'decadence' of officials, he wrote, begins with seemingly trivial matters: gluttony, excessive drinking and womanizing – but also gambling and using prostitutes.[22] Prostitution is prohibited in China, but since the beginning of the reform and opening up era, it has again become widespread. Brothels operate under the guise of hairdressers, massage parlours or karaoke bars, and party officials are among the clients. Some of them take mistresses, some even several – an expensive matter that in turn fosters corruption.

It is possible that Xi Jinping objects to such behaviour on moral grounds, but what really motivates him is the fear that the Communist Party will lose touch with the people – and as a result will lose power. According to an old Chinese saying, it is easier to conquer rivers and mountains than to hold on to them. *The Rivers and Mountains* is also the title of a soap opera broadcast in 2003 by CCTV. A rather turgid story about communist fighters and the victory of the revolution in 1949, its title song was sung by Peng Liyuan:

> The ordinary people are the earth,
> the ordinary people are the heaven
> the ordinary people the forever
> Reminder of the Communist Party
> The ordinary people are the mountains,
> the ordinary people are the ocean
> the ordinary people the resource
> of the life of the Communist Party.[23]

Peng Liyuan made the worries of ordinary people her focus. The Chinese Ministry of Health appointed her as an ambassador for education about AIDS, and she campaigned against the stigmatization of children who had received contaminated blood transfusions because of illegal blood sales. Together with the actor Jackie Chan, she promoted the use of condoms, which had previously been something of a taboo.

The folk singer became the international face of China long before her husband. She performed in many countries, for instance at the Avery Fisher Hall (today the David Geffen Hall) in New York's Lincoln Center, and at the Vienna State Opera. When touring abroad, she wears traditional costume, while at many concerts in China she dons the uniform of the People's Liberation Army, in which she holds the rank of major general. She also speaks out about healthcare on the world stage: since 2011, she has been the WHO's Goodwill Ambassador for Tuberculosis and HIV/AIDS.[24]

The leader of the Communist Party since 2002 and president of China since 2003 was Hu Jintao, a colourless bureaucrat rather than a captivating character. Like his predecessor, Jiang Zemin, Hu did not want to be the focus of a personal cult like the one that developed around Mao. But appearing lacklustre can also be a threat to the Communist Party.

Hu Jintao's time in office was limited to ten years, and after a while it became necessary to line up a successor. His closest colleagues, the members of the politburo, were the same age as he was. In any case, the leadership did not want another high-ranking bureaucrat. They had grander ambitions. Ai Weiwei, whose father, Ai Qing, had lived with Mao, Deng Xiaoping and Xi Zhongxun in the guerrillas' headquarters at Yan'an, knows how the minds of the founding generation of the People's Republic of China work. For them, Jiang Zemin and Hu Jintao were merely transitional figures. 'During the democracy movement in 1989, the old comrades told themselves: if we do not choose our successors very carefully, someone will dig our graves,' Ai Weiwei told us. While no one can dodge the grave, 'here what is at stake is the highest Chinese value: longevity. Blood relations are more important than ideology. Thus, they decided that their legacy would be secured only if the next generation of leaders was made up of their children.' It was against this background that Xi Jinping appeared on the shortlist. But, of course, being a member of the 'red aristocracy' is not enough; relevant experience is equally important. The old guard thus looked to those one rung below them in the hierarchy: who was doing a good job at leading one of the provinces?

Xi Jinping was the party leader in Zhejiang, where in 2006 the economy grew by 13.6 per cent. Clark Randt, the US ambassador in China, invited Xi to his residence for dinner. Afterwards, he sent a secret dispatch to Washington: 'Zhejiang Province Communist Party Secretary Xi Jinping, a contender to succeed President Hu Jintao in 2012/2013, describes Zhejiang as a driving force behind national economic growth. Zhejiang ranks high for income, low for income disparities.' Xi also admitted to being a fan of Hollywood films, for instance Steven Spielberg's *Saving Private Ryan*, and said that some Chinese directors neglected the values they should promote.[25]

It was not only film directors who were out of touch with Chinese values. In August 2006, the central party committee sent 100 investigators to Shanghai. They set up camp in the Hengshan Moller Villa Hotel – people were told it was 'closed for renovation.' One month later, Chen Liangyu, the chair of the Communist Party in Shanghai and member of the central politburo, was removed from power. In July 2007 he was arrested, and in April 2008 sentenced to eighteen years in prison.

How did it come to this? Chen had been embezzling money from the city's pension fund, which was worth about a billion euros, and had used the money to pay friends in business over the odds for various projects, including a motorway between Shanghai and Hangzhou. The friends then returned a share of the profits to Chen. He also accepted bribes worth 270,000 euros, mostly in connection with building projects. He abused his power to manipulate the stock exchange. He was also charged with 'promoting the economic interests of illegal entrepreneurs.' On his orders, Shanghai sold large areas of land to his brother, who then sold them on for ten times the price he had paid. Officials in China are paid only a modest salary, but Chen had the equivalent of 65 million euros in his bank account. He had eleven mistresses, some of whom lived in villas provided by a property tycoon. He also gave hotel employees positions in the city administration in return for sex.[26]

In short, Shanghai, one of China's global economic hubs, with its dazzling skyline, urgently needed someone to carry out a proper clean-up operation. In 2007, a new party leader for the city was appointed: Xi Jinping. The appointment made Xi a household name in China – even if still as 'the husband of Peng Liyuan'. For seven months, Xi dealt with the aftermath of the corruption scandal. Then, he was promoted again: the 17th Party Congress of the Communist Party of China elected him as a member of the Politburo Standing Committee. He was now a member of the party leadership's inner circle. In 2008, he became vice-president of China.

On 17 May 2008, an earthquake shook the Chinese province of Sichuan. There were 70,000 casualties, mostly children crushed in the collapse of shoddily built school buildings. Behind the tragedy were corrupt officials who had misappropriated some of the funds intended for the construction of the schools. The disaster was met with an outpouring of solidarity across China. Teenagers flew to Sichuan to work as volunteers, among them Xi Mingze, Xi Jinping and Peng Liyuan's daughter, who had just turned sixteen.[27]

That year, 2008, was also the year of the Olympic Games in Beijing. For the People's Republic of China, it was more than just a sporting event. It was the largest international event ever staged in the country, and an opportunity to present China to the world. It was also an opportunity for Xi Jinping, as head of the organization committee, to show what he could do. The way he went about it offered a taste of things to come – of the direction in which he wanted to steer the country. Accredited journalists were allowed to witness it all up close.

Sixty minutes is a long time if you have to spend it standing in high heels, balancing a thick English dictionary on your head, clutching a sheet of paper between your legs and clenching a pair of chopsticks between your teeth, as a dog might a bone. That was what Lü Yifeng had to do to prepare to be a hostess at the Olympic Summer Games 2008. She and 1,200 other pupils from the Beijing Changping Vocational School had to undergo this tough and painful procedure daily. It was meant to teach them how to look good when conferring the medals. But why the chopsticks between their teeth? 'So that the smile sits straight', Pan Jie, the school's deputy director, gravely explained. On the lapel of her dark blue suit, she wore the red badge of the Communist Party.

'My parents are not allowed to visit me during the training', Lü Yifeng told us. She eventually wants to become a flight attendant. 'But they support me, send me an SMS: "hang on in there!"'

'Do not talk so much about personal matters', the party activist interrupted her. 'The interview is about how much our country is looking forward to the Olympic Games!' But Lü Yifeng did not need to be told that she was looking forward to the games: she genuinely was. She met the requirements set out by the Beijing organization committee, headed by Xi Jinping: 'The hostesses have to be young and beautiful, between 1.68 and 1.78 metres tall, well-built individuals.' Lü's eyes lit up when she spoke about being in the spotlight during the games: 'a unique opportunity in my life', she said.

Half a million visitors were expected for the games – more than had ever visited China before. The games were designed to be a propaganda spectacle of unparalleled proportions. Xi Jinping was worried that observers might draw comparisons with Berlin in 1936. But he was even more afraid of parallels with Seoul in 1988, where, following the Olympic Games, the military dictatorship came to an end. The Communist Party faced a dilemma: it wanted to present China as a happy and free country, but thought that this was possible only if everything was controlled down to the last detail.

As with all Olympic Games, the Olympic Broadcasting Services company was responsible for the coverage of the events. An OBS employee, who had been part of the team in Atlanta, Sydney and Athens, was puzzled: 'This is a first: the Chinese have sent us employees, and no one knows what they are doing. It very much looks as though their job is to switch off the live coverage if there are protests in the audience.' The Chinese leadership feared that 'hostile foreign elements', 'Tibetan separatists' or 'Islamist extremists from Xinjiang Province' might exploit China's moment in the limelight for their own ends. What they feared most, however, were not foreigners or minority groups, but disaffected Chinese citizens.

For instance, there were the thousands living in decaying huts around the Beijing South Railway Station. These were people, from all parts of China, who had had their houses and land taken away, or their wages withheld by corrupt officials, and who now sought justice in the capital. Any foreign journalist walking nearby would be accosted by dozens of petitioners seeking to tell their stories and hand out leaflets detailing their complaints.

When we visited the area, barely a minute went by before a police car arrived. 'Come to the station, verification of your identity,' a policeman yelled at us. A member of the secret service in civilian clothes – leather jacket, shaven-headed – was quickly on the scene to disperse the crowd.

The huts had neither electricity nor running water, but at the station a police officer was quickly able to tap our passport numbers in and bring up our photographs on a screen. The screen also listed all the dates on which we had entered and left China in the past, and the details of when and where we had stayed during our research trips outside of Beijing. Nothing new there. What was novel was the tone. After half an hour, we were joined by a policeman who was responsible 'for matters pertaining to foreigners,' who told us: 'We respect your right to free reporting, but this is a particularly dangerous area. We are worried about your safety.'

In the old days, we would have been accused of 'illegal reporting.' Back then, every interview had to be approved by the foreign affairs offices. In January 2007, however, in preparation for the Olympics, the authorities implemented a special provision that allowed interviews to go ahead as long as the interviewee agreed – a response to the International Olympic Committee's request that journalists be allowed to report freely. The Chinese leadership wanted to present itself as open to the world. But this tiny Beijing Spring was short-lived. On 17 October 2008, after the Olympics ended, the special provisions were revoked.

Even when we were brought to the police station, China was far from free: 'What leaflets did they give you?' the policeman asked. 'But you said you only wanted to verify our identities,' we replied. 'We have photographs,' he snapped back, 'we know everything! Hand us the documents or we search your bag!' When we were finally released, he addressed us in English: 'Please enjoy your stay in Beijing.' Even the police had got the memo about the Olympics.

Although the policeman had told us to 'leave the area immediately,' we went to meet one of the petitioners in his hut. The place was just big enough for three stools and a wooden plank, serving as a bed. Liu Guocai, eighty-one years old, was wearing a green army uniform. He had taken part in the revolution and the Korean War, he said, but was not receiving the increased pension to which such veterans are entitled. When he complained to the local authorities, the employees in the office beat him up, he said. He showed us his crooked thumb. Other petitioners hammered on the door with their fists, wanting to voice their grievances, too, and hopeful that reports in the foreign press might help their cause. They intended to demonstrate during the Olympic Games. 'But most likely', Liu Guocai sighed, 'the police will drive us out of Beijing before the visitors arrive from all over the world.'

Beijing, a metropolis of 17 million people, would be a different place by then. That was what the leadership had decided. Its appearance was already changing. Hutongs, the traditional alleyways lined by one-storey buildings, had mostly disappeared, the rubble taken away by donkey cart. Next to the demolition work, skyscrapers shot up, each with its own underground car park. Twenty new sports facilities were constructed, and ten existing ones renovated. The new Beijing National Stadium, nicknamed the bird's nest, was built – a skeleton of steel whose bent pillars criss-cross like twigs. The weightlifting hall, built out of aluminium, looked like a UFO. The building in which the gymnasts would compete resembled a melting golf ball.

The German architect Ole Scheeren designed the new headquarters of the state broadcaster, CCTV. It looks like a modern Leaning Tower of Pisa; two L-shaped towers rise up 200 metres at oblique angles. With a total floor space of 475,000 square metres, it is the second largest office building in the world, after the Pentagon.

The building is the object of awe and acclaim – but not for those who were forced to leave their houses to make way for it. Qiu Guizhi, a retired nursery school teacher, was visiting her daughter in south China when her neighbours rang her: 'They want to pull down our house.' Qiu immediately returned to Beijing, only to find the windows of her flat broken and her furniture stolen.

She unfurled a banner from the top of her six-storey apartment building: 'Prime Minister, help me!' Despairing, she tried to jump from the building, but policemen stopped her. Then they laid into her: 'You are shameless.' They accused the old-age pensioner of 'disturbing the traffic and public order', and repeatedly asked: 'Who has incited you to do this?' The old lady was imprisoned for ten days, without trial. When she was allowed to return home, she found that her front door had been ripped out and the heating system destroyed. Later, the building was demolished. 'I feel so hurt', she told us with an apathetic expression on her face. 'I don't know what to do.' Some 300,000 Beijing residents had to make room for the Olympic buildings. Force was not involved in all cases. Many of those who were resettled were satisfied with the compensation they received; many preferred to live in skyscrapers.

The Chinese leadership believed that foreigners would be impressed by the elegant new buildings, and that this new face of China would improve the country's standing in the world. But they also worried that the less than elegant behaviour of some Chinese people would make a bad impression.

Take, for example, spitting. Every visitor to Beijing will be familiar with the sound, typical of that metropolis, of throats and noses being noisily cleared and the results being spat out onto the ground. Little notice is taken of others – spittle hits anyone who can't get out of the way fast enough. In the run-up to the games, the government sought to fight this habit with penalties of 50 yuan – roughly five euros – and with appeals to morality. A special administrative body, the 'Commission on Building Spiritual Civilization', was created for the purpose. The head of the commission, Zhang Huiguang, demanded: 'People should spit into a paper handkerchief or bag, and then dispose of it in a bin to conclude the process of spitting in a civilized manner.'

Shangguang Yue, a full-time official at the Communist Youth League, held up a sign at the Fuxingmen underground station: 'Please join me in forming a queue.' Four more activists stood behind her. Some passengers joined them, but most pushed past them on to the train as usual. 'Please queue,' Shangguang shouted, 'civilization begins with little things.' This was how, in the run-up to the Olympics, the residents of Beijing were taught the virtue of queuing – only once a month, though, on the 11th, 'because the figure "11" looks like two people queuing'.

Among the good people of Beijing we found the taxi driver Liu Shaoshang. An article about him helping the police catch a black-market taxi driver was stuck to the sun visor of his Dongfeng Citroën Elysée. Liu was one of the official Olympics chauffeurs who would drive the athletes around during the games.

There were doctors to look after athletes who were racing through Beijing or trained hard in the open air. The city's ozone levels are two or three times higher than WHO limits. 'During the games, the government will prohibit most car traffic,' Liu told us. There had already been test runs: on some days, cars with number plates ending in an even number were not allowed on the roads, and on other days those with number plates ending in an odd number.

Liu was a card-carrying Communist Party member, but had apparently also been exposed to hostile influences. He had picked up a few words of English from his clients. 'Turn right,' he exclaimed, at an English lesson for taxi drivers. Seventy of his colleagues, all dressed in the same dark blue suit that he wore, repeated after him: 'turn right.' Somewhat surprisingly, he added: '"right" as in "human rights".' Very few taxi drivers spoke English, and the government was keen for everyone to be able to say at least a few words.

Li Yang was another English teacher we met. But his lessons were attended by hundreds – sometimes thousands – of people. In the National Stadium, he was trying to get 100,000 Beijing residents in the mood for the Olympics. He calls his method 'Crazy English.' When we saw him, he was teaching 600 students from the Beijing Institute of Petrochemical Technology, located in the Daxing district. 'In earlier days, foreigners were seen as monsters, were treated like extraterrestrials,' Li Yang told us; '2008 will be a turning point for making our country more open, civilized, and stronger.'

The 'Crazy English' method is controversial in China. To an observer, the lessons resemble the mass rallies during Mao's Cultural Revolution. 'Your resistance gives me strength,' the students shouted, and waved a red flyer showing the portrait of their teacher. Li turned up the heat with some nationalistic jingoism. 'During the Olympics I shall go to Tokyo and torture the Japanese with my teaching,' he bragged. The students cheered. 'The German chancellor is stupid, went to meet the Dalai Lama. Who is more important, the Dalai Lama or 1.3 billion Chinese?'

Most signs in Beijing were bilingual even before the games: in Chinese and English. The same was true of many restaurant menus.

Often, however, the translations were wrong or odd. The China Ethnic Culture Park, for example, became 'Racist Park', or a spring chicken became a 'sexually inexperienced chicken'. An expert team was set up to search for such inadvertently humorous cases and correct them. By the time the Olympic Games began, the government decreed, the capital would be free of any misleading English signs or menus.

'Anyone travelling to Beijing in August 2008 will get a wonderful impression of the city', said the journalist Wang Xiaoshan, who worked for the Chinese edition of *Sports Illustrated*. 'But I can tell you right now: everything you will see will be deception. The traffic will flow because half of the cars are not allowed to be used. The air will be fresh and clean because the factories have been temporarily closed. There will not be a single beggar on the streets because they are all locked up. The sky will be blue because rain clouds are shot down by artificial means before they reach the city.'

During the Olympics there would be nothing but smiling faces. Practising for this was taken very seriously. The sheet of paper between Lü Yifeng's legs dropped a few centimetres. You could sense the impending disaster: as she tried to bring it back into the correct position with her hand, the book slipped off her head. Aghast, she opened her mouth, and also lost the chopsticks. At this point, she could only laugh heartily.[28]

When the Olympic Games finally began, everything went as the sports journalist had predicted. The whole world watched: China was back! The developing country spared no expense. The whole event cost 40 billion US dollars – three and a half times as much as the previous games in Athens, which up to that point had been the most expensive in the history of the event. Not quite as many foreign visitors as had been hoped came to Beijing, but there were no major incidents. From China's perspective, the games were a success – not least because the hosts won the most gold medals. In his role as organizer, Xi Jinping excelled.

It seemed there was nothing to stand in the way of his rise to the top. Inland, however, where the Yangtse and Jialing rivers meet, the city of Chongqing had, following some administrative changes, just become a gigantic metropolis with a population of 30 million. According to some calculations, it was now the largest city in the world. Its party leader was Bo Xilai, a 'princeling' like Xi Jinping. Bo Xilai's father, Bo Yibo, was even honoured as one of the 'Eight Elders of the Communist Party of China'. Bo Xilai prohibited commercials on local television, with the breaks instead filled with edifying communist songs to promote solidarity among the people. He founded a movement for 'red songs', and tens of thousands of people filled the city's parks to sing communist battle songs. Bo Xilai sent Mao quotations via text message to the city's 13 million mobile phone users.[29] He was also believed to have grand ambitions to take these initiatives further. This was a man who could pose a threat to Xi Jinping.

While the German media report every twist and turn of US election campaigns, the battle for what is in fact the most powerful position in the world receives little attention. As early as 2009, however, Xi Jinping was filmed addressing Chinese expatriates on a visit to Mexico. He did not follow a script, and threw diplomatic caution to the wind: he gave us his worldview pure and simple. He praised the progress made by China, a country that provides for almost 1.4 billion people. Then he complained: 'There are a few foreigners with full bellies who have nothing better to do than to point the finger at China.' Referring to someone's full belly is quite impolite by Chinese standards. And he continued: 'First, China does not export the revolution; second it does not export hunger or poverty; and third, it does not cause them any headaches. What else do they want?'[30]

4

The Fight against Corruption

Stalin as role model

After Xi Jinping was elected general secretary of the Communist Party of China at its 18th Congress, he made a very clear statement: 'To dismiss the history of the Soviet Union and the Soviet Communist Party, to dismiss Lenin and Stalin, and to dismiss everything else is to engage in historic nihilism, and it confuses our thoughts and undermines the party's organizations on all levels.'[1]

To understand what this sentence actually means, we need to turn to Joseph Stalin for a moment. Many people believe that Stalin was the successor to the founder of the Soviet state, Lenin. This is not entirely correct. Stalin was the general secretary of the Soviet Communist Party from as early as 1922, that is, two years before Lenin died. Back then, however, the general secretary was not the chairman of the party but the manager of its apparatus – much as the general secretaries of political parties in the West are today. Following Lenin's death, Stalin created a total dictatorship of the party apparatus, thus making the party's general secretary, him, the crucial person. This system was later adopted by other communist parties.

Three years after Stalin's death, the new general secretary, Nikita Khrushchev, delivered a secret speech, which lasted five hours, to the 20th Congress of the Communist Party of the Soviet Union. He spoke about Stalin's crimes and renounced his allegiance to the former leader. Stalin's corpse was removed from the mausoleum, and statues of him were toppled overnight. Mao did not want China to follow the

Soviet example in this respect, which was one of the reasons for the rift between China and the Soviet Union. But the Soviet Union also took a long time before it addressed Stalin's legacy openly. The official *Geschichte der Kommunistischen Partei der Sowjetunion* [History of the Communist Party of the Soviet Union] – referred to by communists around the world, in private, as the 'green book of lies' (because of the colour of its cover) – contains only the following hint: 'Stalin, who exaggerated the importance of his own role and merits and believed himself to be infallible, began to abuse the trust of the party, to violate Leninist principles and norms of party work, and to break the law. The personal cult surrounding Stalin, especially during the last years of his life, seriously harmed the cause of the party and state leadership and the development of socialism.'[2]

In 1978, a leading Soviet historian, Dimitry Volkogonov, began to search the archives for material relating to Stalin, but it was only with the implementation of Gorbachev's *perestroika* and *glasnost* policies that he was able to complete his work. In 1990, his biography of Stalin was finally published in the Soviet Union, under the title *Stalin: Triumph and Tragedy*.[3] According to Volkogonov's research, Stalin's political purges resulted in the deaths of between 19 and 22 million people. The victims were sentenced to death and shot for alleged political deviance, died in the labour camps of the Gulag, or belonged to minorities and did not survive the hardship of forced deportation. Stalinism was characterized by a constant search for 'traitors' and 'spies', the aim of which was to mobilize the people and party in an ongoing battle against 'enemies' within.

The first victims were the leaders of the Communist Party – anyone Stalin thought might pose a threat to his personal power. Of the twenty-one members elected to the central committee in 1927, only two were still alive in 1939: Alexandra Kollontai, who was an ambassador and therefore abroad, and Stalin himself. Three members died of natural causes before the mass persecution began. The other sixteen were shot or tortured to death on Stalin's orders.[4]

Stalin was the leader of the Soviet Union that defeated Nazi Germany. But the same Stalin had decapitated the Soviet army immediately before the outbreak of the Second World War by ordering the murder of three out of five marshals; three out of five top-ranking chief commanders; all of the chief commanders of the second rank; fifty out of fifty-seven corps commanders; 154 out of 186 division commanders; all army commissars of first and second rank; twenty-five out of twenty-eight corps commissars; fifty-eight out of sixty-four division commissars; and 401 out of 456 colonels.[5]

The statement that Xi Jinping made about Stalin positioned Xi as a kind of anti-Gorbachev. In his speech commemorating the seventieth anniversary of the October Revolution, Gorbachev said of Stalin: 'It is sometimes claimed that Stalin did not know about many of the cases of arbitrary despotism. Documents we have at our disposal tell us that this is not true. Stalin's guilt, and that of his most trusted allies, who were responsible to the party and the people for the mass reprisals and arbitrary despotism, is large and irredeemable.'

What accounts for Xi Jinping's fascination with a tyrant like Stalin? Stalin was in competition with people like Trotsky and Bukharin – just as Xi found himself in competition with Bo Xilai and others. In the case of Bo Xilai, Xi was lucky: Bo got himself into trouble. On 7 February 2012, police surrounded the US embassy in Chengdu, the capital of Sichuan Province, where Wang Lijun, the police chief of neighbouring Chongqing – and formerly Bo Xilai's most trusted ally – had sought refuge. The two had fallen out with each other and Wang felt threatened by Bo. Allegedly, Wang had asked for political asylum in the US, which, however, had been denied. On this basis, the Chinese authorities charged Wang with corruption and defection. In a bid to reduce his sentence, Wang provided the police with some explosive evidence showing that Bo's wife, Gu Kailai, had poisoned a British businessman called Neil Heywood. According to Wang, Heywood had been managing money for Bo and Gu's son's studies at Harvard University, and a dispute had developed between Heywood and Gu. Just a few months later, Gu was conditionally sentenced to death, but this was later reduced to life imprisonment. Bo Xilai was arrested on charges of impeding the investigation into the murder. He was also accused of accepting bribes from an entrepreneur to the tune of $2.6 million. After a five-day trial at the Intermediate People's Court of Jinan, he was also handed a life sentence.[6]

Xi Jinping had reached his goal – almost. In early September 2012, something unusual happened: all of a sudden, Xi disappeared without a trace. He stood up the US secretary of state, Hillary Clinton, and was also nowhere to be seen at a meeting of the World Economic Forum's Future of Urban Development Initiative, which took place in the important port city of Tianjin, south-east of Beijing.[7] The suspicion was that Xi's opponents were spreading rumours within the party that Li Keqiang, a fellow member of the Politburo Standing Committee and two years Xi's junior, would be China's new leader. Unlike Xi, Li is not a descendant of the 'red aristocracy' but the son of a peasant. Like Xi, he had made his career in the provinces. At forty-three, he became China's youngest governor – in Henan Province – and later party secretary in Liaoning.

We are no strangers to Li Keqiang. One of us met him in 1986 at the headquarters of the Communist Youth League in Qianmen Dongdajie, Beijing. In spartan offices, party officials scribbled away, working on political papers and designing the layout of the league's journals. The meeting with Li Keqiang, then a member of the league's leadership with responsibilities for international relations, had been billed as a 'courtesy reception.'

Two red armchairs dominated the hall in which the meeting took place. An employee asked the 'foreign honorary guest' to sit down in one; the other was reserved for Li Keqiang. At the time, he was just thirty – a rising star not yet known to the wider Chinese public, let alone to citizens of other countries.

Li Keqiang entered the room. He was slim and bespectacled, with a friendly, modest demeanour. As befits an official reception in China, a hostess appeared, handed us tall Chinese teacups, took off their lids and poured hot water on the leaves.

When asked about the influence of the youth league, Li responded without any of the boastfulness that such questions usually elicit from socialist functionaries: 'China is large. There are companies in which 50 per cent of young workers are our members. But there are also remote villages where hardly anyone has heard of the youth league.'

Li Keqiang presented himself as a pragmatist. He spoke mostly about the economy, and very little about ideology: 'Our aim is to satisfy the people's needs better and better. We are developing our policies according to the principle: seek truth from facts. We have left behind the erroneous "Two Whatevers" principle.' (Namely: 'We will resolutely uphold whatever policy decisions Chairman Mao made, and unswervingly follow whatever instructions Chairman Mao gave.') Li set out what the youth league had contributed to the development of the economy: it was responsible for 230 key projects, among them the construction of a hydroelectric power plant near Beijing. Young workers and employees whose achievements stood out were called the 'trailblazers of the New Long March.' Among the trailblazers were a tailoress who had designed a new fashion collection and a pupil who had saved someone from drowning. Mostly, however, they were young workers who had invented new technologies for their companies or had made proposals for improving the organization of the production process. 'We need to work more efficiently', Li Keqiang conceded. 'We are therefore reforming the system for managing and planning the economy.'

Li also mentioned the concrete problems faced by young people: 'Modernization sounds abstract, but it is about making the dreams of young people come true – for example, the dream of owning a moped. Until a few years ago, mopeds were practically unknown in China; now they are everywhere, rattling through the city traffic. A moped costs ten times the average monthly salary, and thus in most cases a whole family has to put their money together if they want to buy one. But still, at least mopeds are now produced and sold in China.'

At the beginning of 2012, putting Li Keqiang's name about as a possible leadership candidate was a last-ditch attempt to stop Xi. The China expert Jörg Wuttke told us: 'Your average Chinese official might have said: "Well, okay, if you think so. Let's distribute the roles differently." But not Xi. He went off and said: "In that case, I'm not going to do anything, and you can explain to the world that you built me up as the future president and then gave the job to someone else." So he disappeared for these two mysterious weeks, and there was speculation about an attempted attack on him or an illness – until the party realized that they could not really explain this to China or the world. And they gave in and, it seems, asked him to come back.'

What was crucial in this situation was not only that Xi Jinping was a 'princeling', the son of a hero of the revolution. That was also true of others, and in any case China is not ruled by a few families, much less by one family, as in the case of North Korea. In China, it is the Communist Party that rules, and there is a complicated process for determining who is in its top cadre. Orthodox communist parties do not have public disputes about policy, nor do they have electoral competitions for top posts – and certainly nothing like the US primary system. The different sections of the cadres – roughly comparable to the personnel departments of large corporations – promote or demote officials on the basis of experience, ability, performance and party training completed. But most of all, promotion depends on good behaviour. Decisions rest, ultimately, with the senior leadership: the lower levels do not elect the higher level; the higher level chooses who it wants to elevate.

The claim is that, in theory, this procedure selects the best candidates on the basis of 'scientific' criteria. In practice, however, communist parties consist of human beings, and so success in one's career in fact depends to a large extent on being a member of certain cliques and having good relationships with certain individuals. Such relationships may have been built up through having worked with someone in the past, but in China the family is also very important. Descent thus plays a major role. Not that fathers would promote their sons – such nepotism is frowned upon in the Communist Party of China as well – but it may well happen that an official supports someone whose uncle once helped him twenty years ago. This is where Xi Jinping's status as a 'princeling' conferred an advantage.

Of course, if you want to become general secretary of the Communist Party, it is not enough to convince just one person. You need the approval of the most powerful members of the politburo, and some well-connected veterans in the party leadership. The Chinese Communist Party officially prohibits factions, but before Xi Jinping came to power, there were said to be two separate groups within the party leadership: the 'Shanghai clique' around the former general secretary and president Jiang Zemin (who was also once the party chief in Shanghai), and the clique associated with the Communist Youth League and Jiang's successor as general secretary and president, Hu Jintao (who was once chairman of the league). Any further detail about claims of a rift between these two groups can only ever be speculation; such conflict always takes place behind closed doors.

That said, what we were told by people with inside knowledge of Chinese politics seems credible: Xi Jinping's 'strength,' they told us, was that he was seen as not belonging to either group. He was seen simply as a diligent and talented party official who was committed to implementing party policy on, for instance, economic development, and who never caused a stir with any trenchant remarks of his own. Everyone in the party leadership therefore thought that they could happily live with Xi.

And so, on 15 November 2012, Xi Jinping was elected general secretary of the Communist Party of China. He was just fifty-nine: relatively young for a person in this position. He was also the first party chairman to have been born after the foundation of the People's Republic of China. On the same day, he also became chairman of the Central Military Commission, making him commander-in-chief of the world's largest army. On 14 March 2013, he took on the office of president of the republic, while Li Keqiang became prime minister, the second most powerful position in the Chinese hierarchy.

The party leaders who installed Xi Jinping underestimated him, however, just as many foreign observers did. After he assumed office, it soon became clear that he was not just a grey suit but someone who was determined to extend his power – and to realize his vision of China's future.

As president of the EU Chamber of Commerce in China, Jörg Wuttke is one of the few German businessmen who have met Xi Jinping in person. 'The man is charismatic, there's no two ways about it,' he told us. 'He has aura, looks you straight in the eyes. You get the impression that he is focusing on you. This is not someone who shakes hands and then moves on to greet the next person, but someone who will actually remember a face. He is different from other Chinese leaders. Xi speaks little at such meetings. He is someone who unsettles people by always being just a tad calmer and cooler. He is cold-blooded.'

Sigmar Gabriel once sat next to Xi Jinping at a banquet hosted by the government of North Rhine-Westphalia, as his 'dinner partner, so to speak.' At first, their conversation had been stilted, Gabriel said. 'You ask him a question; he answers. Then you think of another question, and another one, all very formulaic.' All this changed very quickly when Gabriel pulled out a football and football scarf that he had received as a present, 'a one-off, a scarf with all the Ruhr area clubs on it, something that is normally impossible – to get them all on one scarf.' Gabriel knew that Xi was a serious football fan. 'From this moment on, it was a relaxed evening. You could talk about all sorts of things – family, children. He was a different person.'

From then on, when Gabriel met Xi in Beijing, the German minister was able to follow up on their earlier conversation – but it was never quite as relaxed again. When previous general secretaries had been in office, Gabriel and other German ministers had been able to meet with representatives of non-governmental organizations, such as environmental activists and lawyers. 'In the case of Xi,' Gabriel explained, 'there were two occasions when we were told such additional meetings would not be possible if I was also meeting Xi on the same day. We were just about able to shift the meetings to the day after my meeting with him, but sometimes the participants cancelled – they had had visitors. One disappeared afterwards, and was released only because the chancellery intervened. Xi Jinping has very much toughened things up.' There is a reason for this, as Gabriel knows well from his conversations with Xi: 'From the party's perspective, its power is being threatened by the dissatisfaction of the emerging middle classes, which is mainly caused by two developments: first, rampant corruption, and second environmental pollution, which is so serious that people are becoming concerned about their health.' Xi combined the fight against corruption with the removal of his competitors in the party. China's Communist Party is not a monolithic bloc. As in all large organizations, the thirst for power and career ambitions lead to competition. There are personal animosities and divergent political opinions, even if Chinese politicians rarely mention them in public.

It was not just that Xi Jinping had a specific opponent, Bo Xilai, whom he wanted to eliminate. In his first speech as general secretary, he said: 'Our Party is a Marxist party, the organization of which relies on revolutionary ideals and strict discipline.' The formulation calls to mind the song by the German communist Louis Fürnberg, 'Die Partei hat immer recht' [The party is always right]: 'Thus from the spirit of Lenin, / It grows, welded by Stalin / The party – the party – the party.' Xi Jinping's speech continued: 'This has always been our Party's fine tradition and unique advantage.'[8]

For Xi, there was a threat to this 'fine tradition': 'Some Party officials have become demoralized, and their faith has been shaken. Their philosophy of life is to indulge themselves in pleasure-seeking,' he complained. 'Some have abandoned their ideals in favor of material comforts, vulgar amusements, revelry, drinking and a life of luxury.' According to Xi, this threatened not only morality but, most of all, power: 'I give these examples to warn all Party members. If we allow these problems to spread like weeds, the consequences will be disastrous, and the tragedy of *Farewell My Concubine*, which Mao Zedong used as a metaphor for losing power, may come true.'[9] This is a reference to a story set in the latter years of the Qin Dynasty (221–206 BC), in which the arrogant warlord Xiang Yu and his concubine commit suicide after being under siege by enemy forces.

China is, indeed, plagued by corruption. There are two possible ways of combating it: either a free press to keep an eye on the dealings of the powerful, combined with independent courts to try suspects in accordance with the rule of law; or the iron fist of dictatorship. Xi Jinping took the latter route. The China correspondent of *Süddeutsche Zeitung*, Kai Strittmatter, followed the early years of Xi Jinping's leadership. Back then, he reported: 'Since the summer of 2013, the state broadcaster CCTV (China Central Television) has presented its viewers with a never-ending stream of arrested or previously disappeared individuals who, in most cases straight out of prison, play the part of the remorseful sinner who confesses his wrongdoings – long before they have seen a lawyer, never mind the inside of a courtroom.'

Here, Xi Jinping has an advantage over his role model Stalin. Stalin could send only a few model workers to attend his show trials of 'enemy agents' and 'Trotskyists'; Xi can use television to reach every living room in China. 'The exhibition of these individuals fits with the pattern of increasing repression we have seen since Xi Jinping took office. Each televised confession is contextualized by the propaganda machinery so that it serves a higher political agenda,' Strittmatter writes. 'And thus we see the famous liberal blogger, the critical publisher and the Swedish NGO employee who has been supporting human rights lawyers. They all present themselves as ready to repent, and they humbly confess, often through tears, to their "criminal" activities, denounce their former colleagues, reveal their backers in hostile foreign countries, thank the party for its benevolence and ask to be given a second chance.'[10]

Stalin's victims were tortured until they confessed in court to their 'counter-revolutionary crimes' and begged the party to shoot them. The communist leadership then used these 'confessions' to justify the terror, against criticism coming from communists and communist sympathizers, both at home and abroad. Xi Jinping's argument is similar: 'While some officials involved in serious cases were being investigated by the Central Committee, some high-ranking officials complained in private that those involved had done a lot of good work and should not be investigated for such tiny mistakes. Is that true? Reading the confessions of those violators, we can conclude none of them was wrongfully accused.'[11]

The German communists who fled the Nazis and emigrated to Moscow lived in Hotel Lux in Gorky Street (today known again as Tverskaya Street), near the Kremlin. When many of them were threatened with arrest during Stalin's purges, they jumped to their deaths – not onto the street in front of the hotel, though, but out of the windows onto the hotel's courtyard, in order 'not to cause disquiet among the Soviet population.' Here, too, there are parallels with today's China. According to a study by the Institute of Psychology of the Chinese Academy of Sciences, the rate of suicide among officials doubled in the first four years of Xi Jinping's leadership compared to the four years before. Between 2009 and 2016, 140 officials jumped to their deaths, forty-four hung themselves, twenty-six poisoned themselves, and six slit their wrists.[12]

Jörg Wuttke is all too familiar with such tragedies: 'A friend of mine, the party's deputy secretary in Chongqing, jumped out of the window of a skyscraper at a meeting of the Central Committee in October 2019. He was killed instantly, of course. Presumably it all happened with Xi Jinping watching,' he told us. 'Recently, many people simply disappeared. What we are seeing is a proper vendetta.'

Since 2012, 1.5 million Chinese officials have been punished, among them seven from the senior leadership (that is, members of the politburo or ministers) and two dozen high-ranking generals. Two leading officials were sentenced to death.[13] Xi Jinping's popularity as the 'tough man' who has at long last cleaned out the Augean Stables is owed to a campaign against corruption that introduced severe measures to tackle bribery and the abuse of office. But it is almost impossible to prove which individuals are truly guilty, for the trials do not proceed in accordance with the rule of law. In China, the conviction rate is higher than 99 per cent – suspects are almost never acquitted.[14]

The show trials follow the logic of an old Chinese saying: 'Kill the chicken to scare the monkey.' The message is: no one is beyond the reach of the party. Not even the party officials themselves – and certainly not lawyers who care about human rights. Since 2015, lawyers have been subject to a wave of arrests. 'CCTV generously peppered its short clips with ample doses of sex and character assassination. These short sensationalist reports transformed the lawyers, who often worked for ordinary people – most of them victims of arbitrary administrative decisions – into dissolute, money-grubbing cheats. The head of a legal office, Zhou Xifeng, for instance, was revealed to have kept six mistresses at the same time, all meticulously listed on a chart.'[15]

The use of language can be revealing. A demand Xi Jinping frequently issues in his public speeches is: 'We should continue to catch "tigers" as well as "flies".'[16] The Beijing-based Foreign Language Press, which also publishes the English versions of Xi's speeches, explains the remark in a note as follows: 'Referring to senior and junior officials guilty of corruption.'[17] They are all, in any case, animals to be hunted down, and presumably shot.

The rule of the party is unassailable but, as with Stalin, persecution begins inside the party at the very moment someone tries to form a breakaway ideological group. 'We need to unite with the great majority, rather than differentiate people in light of personal preference and forge any form of factions,' says Xi Jinping.[18] Even private meetings among officials are eyed with suspicion: 'Some officials group together as fellow townsmen or alumni,' Xi notices. 'Such activities, though seemingly casual, are not healthy. In reality, they have ulterior motives – their real intention is to form a kind of fraternity, in which members may support each other and collude when necessary.'[19]

At first glance, such remarks might seem to be aimed at corruption and wheeling and dealing, but Xi Jinping goes on to condemn any criticism of the senior party leadership – even in the form of jokes. 'Actually, they merely make inappropriate jokes, spread hearsay, or engage in gossip. Some like to disseminate falsehoods through the internet, or gather with their "inmates" to make groundless criticisms of the CPC Central Committee's policies.'[20] Foreign contacts or a divorce can also put someone in danger: 'Some do not report the fact that their children or spouses have stayed abroad for a long time,' Xi Jinping notes disapprovingly. 'Some do not report major changes in their family situation. Even after they have been divorced or remarried for years, the Party organization is still kept in the dark.'[21]

Once the henchmen are let loose, they want to show the ruler how successful they are. When Stalin established quotas for the number of 'enemies' to be arrested in each region, and for how many should be executed, local leaders asked for the quotas to be increased.[22] A similar competition for Xi Jinping's favour can be observed in China: in 2017, the leadership of Zhejiang Province reported an 83 per cent rise in arrests for corruption. The island of Hainan even reported a ten-fold increase.[23]

Given how eager Xi is to fight corruption, we might ask how he himself fares in this respect. One piece of evidence is as follows. In 2014, his daughter, Xi Mingze, completed her degree in psychology and English at Harvard University.[24] A Chinese official's salary is not enough to afford Harvard tuition fees, so, either Xi Jinping has another source of money, or he used his connections to Chinese grant-awarding institutions. Both possibilities would contradict the principles he advocates. Of course, there is a third possibility: that Xi Mingze was accepted at Harvard because she was among the most qualified candidates, and her background was just a coincidence. Her fellow students reported that she studied diligently and did not flaunt her status. In that regard, she differs from Bo Guagua, the son of Xi's competitor Bo Xilai, who drove a Porsche and invited Jackie Chan to a private party.[25]

A bigger headache for Xi Jinping, however, was the dealings of his sister and brother-in-law. His sister Qi Qiaoqiao was given her mother's surname at birth, which is unusual in China and, with her husband, she amassed hundreds of millions of dollars.[26] According to Xi Jinping's official 'profile,' he warned friends and relatives not to engage in any business that related to his own work. He also said that, should they exploit his name for private gain, he 'would be ruthless'.[27]

The billionaire Xiao Jianhua bought some of the assets belonging to Xi Jinping's family from Xi's sister and her husband. And he was open about the fact. He knew a lot – possibly too much. In January 2017, he was staying in his suite overlooking Hong Kong harbour at the luxury Four Seasons Hotel. He was kidnapped, and brought to mainland China. He has not been seen since.[28]

5

Persecuted by Mao – Revered Like Mao

Xi's relationship with China's towering father figure

Mao was a monster – and Xi Jinping knows it. Under Mao, he and his relatives were persecuted, locked up, tortured. His half-sister was driven to suicide. Some in China say that responsibility for the worst crimes of the Cultural Revolution lies not with Mao but with his wife, Jiang Qing, and the three other members of the so-called 'Gang of Four'. But Xi Jinping is clever enough not to repeat this absurd attempt to excuse Mao. Nor does he repeat the well-known statement of the reformist Deng Xiaoping, that 'Mao was seventy percent right and thirty percent wrong', although official Chinese media continue to quote it.[1] We should add that high-ranking Chinese officials repeatedly told us that what Deng wanted to say was the reverse: Mao had been 70 per cent wrong and 30 per cent right. But that could have shaken the people's belief in the party.

It is 9 September 1976. At Sichuan University in Chengdu, lectures are abruptly cancelled. All students are expected to meet at 3 p.m. For Jung Chang, who is studying English, this is nothing unusual; it happens all the time these days. At 3 p.m. the party secretary addresses the students, a pained expression on her face. From the crackling loudspeakers, her halting voice fills the hall: 'Our great leader, chairman Mao, our adorable eminence. ...' At this point, everyone knows, and starts to sob. Mao is dead.

Jung Chang later became famous around the world as the author of the bestseller *Wild Swans*, a family history of three generations, her grandmother's, her mother's and her own, spanning the period from imperial China to the present day. Following *Wild Swans*, she spent twelve years researching Mao Zedong's life, alongside her husband, Jon Halliday. The two interviewed hundreds of contemporary witnesses in China and abroad, and talked to people who had met Mao, among them members of his family, friends and colleagues in the party leadership. They scoured archives in ten countries. The result was the most comprehensive biography of Mao ever written.[2]

Perhaps the most surprising result of their extensive research is that almost nothing of what is generally said about Mao is correct. Many people think, for instance, that Mao fought against the Japanese occupation, but the war against Japan was led mostly by the nationalist Kuomintang, Mao's opponents who later fled to Taiwan. In 1937, Mao ordered his soldiers to stay out of the battles against the Japanese invaders and to wait until the Japanese had weakened the Kuomintang: 'When, after the war, some Japanese visitors apologized to him for Japan having invaded China, he told them: "I would rather thank the Japanese warlords." Without them occupying much of China, "we would still be in the mountains today".'[3]

The Communist Party leaders sermonize about Mao liberating the peasantry. Chang and Halliday's book is full of horrific stories about this 'liberation', stories that almost defy belief. Chang interviewed not only victims but also some of Mao's closest comrades in arms, whom the Chinese government warned not to speak with the dissident author. 'But', she told us, 'they yearned to tell the truth.' A party official who was involved in the 'liberation war' described to her what really happened. In the Yan'an region, Red Army soldiers knocked at the door of every hut and asked the peasants to provide grain for the revolutionary troops fighting the civil war. A young mother, whimpering, replied that she did not have any. Mao's troops took her and three others, and hung them from their wrists: 'They asked her where she had hidden the grain ... I knew she did not have the grain. But they insisted she did and beat her ... Her blouse was stripped off. She had just had a baby and her milk was dripping. The baby was crying and crawling on the ground, trying to lick up the milk.' In other areas, 'entire families from the youngest to the oldest were killed. Babies, still on milk, grabbed and torn apart at the limbs or just thrown into a well.' Mao saw such violence, and approved of it.[4]

After his victory, Mao continued his rule in exactly the same fashion. During the 'Great Leap Forward', between 1958 and 1961, 45 million people starved to death: this was the worst famine in human history.[5] Mao forced the peasants to melt down their ploughs and pots in order to build small 'steel works'; that much was known, but it is only part of the truth. Chang and Halliday provide evidence that Mao extorted grain and meat from the peasants, exchanging it with the Soviet Union and other socialist countries for details of how to build an atomic bomb: 'During the two critical years 1958–59, grain exports alone, almost exactly 7 million tons, would have provided the equivalent of over 840 calories per day for 38 million people – the difference between life and death.'[6]

The GDR was among the countries to benefit from the exports. They made it possible to end food rationing in 1958, while Chinese peasants were living off grass and leaves. Whole villages perished. '"Deaths have benefits", Mao told the top echelon on 9 December 1958. "They can fertilise the ground."'[7] Back then, many in the West believed that, unlike India, China had successfully eradicated hunger. Mao told fairy tales about the great transformation to his admirers, such as the US journalist Edgar Snow, who happily spread the stories in his 1937 *Red Star over China*. The romanticization of revolution became mixed up with the exoticization of the Far East – ignorance with political cunning. The footballer Paul Breitner made a show of reading the Little Red Book, the Mao bible, during training sessions for the German national team. The philosopher Jean-Paul Sartre praised Mao's 'revolutionary violence' as 'immediately and profoundly moral.'[8] The US secretary of state Henry Kissinger called Mao and his inner circle 'a group of monks ... who have ... preserved their revolutionary purity.'[9]

Given this enthusiastic evaluation, it is not surprising that Kissinger is among those who have criticized Chang and Halliday's biography. He said it was 'grotesque that it presents Mao as a man without any qualities.' In his own book *On China*, he calls it 'one-sided but often thought-provoking.' Chang and Halliday's book is controversial among China experts. Critics argue that it presents Mao's private life in an exclusively negative light and claims his visions for China were disingenuous. The facts mentioned above, however, are not controversial. 'Chang and Halliday's work is destined to become a classic, but it's a flawed classic', wrote *The Washington Post*'s critic John Pomfret, for many years a China correspondent and then a senior Fulbright scholar in China. 'Nonetheless, their central point – that Mao was a monster and should be remembered as one of history's great villains – is right on the money.'[10]

No one has the courage to bury Mao. His corpse is still laid out under crystal glass in Beijing, and people queue for hours to pay their last respects. Xi Jinping, too, paid a visit, bowing three times before him. A portrait of Mao, six and a half metres tall and five metres wide, still hangs resplendent at the Gate of Heavenly Peace. At a party congress, Xi explained: 'If we had completely abandoned Mao, the way the Soviet Union abandoned Stalin, we would no longer be in power today.'[11] And just so that no one else can abandon him either, China's National People's Congress of 2018 passed a law that threatens to punish anyone who 'insults or defames heroes and martyrs' of communism – that is, anyone who questions the official historical record.[12]

It looks like a contradiction, and it is: Mao persecuted and humiliated Xi Jinping's father and Xi Jinping himself, yet Xi Jinping clings to Mao's policies, and even intensifies them. This comes as no surprise to the Chinese artist Ai Weiwei, who also grew up in these circles: 'First thing I can say is he believes in and trusts the system. Like my father, who was deeply victimized by the Communist Party, but I think he never really openly criticized the Communist Party, even if he openly criticized many, many tactics or the way they were doing things. In China, we don't have pure communists, so anybody in China still works in the way of this Confucian and feudalistic society. And this provides many principles that every Chinese person would respect – it doesn't matter whether it's under capitalism or whatever. So in that sense I think Xi still feels the power of China's culture, with the goal of the nation to survive. I think that's much more important than the failure of his father's generation.'[13]

It is also striking that Xi rarely talks about Mao. From time to time, he quotes some of his wise sayings, as if he were an old philosopher, but there are no songs of praise for Mao. The personality cult around Mao is gradually being replaced with a personality cult around Xi Jinping. At junctions, there are advertising boards displaying his oversized portrait. Department stores sell plates with his face on them. There are songs that refer to him as 'Xi Dada' (literally: 'Xi bigbig', the equivalent of 'Big Daddy Xi' or 'Uncle Xi'), and his wife is called 'Peng Mama.' There are even rap songs and cartoons that pay homage to him.[14]

Many Chinese people are genuinely enthusiastic about Xi Jinping. They support his fight against corruption. They like the fact that he is the first Chinese president to appear in public with his wife, who also happens to be very friendly and attractive. And they are astounded by television footage showing the party leader, in simple clothes, eating in an even simpler roadside restaurant – unheard of! It is, of course, all just a show: 'figures like Xi live in a world where they never take a plane with ordinary people, or travel by car along roads that have not first been swept of other travellers by a security detail.'[15]

Still, the state takes pains to ensure that such pictures have the desired effect. In 2017, Jiangxi Province, which has a relatively high proportion of Christians, started a campaign under the slogan: 'Turning religious believers into party believers.' In a Catholic church in the city of Ji'an, the picture of the Virgin Mary was replaced with a portrait of Xi Jinping. In the district of Yugan, the authorities forced the 600 residents of a village to replace pictures of Jesus with pictures of Xi.[16] Are these just the bizarre practices of a few far-flung provinces? Since October 2018, students at Chinese universities have had to take compulsory courses on 'Xi Jinping Thought.'[17]

Mao had his Little Red Book: *Quotations from Chairman Mao Tse-Tung*. Xi Jinping has something even better – a little red smartphone app. When it was launched in 2019, it quickly racked up more downloads than any other app in China. Users have access

> not only to the latest speeches and reflections of the chairman. They can also study the party's press publications, and download the classic texts of Marxism and revolutionary films; they can chat with each other and send each other 'red envelopes' containing monetary gifts. But most importantly – and this is the app's genius – they can collect points: for every Xi essay that they read, the users get a point. They also get a point

> for every video they watch. But they get ten times as many points for taking thirty minutes of 'Xi time' (one of the apps rubrics) or answering a Xi quiz correctly. And between 6 and 8.30 in the morning, and after 8 in the evening, all points count double. Long gone are the days when absent-minded party members watched the evening news without really listening, or consigned the *People's Daily* to the bin unread. Now, the smartphone registers every minute the citizen dedicates to the party cause – and every paragraph that they read.[18]

'Thoughts are free' is so yesterday. Today, thoughts are inside the digital cage.

Some of Xi's honorary titles are telling: the party's Central Committee calls him the 'great helmsman' and the 'people's leader', names that were hitherto used only for Mao.[19] Nor was such a personality cult created around any of the other general secretaries and presidents after Mao. People from all over China go on pilgrimages to the village of Liangjiahe, in Shaanxi Province, to visit the cave in which Xi Jinping lived as a young man. In 2017, 'Xi Jinping Thought' became part of the Communist Party's constitution, and in 2018 part of the constitution of China itself. Now, anyone who criticizes Xi is – in legal terms – an enemy of the party and the state.

After Mao's death, to prevent any more abuses of power, the maximum time in office for a head of state was limited to two five-year terms. In 2014, Xi Jinping still spoke of that change as 'decisive progress': 'We have replaced the life-long tenure of officials with limited terms.'[20] This rule, however, no longer applies to Xi. In March 2018, China's National People's Congress removed the limitation for Xi Jinping, who can therefore remain in power until the end of his life – like an emperor.

One might argue that the same is true, *de jure*, for the German chancellor, and some of them – for instance Konrad Adenauer, Helmut Kohl and Angela Merkel, who were in office for fourteen, sixteen and sixteen years, respectively – certainly made good use of this fact. However, the German chancellor has far less power than the Chinese leader, whereas Xi Jinping is more powerful than even the US president, who, for good reason, is limited to two four-year terms. Further, history has shown that in Germany even the most stubborn top politicians can eventually be ousted. But who would be brave enough to try to remove Xi Jinping? He could conceivably leave only of his own accord. However, as Richard McGregor, for many years correspondent in China for the *Financial Times*, points out, Xi's tough crackdown on critics and corrupt officials means that it is highly unlikely he will ever leave willingly: 'If he were to ever step down he knows that he, or at least his family and his close allies, would be vulnerable to being locked up by whomever came after him.'[21]

In November 2021, Xi Jinping joined the pantheon of great Chinese leaders. It was only the third time that the Communist Party's Central Committee had passed a resolution about the party's own history. The official English translation of its title is: 'Resolution of the CPC Central Committee on the Major Achievements and Historical Experience of the Party over the Past Century'. The first resolution was passed in 1945, when Mao Zedong declared himself the revolutionary with the 'correct political line'. In the second resolution, in 1981, Deng Xiaoping cautiously hinted at the crimes committed by Mao during the Cultural Revolution. The resolution of November 2021 speaks about 'resolutely upholding Comrade Xi Jinping's core position on the Party Central Committee and in the Party as a whole', and declares: 'We must educate our people with Xi Jinping Thought on Socialism with Chinese Characteristics for a New Era.' To that end, 'Party members and officials should be educated and guided to have firm belief in Xi Jinping Thought on Socialism with Chinese Characteristics for a New Era and to practice it faithfully.'[22] The document mentions Xi's predecessors Jiang Zemin and Hu Jintao only once, the great reformer Deng Xiaoping, who was responsible for the economic transformation of China and made it a rich country, six times, and Mao Zedong eighteen times. And Xi Jinping? Twenty-four times. The resolution does not put Xi on a par with Mao – it elevates him above Mao. Mao always had to contend with rivals in the party. Plainly, there are none who rival Xi today.

Xi Jinping is not just the new Mao – he has more power than Mao ever did. How does he use it? What are his aims at home and abroad?

6

Confucianism and Communism

How to combine what does not belong together

If there is one point on which Mao and Xi differ, it is in their attitudes to Confucius, and thus to traditional Chinese culture. In 1958, Mao proudly declared: 'The first emperor of the Qin dynasty only buried 460 scholars alive, while we've buried 46,000.'[1] Xi Jinping's speeches, by contrast, frequently contain references to Confucius, as for instance when Xi warned the members of the Central Committee: 'Confucius once said: "People will obey you if you promote righteous men and suppress evil men. And they will disobey you if you do the contrary."'[2]

Who was Confucius? His real name was Kong Qiu, and he was the extramarital child of an impoverished seventy-year-old aristocrat and his sixteen-year-old concubine. The boy was born 551 years before Christ, and half a century before Rome became a republic. His birthplace was Qufu, a city in what was then the state of Lu and which is today part of Shandong Province. His wisdom earned him the name Kong Fuzi: 'Master Kong.' This name was later translated into Latin by Jesuit priests who came to China as missionaries in the seventeenth century, and the pronunciation of the Latin name in the West produced the familiar 'Confucius.'

Confucius's father died when he was two years old. His father's wives rejected the boy, and he and his mother were not allowed to attend the father's funeral. Nor did they get any support from the family. They went hungry. The child had to work, clean and run errands. It is said that he was ugly, and had a misshapen head, but he was a diligent pupil. Confucius's mother died when he was twenty-two, and Confucius had to struggle to find out where his father had been buried, so that his mother could be buried with him, as tradition demanded. He had married at nineteen, but it seems not to have been a happy marriage. Confucius – who stood 1.8 metres tall, a veritable giant at the time – sought fulfilment in education. His childhood experience taught him that education, not family background, should be the measure of all things. He put forward a revolutionary thought: 'In teaching there should be no distinction of classes.'[3]

When he founded his own school, Confucius adhered to this principle. He accepted everyone as his pupil, even if he offered no more than 'a bundle of dried meat', as it says in Analects 7.7.[4] He taught writing, arithmetic and music, and also archery and chariot riding. But most of all, he instructed pupils in the rituals and rules that should guide behaviour. This instruction was not religious or based on appeals to the supernatural. Rather, he explained his ideas with reference to ordinary human life. His educational institution developed into a school of thought, and became the seed for an intellectual tradition. More and more students flocked to Confucius – eventually there were some 3,000, it is said. Half a century before Jesus Christ, he preached brotherly love, telling his followers: 'Do not impose on others what you would not wish for yourself.'[5] More than 2,000 years later, Kant formulated a similar idea in the form of his slightly more convoluted categorical imperative: 'So act that the maxim of your will could always hold at the same time as a principle in a giving of universal law.'[6]

Confucius was the pioneer of reason and enlightenment in the Far East. He developed practical ideas for civilized social life. They were simple suggestions, and their simplicity was their strength: 'The Master said, "Those who are not human-hearted can neither stay long in privation nor stay long in enjoyment. Those who are human-hearted are at ease in human-heartedness, and those who are wise profit from human-heartedness."'[7] Or: 'The Master said, "Exemplary persons are ashamed of letting their speech outpace their action."'[8] Some of Confucius's formulations could have come straight out of a modern self-help book: 'If you set a higher expectation on yourself and demand little from others, you will keep resentment away.'[9]

Like Jesus and Socrates, Confucius did not write his teachings down. His disciples noted down what he said, preserving it for posterity. They brought an order to his remarks. Confucius's main work is accordingly called *Lunyu*: 'ordered words.' It is a collection of quotations from the master, referred to in English as the *Analects of Confucius*. Confucius believed that, in order to live in harmony with each other, people must have humanity (*ren*). They must be just (*yi*), look after their parents and obey their superiors (*xiao*). They must also follow the proven rituals (*li*).

In 2009, Xi Jinping, then China's vice-president, opened the Frankfurt Book Fair together with Angela Merkel. China was the guest of honour. Xi headed a delegation of 2,000 authors and publishers. The previous year's guest of honour, Turkey, had sent a delegation only half that size. The mountain of 10,000 books that the Chinese delegation brought with them was intended as a symbol of China's cultural greatness. But the megalomania of the Chinese officials was tinged with fear. When two critical authors appeared at an event in the lead-up to the fair, the officials left the room.

Among the delegates was Yu Dan, dean of the faculty of education at Beijing Normal University. She was born in 1965, and studied classical Chinese literature before completing a doctorate in film and TV studies – a fine academic background for her current role as a popstar of Confucianism. Her book *Confucius from the Heart* presents the teachings of the ancient philosopher in comprehensible, up-to-date language. The book has sold more than 10 million copies in China – pirate copies included.

Yu Dan's lecture series on Confucius, broadcast by CCTV 10, was a hit with audiences and achieved exceptional ratings. 'People are looking for orientation,' she told us, by way of an explanation for her success. We were sitting in a Beijing tea house. 'Previously everything in our country was strictly controlled; everyone was equally poor. The market economy has opened up new possibilities. But many people feel lost in it.' While the master of the tea ceremony poured water from one vessel into another and back again, Yu Dan asked us about the Munich Hofbräuhaus and Mozart's birthplace in Salzburg. 'I think you might also find something valuable for your soul in Confucius,' she then said. 'After all, we also read your Marx.'

In 1919, the democratic May Fourth Movement demanded that 'Confucius's old curiosity shop' be crushed. Marxism was becoming popular among Chinese intellectuals, who saw in it a modern and scientific worldview. They were convinced by the Marxist critique of imperialism and colonialism. In the Treaty of Versailles, the Western democracies had betrayed China by handing Chinese territories to Japan, Britain and France. The Soviet Union, by contrast, supported China by sending weapons and advisors – to begin with not only to the Communist Party but also to the nationalist Kuomintang. The rebels blamed the backwardness of their country on the philosopher Confucius, for he had preached the importance of hierarchy and stability. For instance, 'Let a ruler be a ruler, a subject be a subject, a father be a father, and a son be a son.'[10] Yu Dan explained what she took to be the reason for Confucius's bad public image: 'The brutal emperor Han Wudi, who ruled between 141 and 87 BC, did something very harmful. He declared Confucianism to be the only true body of teachings and prohibited all other schools of thought. But it is not Confucius's fault that his teachings were abused by later rulers. He demanded self-restraint not only on the side of the subjects, but even more so on the side of rulers. That was later often forgotten.'

There had been criticism of Confucianism before Mao, but the persecution of adherents really began only after Mao came to power – particularly, and especially brutally, when the Cultural Revolution began in 1966. Alleged followers of Confucianism had dunce caps placed on their heads to shame them. Mobs chased intellectuals in the streets, often lynching them. The campaigns became increasingly absurd. Mao started to attack the posthumous reputation of his former deputy Lin Biao, who had been killed when his plane came down in the Mongolian desert. He had been trying to flee to the Soviet Union. In 1974, 'Criticize Confucius and Lin Biao' became the slogan all over China.

'The aim of the Cultural Revolution was to destroy all the evil old values', the sinologist Tilman Spengler told us when we spoke to him in his Berlin apartment – its walls adorned with Chinese ink drawings and calligraphy. 'Despite forty years of socialist dictatorship, Confucianism was definitely the main target in this context.' Many Confucian temples were destroyed. It was a proper socialist plan: they had a target of destroying 90 to 95 per cent of the temples. The Red Guards turned statues into firewood. Confucius represented precisely the kind of evil from which they wanted to liberate society.

The results of the campaign are still visible in Confucius's hometown, Qufu, and in particular in Kong Forest, the cemetery where Confucius's direct descendants are buried. It is twice the size of the city itself – 100,000 trees towering over 100,000 graves. When we visited, we saw three dozen women and men wearing white hoods or caps (in China, white is the colour of mourning) driving to a funeral in an electric bus. These days, the Kongs can bury their relatives peacefully again. Tourists poured through the stone gate, led by guides with little flags and megaphones. Visitors come from mainland China as well as Hong Kong and Taiwan. They take pictures of one another touching a bronze rhinoceros, in the hope that the animal will bring good luck.

Mao sought to eradicate China's Confucian heritage. In 1966, a revolutionary assignment was given to 200 students and lecturers from the very faculty where Yu Dan, the popstar of Confucianism, teaches today. Mao shook hands with Tan Houlan, the leader of the brigade. The Red Guards boarded a train and went to Qufu, a journey of ten hours. In accordance with Mao's orders, they opened Confucius's grave, but there were no mortal remains to be found. Today, people fold their hands in devotion and fall to their knees before the five-metre-tall gravestone.

Back in 1966, the Red Guards compensated for their disappointment by going on an absurd rampage. Wei Jing, an employee of the Historic Conservation Office, shows us the trail of devastation they left behind. They desecrated 2,000 of the graves of Confucius's descendants. There are still split gravestones and broken-off pieces of stone that bear witness to the destruction. 'We now remember this unspeakable story', Wei told us. 'But many people still do not want to touch this period in our country's history, because it was not only cultural treasures that were destroyed. There was also an incitement of hatred for Confucianism. But now the rain has stopped; the sky is clear. The whole world now accepts the ideas of Confucianism, develops them and unfolds them. Here in Qufu, even young children read his works and learn them by heart.'

In the small city of Qufu, the Red Guards tore up 929 historic paintings and burned 2,700 antique books. In the temple dedicated to Confucius, they toppled his statue, tied a rope around the neck and pulled it through the streets, jeering all the way.

The people of Qufu were treated even worse by the Red Guards. Kong Jihuan moved slowly in front of a one-storey concrete building, on which some youths had scribbled their mobile phone numbers. The eighty-one-year-old practises Qigong, a traditional mixture of meditation and movement, in the hope that it will help him forget the memories that still keep him awake at night. 'I don't know how I survived it,' he told us. 'They kept beating me with their hands, with boards, rods and chairs.' Kong Jihuan spent months in hospital. All because he is a sixty-ninth-generation descendant of Confucius.

The battle against Confucianism in Qufu was waged by communists. That today's communist leader, Xi Jinping, visited the memorials in Qufu in 2013 – the first leader of the Communist Party to do so – therefore seems almost a contradiction. During his visit, Xi described Confucius and his teachings as an 'important part of our traditional culture,' and added: 'I come here to mark this fact.'[11] He recommended that people read Confucius's *Analects*. Then he walked through the 'Gate of Respect for the Saint,' which had traditionally been opened only for the emperor. 'This gate was opened for him,' the conservationist Wei Jing told us. 'The general secretary takes the position that previously was held by the emperor.'

In 1912, China's revolutionaries toppled the last emperor, but Xi Jinping sees himself as carrying on the imperial tradition. In 2014, he told the party's Central Committee: 'China's first systematically compiled code of written laws appeared as early as the Spring and Autumn and Warring States periods (770–221 BC). In the years from the Han Dynasty (206 BC–AD 220) to the Tang Dynasty (618–907), China succeeded in establishing what was essentially a fully developed set of written laws. The legal system of ancient China embodied a huge wealth of knowledge and wisdom.'[12]

Xi also draws on ancient China in his fight against corruption. He reminds the Communist Party's district secretaries: 'In ancient times county magistrates were required to encourage and promote good conduct,' and then reads from Confucius's *Analects*: '"Fortune and riches obtained through unjust means are like floating clouds for me", "A man of virtue has a good knowledge of righteousness", "Be true in word and resolute in deed", "A man of high moral quality will never feel lonely" and "If a man does not keep his word, what is he good for?"'[13] When it comes to private matters, Xi combines the morality of Confucianism with that of communism. Members of the cadre should 'set good examples of caring for family members, providing suitable ethical education for their children, and pursuing a wholesome lifestyle. Officials must maintain the noble character and political integrity of Communists.'[14]

How does Xi square this circle? He has given his own answer to this question:

> Shared prosperity is a primary goal of Marxism; it has also been a basic ideal of the Chinese people since ancient times. Confucius said: 'He is not concerned lest his people should be poor, but only lest what they have should be ill-apportioned. He is not concerned lest they should be few, but only lest they should be divided against one another.' Mencius said, 'Do reverence to the elders in your own family and extend it to those in other families, show loving care to the young in your own family and extend it to those in other families.'[15] The Book of Rites gives a detailed and lively description of 'moderate prosperity' and 'great harmony.'[16] According to Karl Marx and Friedrich Engels, communism will eradicate the opposition and differentiation between classes, between urban and rural areas, between mental labor and physical labor; it will adopt the principle of distribution from each according to his ability and to each according to his needs.[17]

In a nutshell: Xi holds that shared prosperity is a goal of both Marxism and Confucianism.

In recent decades, many Western visitors to China and some Western people living there, especially entrepreneurs and managers, have been subject to a kind of optical illusion: seeing the hypermodern skyscrapers and people dressed in the latest fashions, they have assumed that China is now only paying lip service to communism. In truth, the People's Republic of China has always seen itself as a socialist country, a country whose ultimate aim is communism in the

Marxist-Leninist sense. Xi Jinping is simply clearer about this fact than his predecessors.

Ai Weiwei agrees. 'Yes – communism is Confucius's idea.' Confucius stands at the beginning of a Chinese tradition of revering scholars and state officials and despising tradesmen. Ai also thinks that the West deludes itself if it believes that China has renounced the communist ideology and become capitalist: 'From capitalism they only borrowed the tactics. They always still say, "We use them for our own ends." China is like that. We use the practices of Western medicine, but our understanding of our body comes from our Chinese medicine.'

A well-known author once asked: 'Isn't it paradoxical that private capital should be helping socialism?' He immediately supplied the answer: 'Not at all. It is, indeed, an irrefutable economic fact.' The author was Vladimir Ilyich Lenin.[18] He was justifying the New Economic Policy under which, from 1921 onwards, the Soviet Union began to invite capitalists to invest in socialism – just as China has done since 1978. Lenin provided the theoretical explanation for this step: 'Capitalism is a bane compared with socialism. Capitalism is a boon compared with medievalism, small production ... Inasmuch as we are as yet unable to pass directly from small production to socialism, some capitalism is inevitable ... we must utilise capitalism.'[19]

Lenin's position perhaps explains the view of one contemporary witness who understands China far better than many Western managers and business journalists. Egon Krenz was the last general secretary of the central committee of the Sozialistische Einheitspartei Deutschlands (SED), the Socialist Unity Party of the German Democratic Republic. Thus, in the final days of the GDR, Krenz held the same office that Xi now holds in China, and he continues to be a very welcome guest there – for instance, attending the 19th Congress of the Communist Party of China in 2017. Krenz rightly says: 'In China, all land, the most important industrial complexes, mines, motorways, education and health institutions, etc., are the property of the people, including foreign exchange reserves to the tune of more than three trillion US dollars. Property is the crucial question when deciding whether a system should be called capitalist or socialist.'[20]

Foreign companies often form joint ventures with state-owned enterprises. To do so, they must accept the government's condition that they share their know-how – exactly as Lenin envisaged. The driving power behind China's economy is private enterprise. Egon Krenz is aware of this, and is sympathetic: 'But I do not consider the utilization of the laws of the market and the corresponding capitalist methods as a return to capitalism as long as the results benefit the well-being of the people.'[21] He regrets that the GDR failed to pursue a similar path: 'Sometimes I do wonder what our world would be like today if it had been possible to develop a common strategy and to follow the path of "opening up and reform" that China has now been practising for decades.'[22]

The Chinese have a number for the role private companies play in their country: 56789. Each figure, multiplied by ten, stands for a percentage of private sector contribution to aspects of the economy. Private companies are responsible for 50 per cent of the country's tax revenue; 60 per cent of production output; 70 per cent of modernization; 80 per cent of jobs; and they make up 90 per cent of all companies.[23] Obviously, these are not exact figures, but the proverbial number is an accurate reflection of the general tendency. For this reason, Xi Jinping will not nationalize the private companies. But he does want stricter control over them. Jörg Wuttke, president of the EU Chamber of Commerce in China, is the son-in-law of Igor Rogachev, the former Soviet deputy foreign minister for Asia, who later became the Russian ambassador to China for thirteen years. Thus, Wuttke has it straight from the horse's mouth when he says: 'For officials of the Chinese Communist Party, the Yeltsin era was pure horror. As a consequence of large-scale privatization, some people became filthy rich and then tried to transform their wealth into political power.' The famous – and cringe-worthy – picture of Boris Yeltsin dancing with two beauties in short dresses is symbolic of this period. 'Something like that is inconceivable for Xi Jinping. When private entrepreneurs continue to grow and no longer keep their trap shut, they are sent packing, like Jack Ma, for example, the founder of Alibaba – Xi may do it in a nice way, but with a very clear message: private entrepreneurs must not try to take political influence.'

Control over private enterprises is exerted through party cells embedded in the companies. In corridors, display boards with a hammer and sickle symbol bear witness to their activities. In private companies and joint ventures this used to be a formality with little real significance. But, since Xi Jinping came to power, the Chinese state has insisted that communists take part in those companies' strategic decision-making – in the same way as has always been the case in purely state-run enterprises. This also applies to German corporations like Siemens and Volkswagen.[24]

'More than a few companies caved in immediately, not least German ones, the well-known car manufacturers, for instance,' says Wuttke. 'Each time I am again surprised by the anticipatory obedience with which such changes are accepted. The party official simply says, we won't close down the company, we won't lay off the people. This, incidentally, is something that didn't go down well with Chinese private enterprises either; roughly they thought: I am an entrepreneur, I put my money into this. And now this guy is sitting in the room next door, without a clue about anything except party slogans, and wants to tell me what to do – who is he anyhow? So they cut that back a bit.'

Nevertheless, the fundamental approach remains the same. The role of Chinese entrepreneurs and foreign corporations is to drive the economy, while not threatening the Communist Party's monopoly on power. 'Hostile forces at home and abroad constantly try to undermine our Party, attempting to make us abandon our belief in Marxism, communism and socialism,' Xi Jinping warns. 'A number of people, even including some Party members, cannot see the underlying dangers of accepting the "universal values" that have developed in the West over hundreds of years, along with certain Western political dogma.'[25]

Some in the West thought that the collapse of socialism in Eastern Europe marked the 'end of history' and that China would soon follow the lead of Russia, the Ukraine, and the countries of the former Yugoslavia. Far from it. For Xi Jinping, these are cautionary tales: 'Since the end of the Cold War, some countries, affected by Western values, have been torn apart by war or afflicted with chaos.'[26]

One should not, however, make the mistake of thinking that Xi Jinping is on the side of the workers against big business and finance capitalism. The fifty students who were arrested after supporting striking workers in Shenzhen in 2018 know this only too well.[27]

Xi has also suppressed other social movements. When female students at Beijing University started discussing the suicide of a female student who had been raped by a professor, the party initially tolerated the debate. But that all changed as soon as the discussions morphed into a movement against sexual harassment: 'Yue Xin, a female student who had written an open letter on WeChat about the incidents, was collected from her room at university and locked up at her mother's place for a few days. ... Other activists at universities in Beijing were warned that their activities were unacceptable because they were "pre-planned" and "organized". In China, the party has a monopoly on planning and organization – whatever it is.'[28]

Xi Jinping has 'four cardinal principles' that he never tires of repeating: 'keeping to the socialist road and upholding the people's democratic dictatorship, the leadership of the CPC, and Marxism-Leninism and Mao Zedong Thought.'[29] 'People's democratic dictatorship' is the modern version of what the Soviet Union, the People's Republic of China and the German Democratic Republic once called the 'dictatorship of the proletariat'. But, just as the workers never ruled in the Soviet Union, the people do not rule in China – and nor is China a democracy.

Rosa Luxemburg's reflections on Lenin in 1918 are as true today as they were back then:

> Without general elections, without unrestricted freedom of press and assembly, without a free struggle of opinion, life dies out in every public institution, becomes a mere semblance of life, in which only the bureaucracy remains as the active element. Public life gradually falls asleep, a few dozen party leaders of inexhaustible energy and boundless experience direct and rule. Among them, in reality only a dozen outstanding heads do the leading and an elite of the working class is invited from time to time to meetings where they are to applaud the speeches of the leaders, and to approve proposed resolutions unanimously – at bottom, then, a clique affair – a dictatorship, to be sure, not the dictatorship of the proletariat, however, but only the dictatorship of a handful of politicians.[30]

With a membership of 90 million people, the Communist Party of China is the most powerful political party in the world, but it is not a party in the Western sense of the word. It is more akin to a Chinese emperor's army of bureaucrats, all working in the spirit of Confucius – the recruitment process for the imperial bureaucrats included an entry examination in which applicants had to demonstrate their knowledge of his teachings. Becoming a member of the Communist Party is similarly selective. Applicants must be recommended by two existing members, and during a probationary period there are examinations of the candidate's knowledge of official ideology. Full party members must attend frequent training courses where the teachings of Marx, Lenin, Mao and Xi Jinping are drummed into them.

Like Confucianism, communism is a kind of secular religion. Like a religion, communism connects people through shared rituals and songs, offers explanations for everything and promises a paradise to come. Xi Jinping grew up in a family of ardent communists. Marxism is his way of keeping party and country united – just as Emperor Theodosius I made Christianity the official religion to hold the Roman Empire together. 'No theory in history can match Marxism in terms of rationale, truth, and spread, and no theory has exerted such a huge influence on the world as Marxism,' says Xi Jinping. 'Should we deviate from or abandon Marxism, our Party will lose its soul and orientation. We must follow the guidance of Marxism, a faith unshakable at all times and in all circumstances.'[31]

Just as a university theology department and a Sunday School would take different approaches to teaching the Christian religion, so China has advanced courses on Marxism and simple stories for ordinary people. Xi even tells a communist variation of the legend of St Martin, who cut his coat in half and gave one half to a beggar: 'When passing through Shazhou Village in Rucheng County, Hunan Province, three female Red Army soldiers sought shelter in the home of an elderly villager named Xu Jiexiu. Upon their departure, they cut their only quilt in two, leaving half with Xu Jiexiu. The elderly Xu said, "Who are the Communist Party members? The people who have only one quilt, but give half to the people."'[32]

As Xi Jinping sees it, the battles fought by the Red Army continue today in the fight against Covid-19. In one of the makeshift hospitals that was erected in Wuhan, nurses and care staff who wanted to join the Communist Party stood to attention in front of the red flag. They were all wearing face masks. 'You are about to begin your trial period as party members', an activist explained. 'I invite you to follow my words and to pledge allegiance to the party. Clench your right fist' – she demonstrated the correct position – 'and lift your right elbow so that it is level with your shoulder.' Then she turned around so that she, like everyone else, was facing the red flag. All had their arms in the clenched-fist salute. She recited the oath line by line, and the candidates repeated the lines after her in unison[33] – as happens whenever someone joins the party:

> I swear,
> It is my will to join the Communist Party of China,
> uphold the Party's program,
> observe the provisions of the Party Constitution,
> fulfil a Party member's duties,
> carry out the Party's decisions,
> strictly observe Party discipline,
> guard Party secrets,
> be loyal to the Party,
> work hard,
> fight for communism throughout my life,
> be ready at all times to sacrifice my all for the Party and the people,
> and never betray the Party.

'This is really a mafia, only a mafia can do this,' Ai Weiwei mocked. It is not the party members who determine party policy. They follow the leadership, and implement its policies. Lenin called this 'democratic centralism.' Xi Jinping explains: 'The worst mistake a ruling party can commit is to show indecisiveness on matters of extreme importance, encouraging arguments to rage and division to grow. Consequently, those with ulterior motives will fan the flames of discontent, lead the public astray, and stir up trouble. In the end there are bound to be problems.' He concludes: 'we must uphold the leadership of the CPC. Upholding the Party's leadership is the essential feature of China's socialism.'[34]

Another favourite phrase of Xi's is 'socialism with Chinese characteristics.' This socialism includes nationalistic elements, for nationalism is the easiest way to bring together Confucius and Mao – to be able to invoke both of them as great Chinese figures. Even those with little time for either the old philosopher or the communist tyrant can be enthusiastic about Xi Jinping as the strong leader who has made China proud again and shown the world China's true greatness. In this way, Xi's approach is much the same as that of Trump, Putin, Erdoğan or Bolsonaro – but Xi rules over a much larger population.

'The Chinese have become much more nationalistic,' Jörg Wuttke told us. He has worked in China for more than thirty years, and studied Chinese in Shanghai and Taipei. 'This is not only because of Xi. The Tiananmen massacre in 1989 created the breeding ground for nationalism. The rough idea was: young people must never again get it into their heads to take to the streets and demand freedom.' The recipe works. When you talk to young people in China today, they usually seem much more loyal to the state than their elders do. It used to be that Chinese students studying abroad would protest against their own government. Today, they protest against the democracy movement in Hong Kong, or against the Dalai Lama.

Fang Fang, the writer from Wuhan, thinks that left-wing and right-wing extremism are fundamentally the same: 'The reason I say these two radical groups are the same is simply because neither one of them is capable of accepting anyone with views different than their own.'[35] Therein lies a danger for Xi Jinping. The nationalist element might turn against him if, for instance, he sought to improve relations with a foreign country again after a trade war or the closure of a consulate. Or perhaps people will suddenly ask themselves why they are supporting a party whose ideology was developed by Karl Marx and Friedrich Engels, both Germans, by Lenin, a Russian, and by Stalin, a Georgian. Many Chinese people actually believe that their red flags and scarves are Chinese inventions. They had better not find out that they are Western imports.

7

From 5G to TikTok

Xi Jinping's China: between a bright digital future and an Orwellian surveillance state

Hardly anyone has heard of Foxconn, but almost everyone owns one of its products. From the iPad, iPhone and iPod to the Nintendo DS, from Dell and HP computers to Amazon's Kindle, from Nokia and Motorola mobile phones to Sony's PlayStation – most of our electronic gadgets are produced in Foxconn's Chinese factories. Foxconn is a publicly traded Taiwanese company that employs one million people – roughly the population of Cologne – in China. In 2016, Foxconn acquired the Japanese electronics corporation Sharp, and it is currently also expanding in India.

The company has received negative press because of the poor working conditions in its factories: fifteen-hour shifts, no talking at work benches and fixed times for going to the toilet. In 2010, at least eighteen employees took their own lives. They hanged themselves in the factory toilets, or jumped from the windows of dormitories. The management attached nets to the outside walls to catch anyone else who might try the same, and asked employees to confirm in writing that they did not plan to commit suicide – although in response to protests, Foxconn retracted that demand and instead opened a 24-hour hotline staffed by 100 psychologists. The company also replaced part of its workforce with robots – at least robots don't complain about the drudgery of work or commit suicide.

Foxconn is still going strong, but China is developing at such speed that the company seems almost like a thing of the past. Wang

Laichun worked for Foxconn for ten years. Today, she heads her own company, Luxshare Precision Industry, which produces, among other things, Apple's AirPods, and has bought the iPhone manufacturer Wistron. Wang is one of the richest women in the world. In 2020, her company reached a stock market valuation of $52 million – the same as Foxconn.[1]

Foxconn's and Luxshare's products still bear the logos of Western brands, but this is not the case with Lenovo. Lenovo's headquarters in the north of Beijing resembles the campuses of Google and Microsoft: a park with modern buildings and ponds. Visitors are led to a showroom where they can marvel at special effects: a door opens automatically when you throw a paper plane into a hole. But more astounding than such digital trickery is the crumbling façade of a decades-old Beijing house that has been moved into the showroom. It formed part of a one-storey, semi-derelict building where, in 1984, the Chinese Academy of Sciences permitted eleven engineers to work on computers. The state gave them start-up capital of $25,000 dollars – no more. The engineers were registered as a company: Legend. In the People's Republic, just eight years after the end of Mao's reign, a registered company was a sensation. The hut that housed Legend in those early years resembled Bill Gates's garage – or rather an even more stripped-back version of it. The eleven engineers were glad when, a few years later, they were able to sell and service IBM computers in China.

Since then, times have changed. By 2005, the company – now called Lenovo – had acquired IBM's PC business for $1.75 billion. IBM is the American company that pioneered the development of computers and produced the first personal computer, in 1975. In 2011, Lenovo took over the German company Medion AG, which supplies Aldi with consumer electronics. In 2014, Lenovo acquired the mobile communications company Motorola from Google. Today, Lenovo is the largest producer of PCs in the world.

'The first Industrial Revolution, which originated in the UK in the 18th century, made the country the world leader', says Xi Jinping. 'The US took the opportunity of the second Industrial Revolution in the mid-19th century and surpassed the UK, becoming the No. 1 world power.'[2] The next industrial revolution, the digital revolution, Xi says, will push China to the top. A comparison of the figures for broadband connections in China, the US and Germany suggests that the Middle Kingdom is making good headway: in China, 88 per cent of all broadband users have a fibre internet connection,[3] compared to 15.6 per cent in the US and no more than 3.6 per cent in Germany.[4] 'I have no doubt that China will achieve this goal,' the economist Christopher Jahns told us. Jahns is the founder of Germany's first officially recognized higher education institution with a focus on digitalization, the XU Exponential University of Applied Sciences in Potsdam-Babelsberg, which is backed by both American and Chinese investors. Thanks to his Chinese contacts, Jahns has been able to take a close look at the digital landscape in China. 'There is no data protection in China, which is a shame, but it is ideal if you want to use artificial intelligence and digitally based business models in order to be successful.' Under the heading 'Made in China 2025,' Jahns told us, Xi Jinping 'has for many years been launching planning projects that even small-scale businesses in remote areas have been able to implement. This is a controlled process. There is a boundless will to create wealth for the many. China's power, and especially its digital power, is unstoppable.'

Huawei is one of the global faces of China's digital revolution. The company is headquartered in Shenzhen, the Special Economic Zone that was created by Xi Jinping's father, Xi Zhongxun. In July 2020, Huawei became the largest smartphone manufacturer in the world, ahead of Samsung and Apple, and it produces the crucial component of the new mobile communications standard 5G.

Huawei's role in 5G technology has placed it at the centre of a global controversy. The US and other governments have accused Huawei of enabling global digital espionage by the Chinese – an accusation the company vehemently denies. 'Many people do not know that Huawei itself is not a network provider and has no control over mobile phone networks or the data circulating in them; rather, Huawei "only" provides the material for networks,' writes the sinologist Carsten Senz, Huawei's head of corporate communications in Germany. 'As far as the providers of software updates are concerned, there are strict contractual rules regarding access by certified employees who have to follow certain protocols and work under strict observation by the network providers. It is also important to keep in mind that a telecommunications network differs from the internet in that it is a closed system, and a network provider would be able to see any unscheduled extraction of – mostly encrypted – data.'[5] Senz also points out that Huawei's founder, Ren Zhengfei, was a victim of the Cultural Revolution (although that is, of course, also true of Xi Jinping and his family), and that Huawei's shares are owned by its employees, not the Chinese state. Yet Huawei, like any company, is subject to Xi's national intelligence law, which states that 'any organisation and citizen' has the obligation to support the intelligence services.[6] On 1 December 2018, at the request of the US government, Meng Wanzhou, Huawei's head of finance and the daughter of Ren Zhengfei, was arrested in Canada. But this had less to do with China's global ambitions and more to do with the US's: Meng was accused of violating the US sanctions on Iran, by which, according to the Americans, Chinese companies also have to abide.

Will Huawei bring the Chinese intelligence service into our homes? 'In my opinion, that is absolute bullshit,' Christopher Jahns told us. 'Sure, if you use platforms in China, everything is read and overheard; it would be naive to deny that. But I consider it impossible that Chinese companies who operate on the world market would build technology and mobile phones that allowed the Chinese intelligence service to penetrate data networks.' According to Jahns, Chinese companies are like all other companies: they are interested not in politics but in doing business. 'There are many experts who could prove that – and there has never been a single case [of data breach]. In my view, this is simply rabble-rousing directed against China's economic power.'

From his time as Germany's minister for economic affairs and energy between 2013 and 2017, Sigmar Gabriel knows a lot about Chinese companies that seek to invest in Germany. There is no reason 'to go crazy' over the phenomenon, he told us. 'Sometimes people are given the impression that China is wheeling a shopping cart through Germany and buying up the whole country – but that is not the case.'

In 2017, China's direct investment in Germany stood at €3.3 billion, compared to Germany's €81 billion of direct investment in China – that is, Germany invested twenty-five times as much as China![7] Despite the sense that many people have, Chinese investment in Germany has not increased since. In fact, it has decreased, because Xi

Jinping's administration is regulating the capital markets more tightly to ensure more domestic investment.[8] Indeed, according to Gabriel, increased levels of Chinese activity in Germany would be beneficial: 'I know of cases, for instance, in which employees were happy that a Chinese owner had been found, because they knew the investment would be long term, not just short term.'

Jörg Wuttke agreed that the fear of Chinese investment abroad is usually unwarranted. 'Private companies such as the car manufacturer Geely or the machinery manufacturer Sany are interested in gaining access to markets, in profit and technology, like us,' he told us. 'Basically, the flag follows the money.' Wuttke was also relaxed about Huawei's hardware: espionage focuses on software, which, however, 'is upgraded every week or two weeks. All you need to do is have some specialists to monitor the work.' According to Wuttke, the real issue is whether US sanctions make the use of Huawei's 5G technology unviable, as without American microchips, it will quickly become outdated.

Xi Jinping has not failed to notice this problem. 'The fact that our key technology is controlled by others is our greatest hidden danger,' he says. His 'Made in China 2025' plan accordingly stipulates that 70 per cent of China's demand for semiconductors should be met by domestic production.[9] In this context, one of Xi's more recent slogans is 'dual circulation': to reduce China's dependence on foreign countries, strengthening the economic circulation inside China must be given the same importance as developing the international economic circulation.[10]

As part of this agenda, Xi Jinping visits factories to motivate employees. In October 2020, for example, he went to Three-Circle Group, a business in Chaozhou, a city in south-east China. The company produces ceramic capacitors and resistors for electronic equipment, the energy industry and optical telecommunication devices. Footage of the visit shows Xi in front of the factory, surrounded by workers in short-sleeved light-blue uniforms and employees in identical white shirts. 'We are witnessing major changes never seen in a century,' he tells them. 'We need to take the path of domestic innovation and become autonomous.' Everyone listens attentively; some nod. '[You have to] understand the strategic intent of the Central Committee of the CPC, find your place in this great endeavour, and contribute to our nation's prosperity and modernization.' The audience clap enthusiastically.[11]

It is no coincidence that Huawei is headquartered in Shenzhen. Roughly half of all international patents granted in China originate here. The days of China producing cheap knock-offs are long gone; today, China is all about original innovation. 'In the digital economy, copying has completely disappeared', Jahns told us. 'In the digital arena, China is attempting to design novel, up-to-date products that do not exist anywhere else in the world. And it is well on the way to succeeding.' Companies in Shenzhen develop high-tech products, not cheap, mass-produced goods. Some 80 per cent of the global smartphone production is located here. Creative minds meet at the electronics market in the city's Huaqiangbei district, where you can find anything you need to build mobile phones, robots or drones. In the West, each business produces its own products, and fears copy-cats, but in China start-ups share their knowledge with each other – technology is a raw material available to everyone. New products are created quickly, without any drawn-out planning processes. Today, Shenzhen is the 'capital of hardware'.[12]

China is also heavily involved in software development. The video platform TikTok was the fastest-growing app in the world. In the summer of 2020, Donald Trump announced that he would ban it in the US. Until then, it had been largely the preserve of children and teenagers. TikTok provides a simple tool for users to lip-sync to music videos and other short clips – a tool employed very successfully by the American comedian Sarah Cooper, who produced popular videos in which she used Trump's words and parodied his absurd statements with her accompanying gestures. In Germany, reacting to Trump's attempts at censorship, the former Green Party minister Jürgen Trittin and the former parliamentary state secretary Friedbert Pflüger of the Christian Democratic Union wrote: 'The threat to US national security posed by dancing teens on mobile phone screens has not been demonstrated, just as no one has proved that Huawei is carrying out espionage on the mobile networks of other countries. This is the difference between Huawei and the US. The NSA did not hesitate when using the Patriot Act to spy on the German chancellor.'[13]

TikTok is owned by the Chinese corporation ByteDance, and operates on the international market. Inside China, users have access only to a censored version of TikTok called Douyin, which does not permit any content that could threaten 'national security'. In the Xi Jinping era, 'national security' has become a very flexible concept. Users who want to upload videos to Douyin must first register with their ID cards. If the app detects the face of an unregistered user, it stops working.[14]

The censorship applied to Chinese internet platforms prohibits not only any criticism of Xi Jinping and the Communist Party but also any mention of contemporary or historical facts that the party considers 'controversial'. Among the content that the censors deem unacceptable are not just obvious candidates such as references to the 'Hong Kong democracy movement' or reports about the 'Dalai Lama', but also discussions about 'MeToo', which do not sit well with the old men of the politburo, and any mention of 'Winnie the Pooh' – some Chinese internet users have joked about similarities between Xi Jinping and the cartoon bear.[15] Humour is not exactly Xi's forte.

Xi is full of praise, however, for patriots such as the model blogger Zhou Xiaoping. Zhou has little time for criticism of the government, telling his followers: 'The tone of positive energy should become the main tone on the internet.' When Xi Jinping met the thirty-something blogger at a conference, Xi told him: 'Keep spreading positive energy on the internet!'[16] 'Positive energy' has since become a recurring phrase in party propaganda.

The Chinese internet is, in truth, a large intranet. The state seals it off from the external world through its 'Golden Shield Project', commonly referred to as the 'Great Firewall', in allusion to the Great Wall of China. Chinese internet users cannot access Google, WhatsApp, Twitter, Facebook or Instagram. Donald Trump's announcement that he was going to ban TikTok not only annoyed millions of kids but handed a gift to the Chinese Communist Party, which could now claim that it was perfectly normal for a state to block access to certain sites 'in the interest of security'. Foreigners living in China and Chinese people with a lot of contacts abroad circumvent the firewall with virtual private networks, but in 2019 Xi Jinping prohibited those too. Some still continue to use VPNs – they are difficult to police – but those who are caught face up to five years in jail, even if such severe sentences are rare.

However, most Chinese people do not even try to use VPNs, as they see no need for them: for every foreign platform, there is a censored Chinese counterpart. Instead of Google, the Chinese use the search engine Baidu. If you enter 'Massacre at the Gate of Heavenly Peace' into Baidu, the result is an error message. On the microblogging service Weibo, everyone can air their opinion, just as they can on Twitter – at least in principle. In its early years, Weibo allowed a colourful hotchpotch of ideas to develop on the platform, but after Xi Jinping's 2013 order 'to retake the commanding heights of the internet' and delete critical accounts, some of which had millions of followers, it has become a rather sad affair.[17] WeChat may look like the equivalent of WhatsApp, but is in fact an app for everything: it allows users not only to chat but, as with Facebook or Instagram, to post links, pictures and videos, and to voice opinions. The maximum size of a group is 500, which is an advantage from the perspective of the censors: unlike Weibo, no mass audiences can emerge. And despite the large overall number of WeChat users, critical comments are quickly detected, as became clear during the Covid-19 crisis. WeChat also allows users to order food, call taxis, buy cinema tickets, make doctor's appointments, pay their electricity bills and even rent flats. What would require twenty or thirty apps in the US or Europe can be done with one in China. Using a WeChat QR code, you can pay at the supermarket, or even at a grocery stand in the street. In China, even beggars receive money in this way.

This makes life in China very easy. As well as WeChat, you can also use Alipay to pay for things. Alipay is comparable to PayPal – albeit with an overall volume of transactions twenty-four times that of the latter.[18] Alipay is part of the online trader Alibaba, founded by Jack Ma. He began his career trying – and failing – to get a job in a branch of KFC; he was told that he would not make a suitable salesperson. Today, anyone can pay for a meal in a KFC in China with Alipay, and Alibaba has a larger turnover than Amazon and eBay combined.

The competition between Tencent (which runs WeChat) and Alibaba benefits Chinese internet users. Their services overlap in many areas, and thus they are forced to compete on quality. Most Chinese people use the products of both. And, while in Germany people face the hassle of cookie popups, and have to sign data protection agreements at the doctor's office or when communicating with a building management company, Chinese companies already know everything about their users.

Christopher Jahns has seen many of the pilot projects of Chinese tech companies at first hand. Some have already been implemented: 'When you approach a shelf in the food market, artificial intelligence recognizes via your mobile phone what you bought there in the past. The price tags are adaptable: if the market wants to sell you something you didn't purchase before, it becomes cheaper; what you buy regularly may become more expensive. You don't have to pay at the checkout – your account is automatically debited. Next, you can decide whether to take the food home or have it prepared for you there and then. If you decide to eat at the market and a neighbour places an online order with the market at the same time, you receive a notification: if you decide to take their food to them, you will receive a voucher covering your meal.'

These levels of customer service in China are made possible by the fact that companies collect enormous amounts of data about their users. That may strike many Westerners as unacceptable, but it often makes life easier for Chinese consumers.

It is also good for business, even for bookstores, as Jahns told us. 'The surveillance camera knows where you are standing – and identifies you via your mobile phone signal. There are screens above the book shelves. Suddenly a film starts, and a writer addresses you by name and tells you about his book.' In a clothing store, the mirror is not a mirror – it is a monitor that not only makes the customer look younger but also suggests skincare products and lipstick: 'The artificial intelligence recognizes the skin colour, the contours, the nose. The system learns by itself and becomes better and better. It is not really controlled by any data protection. The result is that China is emerging as the clear winner in this new industrial revolution.'

'China has countless internet gurus,' the official news agency, Xinhua, states, 'but none of them can hold a candle to the "wise man of the internet" Xi Jinping.'[19] Xi's idea is to use internet censorship, video surveillance and artificial intelligence to create what he thinks is the perfect society. This idea came to him when he was in charge of the preparations for the Olympic Games in Beijing, and had to think of a way to prevent demonstrations. His solution was a dense network of surveillance cameras, equipped with facial recognition software, to identify suspects in the crowds.

Xi then decided to expand this system across China. When he became president in 2013, the country had about 100 million surveillance cameras. By 2020, that figure had risen to 600 million: one for every two citizens.[20] 'The surveillance cameras are everywhere; the government sees absolutely everything', says the young Chinese artist Ge Yulu. 'They know your daily routes, what you do and what you did today.'[21]

Ge's critical standpoint is the exception rather than the rule in China. Many point to the positive impact of surveillance. For instance, in 2017, in the Longgang district of Shenzhen, a three-year-old child, Xuanxuan, was kidnapped. The kidnapping was caught on a surveillance camera, and it took the facial recognition software exactly two seconds to identify the kidnapper. With the help of other surveillance cameras, the police were able to track his movements; he was quickly arrested on a train, and the child freed. Everyone's movements are tracked on a giant monitor at the so-called 'Smart Centre' in the Longgang district administration: at 8:23, an illegal street vendor is spotted; at 8:59, someone is seen illegally dumping construction waste; at 9:01, a suspicious heap of rubbish is discovered. Within six months of the system's introduction, the number of thefts in the district halved. The Smart Centre solves 85 per cent of all cases, from traffic offences to pick-pocketing.[22]

Xi Jinping wants to go a step further. It is not enough for the Orwellian surveillance state to solve criminal cases; it is also meant to persuade citizens to behave better and show consideration for others. While Western politicians see data collection first of all as a danger, Xi sees digitalization as a way of improving the communal life of the people.

There is also widespread data collection in the West, but there it mainly serves commercial purposes. The European Union's General Data Protection Regulation was intended to counteract these activities, but it impedes the work of police, journalists and associations, while big corporations like Google and Facebook circumvent it by making data access and collection a condition for using their services. There are similar corporations in China, but there the state also collects data and analyses it with the help of artificial intelligence. Unlike in the West, there is no particular value attached to the private sphere – indeed, making misbehaviour public is seen as desirable because it is supposed to have an educational effect.

The goal is no less than the creation of a new kind of human being. This idea, by the way, is nothing new. Paul's letter to the Ephesians in the New Testament says: 'That ye put off ... the old man ... And be renewed in the spirit of your mind. And that ye put on the new man, which after God is created in righteousness and true holiness.'[23] Tyrants like Stalin and Mao sought to impose a secular version of this new man. And even the great German poet Heinrich Heine wrote:

> A different song, a better song,
> will get the subject straighter:
> let's make a heaven on earth, my friends,
> instead of waiting till later.[24]

In pursuit of this noble goal, Xi Jinping decided to evaluate his subjects in a so-called 'social credit system.' Points are awarded for good behaviour, and one's score can be crucial when it comes, for instance, to promotion at work. The system was first trialled in individual cities, including Rongcheng, which has a population of 670,000. Rongcheng is part of Shandong, the home province of Xi's wife, Peng Liyuan. The scores achieved by the citizens are publicly displayed at the centre of each of the city's districts. To begin with, every citizen has 1,000 points. If you reach 1,050 points, you are awarded the title of 'model of honesty.' Helping others to move house, or leading neighbours in a communist singalong, earns you five points. Illegal harvesting, by contrast, results in five points being deducted. Burning household waste or leaves, or not cleaning up after your dog, also reduce your score by five. 'Illegal religious activities' will lead to a full 100 points being deducted (this is mainly aimed at the Falun Gong sect, which is forbidden in China). Anyone whose score sinks below 850 points receives a warning. Below 600, you will be publicly exposed as 'dishonest' and will become, according to the city's handbook, 'an object of significant surveillance.' Some of the rules openly encourage denunciation. Anyone who reports members of a religious sect receives five points. Many citizens welcome the point system. 'For peasants like us who want to move to the city, it is useful. It makes us think how we may improve ourselves,' one of them says. 'With this, anyone can work his way up. Everyone wants to have more points so that they become model citizens. Everyone is responsible for their own behaviour and is careful. A good attitude and good habits are important.'[25]

Although the government planned to implement the system nationwide by 2020, many Chinese people still have not heard of it. Covid-19 may have delayed many things, but in general it intensified surveillance. Each place pursues surveillance in its own way. Sometimes, there is resistance. In Suzhou – a popular tourist destination that is often called the 'Venice of the East' because of its many canals – people took to social media to criticize the hefty penalties for driving infractions. After only three days, the government retracted the provisions and promised to revise them.[26] Since May 2019, anyone caught on camera eating on the Beijing subway has had points deducted.[27] Here, too, omnipresent facial recognition technology is helpful.

The inventor of the social credit system is a sociologist and esteemed member of the Chinese Academy of Sciences: Lin Junyue. 'Education is necessary,' he says. 'The social credit system is the best means to guide a society. It not only allows us to control financial risks, such as bank loans, but also to guarantee moral education: decency and honest behaviour. The social credit system does not solve problems by locking up those who break the law, but by way of the disapproval shown by the rest of society.'[28]

Photographs of those with the highest scores are displayed on a board of honour in front of the local headquarters of the social credit system in Rongcheng. Among them is the teacher Yuan Chuang. 'This expert in psychological health is an honest worker who helps pupils,' the caption reads. 'She treats the children of others like her own. Her pupils even call her "Mama teacher". She was elected the fifth moral role model in Rongcheng.' Photos of 'bad citizens' are shown on screens in some shopping centres – an effort at public humiliation. In the coastal city of Ningbo, pedestrians who cross the road before the light turns green appear on LED screens next to the road, with their name and identity card number automatically generated by facial recognition software. In Henan Province, the authorities have even installed an automated telephone message that comes up if you dial the number of a person with a bad reputation: 'The person you are trying to call has received a bad evaluation from the court of the city of Dengfeng. Please encourage them to show responsibility and help them to obey the law.' There are now said to be more than 20 million Chinese people on the social credit blacklist. Because of their bad scores, many jobs are not available to them, and they are not permitted to travel.[29]

In an interview with the Franco-German broadcaster *arte*, Lin Junyue, the inventor of the system, suggests that France adopt it too: 'With the social credit system in place, the *gilets jaunes* movement would have been impossible. They would have been identified before they could have acted.'[30]

8

The Dalai Lama and the Uyghurs

How friends of the Xi family became their enemies

After Lady Gaga met the Dalai Lama for a philosophical discussion about wealth and compassion, Xi Jinping banned her songs, despite the singer's great popularity in China. On Instagram, Mercedes-Benz quoted the Tibetan spiritual leader: 'Look at the situations from all angles, and you will become more open.' This led to an outpouring of anger from Chinese nationalists on the internet, and Mercedes was forced into an embarrassing apology for the innocent quotation – after all, China is by far the car company's most important market. Profit trumps morality.

One could be forgiven, therefore, for thinking that the Chinese are quite sensitive about people meeting or quoting the Dalai Lama. But it was not ever thus. Even Mao Zedong sat down with him. There are photographs, from 1954, of the two enthusiastically shaking hands, and smiling in conversation. The Dalai Lama, then nineteen years old, even wrote a poem for Mao, and wanted to join the Chinese Communist Party.[1] He went to Beijing for six months to study Chinese and Marxism. The communist official assigned to him as a mentor met him many more times than Mao did. The official was none other than Xi Zhongxun, Xi Jinping's father. In 2012, the Dalai Lama recalled the elder Xi as 'very friendly, comparatively more open-minded, very nice.'[2]

However, the relationship between Tibet and China remained complicated, to put it mildly. Tibet was part of the Chinese empire at various points throughout history, without this really changing anything about everyday life in the remote mountain region. Tibet lies 4,500 metres above sea level – hence its description as the 'roof of the world'. Most Tibetans were followers of a fundamentalist Buddhist religion, and the rule of the Dalai Lamas was a kind of theocracy. In 1903, the British occupied the territory – another humiliation of the Chinese by a colonial power, and an important reason for China's sensitivity regarding all matters concerning Tibet. Tibetan independence began in 1913, by the grace of the British, and ended in 1950, when the People's Liberation Army entered the region to liberate it from the 'British imperial yoke'.

During the Cold War, the CIA trained Tibetan guerrilla fighters and provided them with weapons. Everywhere in China, peasants were suffering under the coercive measures of the 'Great Leap Forward', but in Tibet the conflict also had a national component. The measures were experienced as a repression not only at the hands of the Communist Party but at the hands of 'the Chinese'. In 1959, the Dalai Lama led the Tibetans in an uprising, which was violently put down by the Chinese government. The Dalai Lama fled to India.

When Deng Xiaoping began his project of reform and opening up decades later, he initially intended to restore a good relationship with the Dalai Lama and find a peaceful solution. Gyalo Thondup, the Dalai Lama's brother, went to Beijing for the negotiations. His opposite number was, again, Xi Zhongxun. The Dalai Lama was particularly touched that at the meeting Xi wore a watch that the Dalai Lama had given him as a present in 1954. A photograph of the meeting, dated 1987, shows Xi in friendly conversation with Gyalo Thondup, with the customary tall, lidded teacups on a small table between them.[3]

Just twenty years later, in 2006, foreign journalists were no longer welcome on the roof of the world – the Chinese administration considered any reporting about the tense situation in Tibet too risky. It was all the more surprising, then, when the Chinese leadership agreed that the Tibetan party leader could be interviewed – by *Der Spiegel*. Zhang Qingli, the Communist Party chief in Tibet, received us strictly according to protocol. One after another – and precisely on time – we filed into the magnificent hall of the heavily guarded Communist Party headquarters. Nineteen high-ranking officials had been ordered to attend. Zhang agreed to give us more time than had originally been planned.

Marx famously called religion the opium of the masses. We began by asking Zhang how the atheistic Communist Party of China rules in Tibet, traditionally a deeply religious country. 'First, we have religious freedom,' he claimed. 'Second, religious communities must make their own decisions, and we cannot have interference from abroad. Third, they must be conducted and managed according to the laws. And, finally, we show them how to become integrated into socialist society. You can see the way it is in Tibet, where people make pilgrimages to the temples, turn their prayer wheels and pray to Buddha.'

Then we turned to the subject of the Dalai Lama. Zhang had the following to say on him: 'Our policy towards the Dalai Lama is clear and consistent. After the founding of the People's Republic and the peaceful liberation of Tibet, he was elected to a leadership position in the National People's Congress in 1954. In 1956 he was named director of the preparation committee for the Tibet Autonomous Region. All of this was done so that religious freedom could be guaranteed, and so that Tibet could be integrated into the great family of socialist nations. He fled the country in 1959. There is no doubt that at that time he was a widely respected religious leader.'

And is he no longer that today, we asked.

'He did many bad things later on that contradict the role of a religious leader. The core issue is this: everyone must love his motherland. How can it be that he doesn't even love his motherland? We have a saying: "No dog sees the filth in his own hut, and a son would never describe his mother as ugly."'

The Dalai Lama doesn't love Tibet?

'Tibet is the home of the 14th Dalai Lama, but China is his motherland. He deceived his motherland. He rebelled in the 1950s, and in the late 1980s he incited unrest in Lhasa that was directed against the people, the government and society. He destabilized Tibet.'

When confronted with the fact that the Dalai Lama had dropped his demand for an independent Tibet, Zhang replied: 'The problem is that his behaviour and his statements contradict one another. ... He wants to integrate Tibetan settlement areas in the provinces of Sichuan, Yunnan, Qinghai and Gansu into Tibet. He wants to be in charge of this "Greater Tibet" and he demands that the People's Liberation Army be withdrawn from the region. Besides, he wants to see a return to an earlier, theocratic feudal realm, as dark and gruesome as it was. In those days, government officials, noblemen and monks ruled 95 per cent of the population. And he wants even more autonomy for Tibet than has been given to Hong Kong and Macau. That is splittism.'

China and the regional state of Lower Saxony have a special relationship. The reason is that the most important company in Lower Saxony, Volkswagen, was one of the first foreign companies to build a factory in the People's Republic – a joint venture with a Chinese partner, of course. In 2002, the then general secretary of the Communist Party and president of the People's Republic of China, Jiang Zemin, visited Wolfsburg with Lower Saxony's premier, Sigmar Gabriel. From Wolfsburg they went to Gabriel's home town of Goslar, a town with a population of 50,000. In hindsight, Gabriel realized, people were none too happy about the visit: 'Marksmen on the rooftops; manhole covers welded to the ground; for some time people were not allowed to walk the streets,' he told us. 'I thought I was doing something extraordinary for my town, but afterwards letters from citizens arrived, saying, "Next time he invites his friends, he should take them to Berlin or Hanover – not here."'

The visit went down much better with the Chinese – so well, in fact, that Sigmar Gabriel was invited to China, and told he could go wherever he wanted. He said that he and other Social Democratic Party members of the Bundestag would like to visit Tibet.

He told us what he had witnessed there. 'During the day, I saw children who repeatedly prostrated themselves on the ground in front of the temple in Lhasa. My Chinese guide noticed that this seemed somewhat strange to me. "Well," he said, "what do you want us to do? When we force them to go to school, you tell us that we are destroying Tibetan culture. Or should we leave the children alone? Then in 200 years they will still be living in the Middle Ages." And then he said: "Just look at the history of the Native Americans. Of course, there is this battle of cultures." He was quite a smart guy. I couldn't think of a response.'

It is 2008, a few months before the Olympic Games are due to take place in China, with Xi Jinping at the helm. In a Tibetan area of China, there is a tailback of lorries carrying pigs, behind a line of green trucks. In the beds of the trucks stand elite paramilitary policemen holding machine guns. A sign saying 'Safe Road' dangles above the pothole-riddled stretch of highway. Against the grey horizon, a red flag can be made out; it is moving uphill, past fields of tea plants, followed by some indeterminate shapes. As we approach, the shapes turn out to be about fifty peasants. They are beating drums and bells, singing: 'There will be no new China without the Communist Party.'

The flag bearer is Zhang Bin, a worker in the village's aluminium factory. He is wearing a light grey suit. He shouts: 'Down with the Dalai Lama clique! No to Tibet's independence!' The procession ends in front of an abandoned house – one of the many in China that seem to be either not yet completed or not yet fully demolished.

A crackly sound system plays the Chinese national anthem, followed by *The Internationale*. By now, more than a hundred peasants have shown up. There are mothers with their babies tied to their backs, girls dancing. It's a very long time since we had such a lively event, they say. Most of them are Han Chinese, the ethnic group that constitutes more than 90 per cent of China's population. One of the village leaders stresses that some of the villagers protesting against the Dalai Lama are Tibetan.

One of them is He Wenying, a twenty-five-year-old peasant woman. Her father, she says, is Tibetan, her mother Chinese. She no longer goes by a Tibetan name. Asked why she is here, she answers: 'Because I like to dance.' An activist standing behind her is not happy with her answer, and speaks in her stead: 'Because she is of one heart and one soul with the party.' The half-Tibetan, half-Chinese woman stands there shyly, silently.

Yang Yin is a very different character. She is dressed in modern clothes, wearing her hair in a ponytail. 'For my whole life, I have never been interested in politics,' the twenty-two-year-old says. She moved to the city as a migrant worker, but is back visiting her village. 'Abroad, our country is presented in a bad light and there is one-sided support for the Dalai Lama. The Tibetans have launched violent attacks on us, but now they pretend it was the other way around.' Just a few days ago, angry young Tibetans had attacked Chinese shops and restaurants in Lhasa, the capital of the Tibet Autonomous Region. Shop owners were burnt alive. Female pedestrians were chased in the streets and stoned to death because they were Chinese, or looked Chinese. During this unjustifiable racist violence, the supposedly gentle Buddhists also attacked Hui Muslims and destroyed mosques.

The Communist Party was mobilizing because the village of Xuankou in Sichuan Province is part of the 'Greater Tibet' claimed by the Dalai Lama. 'Greater Tibet' accounts for a quarter of China's territory – another reason why the leadership in Beijing gets nervous when it comes to the Dalai Lama. Xuankou lies on the road to Aba, where Tibetan protesters were demanding the return of the Dalai Lama and had become embroiled in battles with the police. Thirty semi-automatic weapons had been found in a monastery there, according to a police statement broadcast on Chinese television. There are 1.1 million Tibetans living in Sichuan. Only the neighbouring Tibet Autonomous Region is home to more Tibetans – 2.8 million.

When we arrived at the village, plain-clothes policemen took our passports. They were suspicious: 'What do you want here? Where will you be going next?' We were allowed to continue with our work only after we showed them a text of the Chinese government regulation that, in the run-up to the Olympic Games, granted foreign journalists the right to conduct interviews without the permission of the authorities. After the games, this right was revoked and it again became very difficult for foreign journalists to get permission to travel to Tibet.

On the way to Aba, we saw three Buddhist monks sitting at the side of the road. We asked them what they knew about the unrest, and what they thought of the Dalai Lama. One of them answered each question with the same mantra: 'What do you yourself think?' One of the others finally said: 'It is dangerous to speak.' He then took us with him to his house. A dozen boys were sitting on the floor. 'Please do not take photographs. What the boys are doing is illegal,' the monk warned us. They were learning Tibetan, and probably also receiving religious instruction. They were truanting. The monk then showed us something even more illegal. Rummaging around in a wardrobe, he pulled out a picture of the Dalai Lama. Unrolling it, he said: 'Unfortunately, we cannot put it up on the wall. That's too dangerous.'

'Previously, this area was not China. It was Tibet,' the monk said. 'We hope the Dalai Lama will return, but at the moment this is impossible.'

He had heard that young Tibetans had attacked Chinese people and Muslims with knives, and had set their shops on fire. He disapproved of such actions: 'The Dalai Lama cannot be in favour of this; he is against violence.' Monks are prohibited from gathering in large groups, he lamented. Leading lamas, that is, spiritual teachers, are not allowed to travel in the country. 'But it is much better than before', he said. 'We are 80 per cent free.'

Suddenly, the boys were shouting. 'Police, police!' Two officers opened the door. They took down our passport numbers. 'Why?', we asked. 'It's for your safety.' 'Is this area still unsafe?' we asked. 'No, but we are here for your safety.'

On our way to the monasteries in Aba county, we were stopped at a police checkpoint. It was not the first control, but it was the first that was thorough. At previous checkpoints, the police had not noticed us sitting in the back seat of the Jeep. The policemen, carrying machine guns, asked us to get out of the car. Because of the unrest, they said, we could not travel any further in this direction – even Chinese people required a special permit. Again, our passport details were noted down. Inside the police station, we were treated with courtesy, but outside policemen were threatening our Chinese driver: if he did not take us somewhere else immediately, he would be in trouble.

The driver was at his wit's end. First, he had faced all the hatred from the Tibetans, and now he was in trouble with the Chinese police. 'And I have always tried to help the Tibetans. I donated three bags of my daughter's old clothes.' Now, he said, everyone was suffering; there were hardly any tourists, and the people here lived off tourism.

The Communist Party tries to solve today's problems with yesterday's methods: repression and propaganda. At the party event in Xuankou, a teacher from the village shouted into a microphone: 'Are the people who sing "socialism is good" ready for their performance?' A dozen women in traditional Tibetan costume appeared. Only two of them, however, were actually Tibetan; the others had merely dressed for the part. 'We are happy about the liberation of Tibet, thank chairman Mao', they sang. 'Mao shines above the country like the sun, warms us up.'

The peasant women's colourful dresses covered their bodies up to the neck. They were followed by young female dancers wearing crop tops bearing a nonsensical Chinglish slogan: 'A sexy spiral girl products.' The climax of the performance cum party rally returned to Mao: girls in red silk blouses waved red handkerchiefs, formed a pyramid of human bodies, and held up a picture of the 'great chairman.' It all seemed like the old days, until some people from the neighbouring village who also took part in the event began to grumble. Their village, they said, was poorer than this one: 'Look at our street, full of potholes,' one of them said. 'We do not even have the money to buy the Tibetan costumes for our performance today, we had to hire them.' A member of the village cadre stares at her disapprovingly. She stops talking.

Even though the vast majority of Chinese people are in favour of a united China, the Communist Party practises a unique form of control over the population. A segment of the Tibetan population is against the separatists – and not only when there are police or members of the village cadres about. 'I am a Buddhist, but I do not pray to the Dalai Lama,' a Tibetan woman named San Langtou told us. Her suntan made her look much older than her thirty-three years. 'My grandmother was a serf under the former Dalai Lama, and had to work in the fields as a shepherdess when she was eight.' When Tibet was ruled by the Dalai Lamas, 95 per cent of the population were serfs. A Tibetan man, Zelang Luo'er'ri, wearing a traditional dark red robe, lit oil lamps, poured three cups of tea for the Buddha and prostrated himself. 'I have bad feelings when I think of the Dalai Lama,' the sixty-two-year-old said. 'The government is good to us, brought us water and electricity; now it has even had the street tarmacked.' He had ninety yaks, ten cows and two horses. In front of his two-storey house there stood a pole that was meant to bring good fortune and health. There was a satellite dish the size of a car.

In recent decades, everyday life has improved dramatically for Tibetans. That, at least, is the message China wants to convey to the world. 'In the 1950s, only three per cent of Tibetan children received schooling. Today it is more than ninety per cent,' Hong Kong's former head of government Tung Chee-hwa explained in a speech at New York's Columbia University. 'Back then, the average life expectancy of a Tibetan was thirty-five. Today it is sixty-seven.'[4]

'The Dalai Lama does not represent our kind of Buddhism,' Zelang Luo'er'ri told us. There are four main schools of Tibetan Buddhism.

The Dalai Lama belongs to the Gelug school, and he is accused by some of looking down on the other branches. For these reasons, Zelang Luo'er'ri preferred the Chinese to the Dalai Lama: 'During the Cultural Revolution, we were persecuted, but now we can freely practise our religion.'

This was also the view of one of the Dalai Lama's inner circle, a monk who lived outside China and frequently visited the Indian city of Dharamsala, the seat of Tibet's government in exile. 'Today we have more or less complete religious freedom. The Chinese government simply wants to ensure that monks do not intervene in politics,' he said. The monk preferred quiet conversations with Beijing to open confrontation. 'We have wasted a great opportunity because, ahead of the Olympics, China wanted to present an open and civilized image of itself. Had we not opted for confrontation, we could have achieved more: for instance, Tibetan becoming the first language taught at school, rather than, as now, the second.'

The monk wished to remain anonymous in order to protect himself and his family – not from the Chinese state, however, but from the Dalai Lama: 'Those who express opinions that differ from those of the Dalai Lama are completely ostracized – they may even get stabbed or have their houses burned down.' How does this fit with the Tibetans' commitment to non-violence? A gentle smile crept across the monk's face. 'That is a myth that circulates in Europe and the US. In some regions of Tibet, there are still blood feuds. Many families keep a rifle at home.'

The dispute between Xi Jinping and the Dalai Lama is about Tibetan autonomy. Xi claims that the rights that Tibet already has amount to autonomy. While some more radical voices in Tibet demand full independence, the Dalai Lama's aim is Tibetan autonomy within China – something that he believes presently exists only on paper. The Chinese leadership, in turn, think that the Dalai Lama's commitment to Chinese unity is only a pretence, and that in fact he is a separatist striving for full independence. And on separatism, Xi Jinping takes a pretty strong line: 'We should make an all-out effort to prevent and fight terrorism, ethnic separatism and religious extremism.'[5]

Xi Jinping also sees separatist forces at work in the Xinjiang Uyghur Autonomous Region in north-west China – at present, a region even more controversial than Tibet. Xinjiang is also another place where Xi Jinping's father was active in the past. Here, too, he adopted a relatively moderate political position. In the early 1950s, he successfully worked for the release of several thousand shepherds who had been imprisoned during a 'class struggle campaign'. Prior to Xi junior taking office, his father's moderate stance had led some to hope that Xi Jinping's leadership might be more open and flexible towards Tibet and Xinjiang than his predecessors. In 2012, even the Dalai Lama himself expressed this view: 'I can't say for definite, but according to many Chinese friends, they say the new, coming leadership seems more lenient.'[6] So far, however, there are no signs of any such lenience – quite the contrary. In the years before Xi Jinping took office, Chinese government representatives were still occasionally meeting with representatives of the Dalai Lama. Xi put an end to that.

The name 'Xinjiang' can be translated as 'new border' or 'new region'. China first conquered the region under Emperor Han Wudi (141–87 BC), but it was repeatedly recaptured by various nomadic tribes. As in all places where there are independence movements – from Catalonia to Kurdistan – the two sides can look back to different points in history to find historical evidence that backs their cause. As a matter of international law, however, all countries that have diplomatic relations with China (that is, almost all states) recognize that Xinjiang and Tibet are parts of China. The majority of Xinjiang's population belong to Turkic peoples (so called because their languages are related to Turkish), such as the Uyghurs and the Kazakhs. But, most importantly, they are Muslims, and for Xi Jinping, that is a problem. Xinjiang borders Afghanistan, Pakistan and Kashmir, a disputed territory claimed by both India and Pakistan, and Xi's fear is that conflicts in and between these countries could spill over into China. (Xinjiang also borders Russia, Mongolia, Kazakhstan, Kyrgyzstan and Tajikistan.)

Xi Jinping has reason to be concerned. In 2013, a Uyghur extremist steered a car into a crowd at the Gate of Heavenly Peace in Beijing, killing five people. Four months later, hooded Uyghurs appeared at a train station in Kunming, a city of a million people, and began stabbing travellers indiscriminately, killing thirty and injuring more than 100. Several hundred Uyghurs joined Islamic State.[7] And there was one incident that was particularly personal for Xi. When he visited Xinjiang in April 2014 – with all the intense security measures that such a visit entailed – two suicide bombers blew themselves up at the southern train station of the province's capital, Urumchi, while accomplices attacked people with knives. Three were killed and more than eighty injured. At that point, the new Chinese president had had enough. He declared: 'The population must be aware that the fight against Xinjiang's separatists will be a protracted, complex and difficult one.' He added that 'decisive measures' would be needed 'to destroy the terrorists' pure arrogance'.[8]

With that, China's 'war on terror' had begun. After the 9/11 attacks, the US killed half a million Iraqis in its 'war on terror' (according to a study by the University of Washington, in Seattle),[9] even though Iraq had nothing to do with the attacks. Bombing his own country was hardly an option for Xi Jinping, so he decided to employ another, very special form of 'war on terror'.

It is November 2017. In the centre of Zhaosu, four policemen armed with machine guns pounce on Sayragul Sauytbay. They pull a bag over her head and shove her into a car. Sayragul Sauytbay is a Kazakh – one of the Muslim ethnic groups in Xinjiang. But she is also a model Chinese citizen, speaks perfect Mandarin, works as a head teacher and is a member of the Communist Party. She has no idea what she might have done. The car journey takes two hours. Finally, the bag is removed, and she finds herself sitting across from a People's Liberation Army officer. Wasting no time on greeting her, he gets straight down to business: 'You are in a re-education camp, and you will work here as a teacher.' Her job is to teach the inmates Chinese.[10]

As an instructor, Sayragul Sauytbay enjoys certain privileges denied to the inmates, but she is not allowed to leave the camp, or to contact her family or other people on the outside. In a small hall, there is a glass sentry box, and beyond it a corridor, about twenty-five metres long. The corridor has twelve cells on each side – one side for women, the other for men. Each cell door is triple-locked, and watched over by two guards. When the doors open automatically at precisely 6 a.m. each morning, a stench of sweat, urine and excrement comes from the cells. There are up to twenty people crammed into each 16 square metre cell. Between them, they have just one plastic bucket with a lid that serves as a toilet. Every twenty-four hours, one of the inmates is permitted to empty it.[11]

Teaching begins at 7 a.m. The instructor stands in front of fifty-six people, who sit on tiny plastic stools in clanking leg irons. They shout: 'We're ready!' They wear a uniform of blue shirts and trousers. Their heads have been shaved – the women's and men's alike. Some have black eyes from beatings; some have mutilated fingers. 'Roughly 60 per cent were men between the ages of eighteen and fifty,' Sayragul Sauytbay will later remember. 'The rest were girls, women, and elderly people. In the first row was the youngest, a schoolgirl thirteen years old – tall, thin, very clever. With her bald head, I'd first taken her for a boy. The eldest, a shepherder who joined us later, was eighty-four.'[12]

Many Uyghurs and Kazakhs speak no, or very little, Chinese. Here, they are taught the language. Despite having little Chinese, the inmates are forced to learn about topics ranging from Chinese wedding customs to Xi Jinping's speeches. It is, in effect, the Chinese version of an integration course in Germany – but under severe compulsion. The Muslim inmates repeat together: 'I'm proud to be Chinese!' And 'I love Xi Jinping!'[13]

One million of Xinjiang's citizens are currently interned in such re-education camps.[14] Some estimates even put the figure at 3 million.[15] Given that there are only 13 to 14 million Muslims living in Xinjiang, babies included, this means that a substantial proportion of the Uyghurs, Kazakhs and members of other Muslim ethnic groups are imprisoned. The Chinese government initially denied this. But Sayragul Sauytbay is not the only witness. After a five-month stint as an instructor, she was released from the camp. She managed to flee to neighbouring Kazakhstan using false documents, and later teamed up with the German journalist Alexandra Cavelius to write a book about her experiences. Cavelius had previously published work on the plight of the Yazidis and other victims of Islamic State.

In 2019, Harald Maass, the long-serving China correspondent of *Frankfurter Rundschau*, was able to travel through Xinjiang and talk to former inmates of the re-education camps. 'They claimed I was not loyal towards my fatherland,' said one, a greengrocer named Kairat Samarkhan. 'They tied my hands and feet and pulled a black bag over my head. Then they brought me to the camp.' His description of the daily routine at the camp resembles that provided by Sauytbay: 'Getting up at six, breakfast, tidying the beds. Then teaching: learning the outcomes of the party congress by heart. Singing the national and party anthem. In the evening, we had to write essays on what we wanted to do better in the future.'[16] The BBC has also interviewed former inmates.[17]

In response to these reports, the Chinese government adopted a different position: yes, the camps do exist, but they are 'professional training centres', 'boarding schools' at which Islamists are persuaded to give up their extreme ideas while learning Chinese and other skills that will help them have a brighter future.

China's government invited the BBC to visit one of the camps. The British broadcaster compared the visit to the press tours around Abu Ghraib, where American soldiers abused imprisoned Iraqis, and to the international press visits to Theresienstadt and Sonnenburg during the Nazi era, when the allegedly wonderful life in these concentration camps was advertised to the world. The prisoners at the Chinese model camp, many of them good-looking young women, do not have shaved heads; instead of uniforms, they wear traditional dress. They happily sing Chinese songs. 'They are influenced by religious extremism', the instructor says. 'It is our task to get these extremist thoughts out of their heads.' The BBC journalist John Sudworth asks one of the prisoners whether they have been convicted of a crime. 'I haven't committed any crime', a young woman answers. 'I have made a mistake.' How often are you allowed to pray, the journalist wants to know. 'Chinese law defines schools as public spaces', a young man explains, 'and we are not allowed to engage in religious activities in public spaces.'[18]

Chinese propaganda sometimes claims that the People's Republic guarantees religious freedom. This is true on paper. However, Xi Jinping's understanding of religion is somewhat idiosyncratic:

> In order to encourage religions to adapt to our socialist society, we need to lead believers to love the country and the people, maintain the unification of the country and the solidarity of the Chinese nation, follow and serve the highest national interests and the common interests of

> the Chinese nation, embrace the leadership of the CPC and the socialist system, adhere to the Chinese socialist path, practice core socialist values, promote Chinese culture and endeavor to integrate religious tenets with Chinese culture.[19]

Believers must also 'participate in reform and opening up and socialist modernization, and contribute to the realization of the Chinese Dream of national rejuvenation.'[20] It is no wonder, then, that banners praising the Communist Party and Xi Jinping adorn the façades of mosques in Xinjiang.

When the BBC team sought to look elsewhere around the camp, one of the guards covered the camera with his hand. Instead, there were further interviews with prisoners, the interviewees always flanked by several guards. The journalist asks a young man with a black eye: 'Is it your choice to be here?' He responds: 'Yes. I had weak awareness of the law. I was influenced by extremism and terrorism. A policeman at my village told me to get enrolled in school and transform my thoughts.'[21]

There is a long tradition of re-education camps in socialist states. In the Soviet Union, there was the Gulag – an acronym that, translated into English, stands for 'Chief Administration of Penitentiary Labour Camps and Colonies.' In Vietnam, following victory over the US, the prostitutes were re-educated. And in China, as we know from Bernardo Bertolucci's monumental, but historically accurate film *The Last Emperor*, even the last of the Chinese emperors was forced into a re-education camp. Under Mao, the name for these practices was 'xi nao': 'washing the brain.' 'Brainwashing' is one of the few Chinese expressions that has made it into Western languages.

The BBC documentary shows inmates writing 'I love the Communist Party of China.' None of the prisoners knows how many months or years they will spend inside, or when they will be allowed to see their families again. 'When the thoughts have been transformed,' say the authorities. How does that fit with the claim that the inmates have chosen to be there? Can they go home once they feel they are rid of their incorrect thoughts? And what happens if they don't want to come in the first place? Mahemuti, the head of the 'Education and Training Centre' in the Hotan district, is visibly irritated by the BBC correspondent's questions. He replies: 'We've never encountered that before.'

Satellite pictures show that everywhere in Xinjiang there are such camps, surrounded by high walls, barbed wire and watchtowers.[22] The pictures also prove that, at some of these camps, the fences and watchtowers were dismantled prior to the arrival of foreign journalists. When there are no journalists present, conditions in the re-education camps are much tougher. It is also possible that different camps have different levels of strictness. 'They put cuffs on my legs for a week,' says Rakhima Senbay, who managed to escape to Kazakhstan. She had been sent to the camp because she downloaded WhatsApp to her mobile phone. 'There were times when we were beaten. Once, I was struck with an electric baton.'[23] Sayragul Sauytbay also reports that inmates were tortured in the camp where she worked as an instructor: 'Many inmates, bound at the wrists and ankles, they strapped into chairs that had nails sticking out of the seats. Many of the people they tortured never came back out of that room – others stumbled out, covered in blood.'[24] She also mentions cases of rape: 'When I was working as a sentry or cleaner in the evenings, I often noticed the guards fetching the youngest and prettiest girls from the cells, most of them eighteen or nineteen years old.'[25] It is not yet clear whether these were cases of individual men abusing their power, or whether they were part of a systematic campaign to humiliate Muslims, like in the Bosnian War.

The reasons for which people are locked up in these camps are trivial. Just one of the following 'suspicious factors' will suffice:

- meeting with foreigners, for instance relatives from Kazakhstan
- taking selfies with artists from Kazakhstan who previously, during more liberal times, were allowed to perform in Xinjiang
- making a donation to a mosque[26]
- having WhatsApp, Facebook or other banned apps on your mobile
- wearing a beard or traditional dress
- regular prayer
- not drinking alcohol
- fasting during Ramadan

- frequently filling up your car (the petrol might be used for bombs)
- having an 'extremist name', such as Mohammed or Fatima.[27]

This recalls the Stalinist quota system, or more generally the kind of anticipatory obedience that is typical for dictatorships: every district and police department competes to detect as many 'suspects' as possible. But the responsibility lies with Xi Jinping: it was he who ordered the introduction of the re-education camps, and he has not condemned any of the excesses. In a one-man dictatorship, as long as the leader remains silent, nothing will change. 'I know President Xi. I've talked with President Xi', says Leon Panetta, US secretary of defense under Barack Obama. 'I just cannot for the life of me understand why someone who generally has a pretty good sense of things is making such a devastating decision.'[28]

It should be stressed that it is only the Muslims of Xinjiang who are subjected to these harsh and arbitrary measures. Ethnic Chinese (Han) people in Xinjiang, and other Chinese citizens outside Xinjiang, do not suffer anything remotely comparable. But that is part of the problem.

The founding father and long-serving prime minister of Singapore Lee Kuan Yew, who died in 2015, once compared Xi Jinping to Nelson Mandela.[29] But in quite a few respects, Xinjiang rather resembles South Africa under the apartheid regime.

'After a few kilometres, policemen stop our bus, security control', writes Harald Maass. 'The four Han Chinese people can remain seated. All other passengers, about a dozen Uyghurs, ethnic Kazakhs and myself, have to get out and are directed into a hall by people in uniform.' The same happens in Kashgar, for centuries the cultural centre of the Uyghurs, and today popular with Chinese tourists: 'Han Chinese to the right, where they can walk through a separate entrance without any further controls. Uyghurs and other minorities to the left: queuing for the police checkpoint.' Uyghurs and Kazakhs have also had their passports taken away, but not so for the Han Chinese.[30] Sayragul Sauytbay describes similar experiences. 'As of 2014, nearly all five-star hotels were reserved solely for Chinese: it didn't matter how much money indigenous people had', she writes. 'It reminded me of apartheid in South Africa and the racist Jim Crow laws in the USA, when white people and people of colour were strictly segregated.'[31]

Some Chinese people welcome the state's approach. 'The cities are now safe', a teacher tells Harald Maass on a train. 'The Uyghurs have four, five children and don't care about education. That is the problem.' In Hotan, a city on the route of the former silk road from China to Europe, a shopkeeper says of the Uyghurs: 'We can improve the infrastructure and build up the economy, but to raise the quality of the people is much harder.' By contrast, Zhang Haitao, a Han Chinese man living in Xinjiang's capital, Urumchi, posted on social media: 'The so-called ethnic and religious problems are fundamentally a problem of human rights. It is shameless when China's communists play the saviour and declare that they have lifted the Uyghurs out of poverty.' For these two sentences, Zhang was arrested. His post was considered an 'incitement to undermine the power of the state'. A court sentenced him to nineteen years in prison.[32]

People may be referred to a re-education camp without a court order – the police make these decisions at their own discretion. Zhang Zhisheng, from the foreign affairs office of the Xinjiang Uyghur Autonomous Region, explains the rationale behind this: 'Some people before they commit murder already show they're capable of killing. Should we wait for them to commit the crime? Or should we prevent it from happening?'[33]

It is possible that Xi Jinping thinks that his tough approach has been vindicated. There have been no Islamist terror attacks in China since 2015. 'There is no doubt that intense control contributes to Xinjiang's peace today', writes the *Global Times*, the English-language arm of the Communist Party's main newspaper *Renmin Ribao*. Xinjiang has been prevented from becoming 'China's Syria', it claims.[34]

We asked Sigmar Gabriel, as a former foreign minister and someone who has held talks with Xi Jinping, how he saw the situation in Xinjiang. He said: 'I think the international reports on it are true. I think that they have this kind of Gulag system there – and for the simple reason that they are worried that without it they will not be able to control the Muslim movement, Islamic fundamentalism, the Muslim Brotherhood.'

So is Xi right to claim that he is acting simply to prevent terrorism?

'That is also Putin's argument for throwing his military weight around in the Caucasus. It sets up a simple alternative according to which there is no other way of dealing with Muslims, with religions, apart from repressing them. That is an enormous problem, of course, when in China, with its population of 1.4 billion, something like this affects one million Uyghurs. But if you were to ask people in any of the anonymous cities in China with their 10 million residents what they think about it, they probably wouldn't even know that it is happening, or it would not interest them. Therefore, I don't think this can be changed from outside.'

Should we just not talk about it, then?

'No, we should continue to make this a topic of discussion, but without always having a debate about economic interests on the one hand and human rights on the other.'

Incidentally, the naive comments of Western tourists, whom Chinese state-run media very much like to interview, are also quite unhelpful. 'We drove through Xinjiang,' they say, 'and it was actually all very nice there.' Such remarks recall those of Berti Vogts, who captained West Germany at the 1978 World Cup in Argentina, and had nothing but praise for the military dictatorship: 'Argentina is a country where order reigns. I haven't seen any political prisoners.'[35]

9

Xi for Future

The eco-president

Many Europeans believe that the whole world is talking about Greta Thunberg and the 'Fridays for Future' movement. But this is Eurocentric. In China, hardly anyone has heard of the Swedish schoolgirl. The handful of intellectuals who know her name mock her as the 'heroine of the blank answer sheet', an allusion to the student Zhang Tiesheng, who, during the Cultural Revolution, handed in a blank paper at an examination, saying that it was more important to fight for Mao's revolution than to learn. All those Westerners who think that the apocalypse is nigh would probably also be surprised to learn that even the well-known Chinese environmental activist Wang Yongchen believes that, 'for young Chinese people, other problems are more urgent than climate change'.[1]

That attitude is not due to China making a limited contribution to global CO_2 emissions. With a share of 29.7 per cent of global carbon emissions, China is way ahead of the rest of the pack – the US, in second place, accounts for 13.9 per cent. The picture changes when we look at emissions per capita, which for China are slightly lower than those of Germany and about half those of the US.[2] One reason why the Chinese talk less about climate change is the presence of other, everyday dangers: polluted air and poisonous water.

'Humanity was born in nature, lives in coexistence with nature, and will finally incur harm by damaging nature.' These words read like a line from a poetry collection for environmentalists, but they are from

Xi Jinping. He even invokes Confucius: 'Our predecessors understood the significance of the eco-environment. The *Analects of Confucius* says, "The master fished with a line but not with a net; when fowling he did not aim at a roosting bird."' Xi Jinping waxes lyrical as if he were Confucius reincarnated: 'Environment is livelihood, green mountains are beauty, blue sky is happiness, and clear water is wealth.'[3]

It is 2005, before the Xi Jinping era.[4] A dead fish washes up on the bank of a poisoned river. Crowds of people trying to escape the deadly water throng the train station. The trains are fully booked. In the supermarket, people come to blows over the last bottles of water. A slick of carcinogenic benzene, 80 kilometres long, is moving downstream. When it reaches the north-eastern city of Harbin, the government shuts off the water supply for the 4 million people living there. The Songhua River, from which the water supply is drawn, has a benzene concentration 100 times the permitted limit. Anyone who comes into contact with the water risks immediate death. Later that week, the poison reaches Khabarovsk and other Russian cities along the Amur. The Chinese call this river the 'black dragon.'

On that occasion, the Chinese government reacted quickly, by its usual standards. Residents were informed ten days later that a PetroChina factory in Jilin had exploded, polluting the Songhua River with benzene. PetroChina is 90 per cent state-owned and, especially after it was floated on the New York and Hong Kong stock markets, depends on good performance figures. A year earlier, another of its factories had exploded in Chongqing, a city of 32 million people, killing 243 and poisoning more than 10,000.

Chinese people rarely even hear about such events. Take, for instance, the 1,000 residents of the village of Xiakang in Shanxi Province. One day, their water tasted salty. Then, pots were stained red after cooking. 'I had diarrhoea; it didn't stop,' said Mrs Chen. 'When I talked to the neighbours about it, they told me they had the same problem.' A few months later, she was unable to move her legs. Today, she spends her days lying on the boards that serve as her bed. Syringes in plastic bags hang on the bare walls. She suffers from cerebral thrombosis and hemiplegia – as do dozens of the other villagers. Twenty-seven have already died, among them a fourteen-year-old girl.

The village resembles a sanatorium. Almost everyone you come across on its dusty paths limps along on a stick, if they can still walk at all. Despite being ill himself, Mrs Chen's husband carries her to the doctors; they cannot afford a wheelchair. 'Had I known that our water was poisoned, I wouldn't have drunk it', she says, in tears. 'But no one told us anything.'

For years, they have fetched water from the well, despite the groundwater being polluted with chlorides, potassium sulphate and nitrates. The steel and iron works and the paper mill in the neighbouring city of Linfen pour untreated waste water into the Fen River. Both factories have increased the volume of waste emitted tenfold over the past ten years.

There are many cases like Xiakang. One is Huangmengying, on the Huai River, which is covered with white foam where it runs through the village. The nearby Lotus glutamate factory pollutes the water. Over a period of ten years, 110 of the 2,400 residents have died of cancer. Kong Heqin, thirty-one years old, showed us the ileostomy next to her navel. She had had four operations for her bowel and thyroid cancer in the past five years, and had undergone twelve courses of chemotherapy. 'I cannot afford another one', the mother of two sons, aged seven and nine, lamented. 'All that's left for me now is to die.'

Huo Daishan, who used to be a photographer at the local newspaper and is now the head of the environmental group 'Guardians of the Huai River', said: 'The dirty water makes people sick, the sickness makes them poor and now they are poor and sick.' Others have made a nice profit. The glutamate factory is run by local party cadres, and is backed by Japanese investors. 'Power and money have formed an alliance', Huo told us. This is how corruption in the Communist Party can threaten both humans and nature.

China's economy grew by 9 per cent in 2005. Exports were up by 30 per cent. 'But this miracle will soon be over because the environment can't take it any longer', a man with a buzz cut, pulling deeply on his cigarette, told us. When we spoke to him, Pan Yue was the deputy director of the State Environmental Protection Administration. 'I've never minced my words', he said, smiling. 'Half of the water in our seven large rivers is completely unusable. A quarter of our citizens do not have access to clean drinking water.'

In 2005, more than 80 per cent of waste and waste water were not properly disposed of or treated. The same year, 400,000 Chinese people died from air pollution. Sixteen of the world's twenty worst cities for air quality were in China – among them Beijing. According to satellite measurements from the European Space Agency, Beijing was 'the most polluted capital in the world.' An air show has had to be cancelled because the smog in the capital limited visibility to 200 metres.

Beijing is moving factories out of the city, but at the same time more and more cars are polluting the air. The relocation of factories to rural locations is also leading to increased pollution in villages, where investors appreciate the low cost of land and the corrupt village cadres, who are even more lax about the enforcement of environmental laws than the officials in the big cities.

The faces of the residents of Beishan, a village of 400 people in the north of China, are often as black as soot. Since 2001, more than 100 coking plants and iron works have been built in this area. They produce not just for the domestic market but also for Japan and South Korea. The residents call their region the 'black triangle.' Black, yellow and white smoke belches out of the chimney stacks. The stench makes breathing difficult. Your eyes hurt.

The carcasses of goats rotted in the grey grass. A shepherd, Zhuan Longhai, had his baseball cap pulled over his face. 'The factories have bewitched the grass,' the Mongolian man told us. 'Thirty of my 370 sheep and goats have died this year. And the wool is black!'

Yang, a fifteen-year-old boy, had tied nylon cloth over his eyes, over which he wore sunglasses. His job was to crush limestone into small pieces, pour it into sacks and carry it to a carbide factory. 'With just the nylon, large pieces of limestone would destroy my eyes. And the sunglasses by themselves would not protect me against sand and splinters.' Unlike the shepherd, he did not complain about the air quality. 'I got used to it,' he told us, 'and apart from that, I earn well here.'

After the poisonous fumes damaged their grain and halved their harvest, the farmers of Beishan went to the regional government for help. The police arrested them in their dozens. Next time, the villagers blocked the road, holding signs saying 'Stop the pollution.' Hundreds of policemen arrived on the scene. 'Can you not understand us?,' the twenty-year-old Xue Jun shouted at the security forces. 'Even when we close our windows and doors, our faces still turn black!' Xue was thrown into prison for these words.

That same year, 2005, discontent was bubbling up all over China. In the Huaxi region, villagers protesting against a chemical factory set fire to a police car. A demonstration outside a pharmaceutical plant near Shanghai ended in a battle with the police. In Meishan, thousands of farmers stormed and burned down a battery factory that was poisoning the water with lead.

This is part of the prehistory out of which one of Xi Jinping's core ideas emerged. He understood early on that, if he wanted to keep the Communist Party in power and make China the world's leading nation, he had not only to fight corruption but also to tackle China's serious environmental problems. He dedicated one of his first speeches as party chairman to the topic: 'Usher in a New Era of Ecological Progress'. In the speech, Xi declared:

> We will launch major projects to restore the ecosystem, and increase our capacity for producing eco-friendly products. A sound ecological environment is the basic foundation for the sustainable development of humanity and society. The public are greatly concerned about the environment. So we should place emphasis on serious environmental problems that pose health hazards to the people, and take a holistic approach to intensifying the prevention and control of water, air and soil pollution, with the focus on water pollution in key river basins and regions, and on air pollution in key industrial sectors and areas.[5]

Stronger environmental regulations – this was more or less the diametrical opposite of the programme pursued by Donald Trump in the US a few years later. Trump boasted about deregulation. Xi, by contrast, not only introduced stricter laws but also called for stricter controls, because he knew that local officials were often more interested in profit than in the environment: 'Some places value development far above environmental protection and intervene in the monitoring and supervision over law enforcement by environmental protection agencies. As a result, it is difficult to implement the environmental protection responsibility system, or laws are not properly observed or strictly enforced, or lawbreakers are not prosecuted by some local regions and government agencies.'[6]

This was not just lip service. In 2015, China changed its environmental protection law and introduced a new system of penalties. Before, violators of air or water pollution regulations were punished once (in practice, often not at all), but now the fines increase with every day the pollution continues. In the first year, 715 violations were identified, and penalties totalling $95 million were handed out. The new law led to 456 court cases.[7]

Even when he was in charge of the preparations for the 2008 Olympics, Xi Jinping was already championing a 'green games'. He moved 2,000 factories from the city. Coal heating was replaced with gas heating.[8] To limit traffic, cars with number plates ending in even numbers were not permitted on the roads on one day, odd numbers the next. At the same time, he expanded local public transport. Before the Olympic Games, Beijing had just two subway lines, one circular route and one straight. Today, the network comprises twenty-three lines and 405 stations, and has a total length of 699 kilometres, making it the largest subway in the world.[9] Unsurprisingly, the second largest is also in China: Shanghai's, with a total length of 676 kilometres.[10]

Xi Jinping has modernized transport not only within the big cities but also between them. The Chinese network of high-speed trains is by far the largest in the world. The trains travel at a top speed of 400 kilometres per hour along 20,000 kilometres of track, and there are plans to add a further 10,000 kilometres by 2030.[11] The total length of high-speed track in Germany, by way of comparison, is 2,635 kilometres, and speeds of more than 250 kilometres per hour are rare exceptions. What might come as a particular surprise to customers of Deutsche Bahn is that 98.8 per cent of China's fast trains arrive right on time.[12] The reason for this has as much to do with good organization as with good infrastructure. The high-speed trains run on separate tracks. Passengers sit in waiting rooms and are only brought to the platform when their train is ready to depart. Unexpected platform changes are unknown in China.

'If we are to consume as much energy in production and daily lives as the present well-off people do, all the existing resources in the world would be far from enough for us!' says Xi Jinping. 'The old path seems to be a dead end.' So far, it could be Greta talking. But Xi does not see the solution in sailing boats: 'Where is the new road? It lies in scientific and technological innovation, and in the accelerated transition from factor-driven and investment-driven growth to innovation-driven growth.'[13]

While other countries talk a good game about electric cars, China has actually introduced targets. By 2020, 12 per cent of all new cars had to be electric, plug-in hybrid or hydrogen-powered. The target rises by 2 per cent each year – meaning 18 per cent by 2023.[14] In 2019, 3.81 million electric cars were already registered in China, by far the largest number in any country. The US took second place with 1.45 million, while Germany had no more than 231,000.[15] However, 69 per cent of the electricity for China's electric cars was still generated from fossil fuels, mainly coal; 18 per cent came from hydropower, 6 per cent from wind farms, 5 per cent from nuclear power plants and only 2 per cent from solar energy.[16]

Not all coal-fired power plants are the same, however, as we saw for ourselves in Shanghai. Shiny, immaculately clean pipes run through the halls of Coal-Fired Power Plant No. 3 in the suburb of Waigaoqiao. There are no soot-stained workers here. Instead, there are engineers huddled in front of a monitor. 'With our technology, we can filter and catch most of the pollutants', one of them told us. 'Therefore, only very little pollution comes out of the chimneys. We are already pretty advanced here. We feel responsible for helping other power plants in China. We also are very happy to help other countries, including Germany.'

Coal-Fired Power Plant No. 3 provides a third of the electricity for the mega-metropolis Shanghai. 'China depends mainly on coal. We have no other resource in such abundance', Feng Weizhong, the plant's chief engineer, told us. 'Our main path must therefore be to make coal more environmentally friendly.' To meet the growing demand for energy, China is also investing heavily in renewables, more than any other country. By themselves, however, they would not be enough, which is why coal remains the major element in the mix. 'Solar power and wind are not reliable', Feng told us. 'When the sun shines, it can be used for generating energy. When it's cloudy, it can't. The same with wind. If it's strong, it produces electricity, but when it dies down, it doesn't. Imagine: you are hungry, but just at this moment, there is nothing to eat.'

China is far ahead of all other countries when it comes to efficient and clean coal power. The very fact that it is building so many plants gives the People's Republic an advantage – having built a great number, the Chinese have learned a great deal. As early as 2010, the US magazine *The Atlantic* called China the world leader in 'clean coal', that is, low-emission coal: 'If you want to learn how the power plants of the future will work, you must go to Tianjin – or Shanghai, or Chengdu – to find out.'[17]

Aerodynamically rounded at front and back – inspired by the shape of a dolphin – the buses of Beijing's No. 1 line float through the metropolis almost without a sound. They are quiet because they are powered by lithium-titanate batteries. Some 99 per cent of the world's electric buses run in China, and e-buses are big business: 'In 2017, about 90,000 e-buses were sold, almost all of them produced by Chinese manufacturers. The frontrunners are Yutong (25,000 vehicles), BYD (13,000 vehicles) and Zhongtong (8,000 vehicles). The largest manufacturers outside China, Volvo and Proterra, produce only a couple of hundred e-buses.'[18] There is no trade-off between economy and ecology here; each one benefits the other. As Xi Jinping points out:

> Green, circular and low-carbon development, which is the most promising sector, guides the direction of the current revolution in science, technology and industry. We have huge potential in this regard which could give rise to many new engines of growth. While we are constantly faced with ever-tighter resource constraints, serious environmental pollution, and ecological degradation, we are also faced with people's growing demands for clean air and drinking water, safe food, and a beautiful environment.[19]

China's adoption of electric vehicles is driven less by concerns about climate change and more by the need to reduce air pollution. If the residents of cities with a population of 10, 20, or 30 million all drove a petrol or diesel car, the cities would be choked with smog. In the long term, electric cars also contribute to the reduction of CO_2 emissions, but in the short term they raise them. Taking emissions from the production of batteries into account, a new electric vehicle produces more CO_2 emissions than a new conventional vehicle. Only once it has been on the road for a long time are its total emissions over time lower than those of a normal vehicle.

For the Chinese leadership, the electrification of transport has a strategic as well as an environmental benefit. The production of electric motors requires rare-earth elements, by far the largest reserves of which are to be found in China.[20]

'Protecting the environment, addressing climate change and securing energy and resources is a common challenge for the whole world', says Xi Jinping. 'China will continue to assume its due international obligations, carry out in-depth exchanges and cooperation with all other countries in promoting ecological progress, and work with them to promote the sharing of best practices, and make the earth an environmentally sound homeland.'[21] Are these just so many fine words?

Barbara Finamore is the director responsible for Asia at the Natural Resources Defense Council, a US environmental group. A Harvard-educated lawyer specializing in environmental law, she created the NRDC's China programme in 1996. She says: 'As far as the climate and clean energy are concerned, China often makes modest announcements and then surpasses itself – at least this is my experience. Under the Paris climate treaty, China made a commitment that its CO_2 emissions would continue to rise only until 2030 and would then begin to fall. I consider it very likely that they will already have reached this goal by 2025, and some experts believe even earlier.'[22]

China's target for expanding solar power by 2020 was reached ahead of schedule – and exceeded by 50 per cent. In 2017, China invested more money in renewable energy than the next three biggest investors – the US, the EU and Japan – together. Today, more Chinese people work in the clean energy sector than in coal mining. Nine out of ten of the world's largest producers of solar panels and five out of the ten largest producers of wind turbines are Chinese.[23]

For Barbara Finamore, all this is cause for optimism. She even wrote a book, *Will China Save the Planet?*, in which she says of Xi Jinping's vision of an 'ecological civilization':

> This emphasis on ecological civilization coincided with a period of slower economic growth that China's leaders dubbed 'the new normal'; rather than emphasizing double-digit growth, the government began to focus on slower, but higher-quality and more balanced, economic growth. Under President Xi, China began to accelerate its efforts to transform its economic structure from one reliant on fossil fuel-driven heavy industry and manufacturing to one based on services, innovation, clean energy, and environmental sustainability.[24]

In putting this agenda into practice, party officials sometimes overdo it. In 2017, Xi Jinping's ambitious environmental targets led to millions of people in north China freezing. Because of the uncoordinated way in which the old coal heating system had been dismantled in the transition to natural gas, gas supplies were running out.[25] In December 2013, the Chinese government had announced that increasing GDP would no longer be the most important factor in judging the performance of officials; the quality and sustainability of economic development, including reductions in emissions, would also be taken into consideration. Hainan Province, an island, went a step further, making environmental achievements the main criterion for promotion. In January 2015, Shanghai was the first major region in China to drop targets for increases in GDP altogether.[26]

As Sigmar Gabriel is also a former environment minister, he follows these developments very closely. 'China's government calculated, and also made public, that the environmental destruction of the country was more or less neutralizing annual economic growth – that is, about 10 per cent of the economy,' he told us by way of an explanation for Xi Jinping's new strategy. 'The Chinese debate, however, is still problematic. It says, "You, the historical polluters, first have to reduce your per capita consumption down to our level." We won't have the time to do that.'

Xi Jinping does not want climate protection to come at the expense of the world's poor. In a speech at the UN climate conference in Paris in 2015, he said: 'Addressing climate change should not deny the legitimate needs of developing countries to reduce poverty and improve their people's living standards. The particular needs of developing countries must be given due attention.'[27] The rich countries that have been the main polluters throughout history cannot simply be let off the hook: 'China will shoulder its share of responsibility and continue to play its part in this common endeavor. We also urge developed countries to fulfill their historical responsibilities, honor their emission reduction commitments, and help developing countries mitigate and adapt to climate change.'[28]

With China having made good progress in recent decades, Xi Jinping now wants to support other countries in combating climate change – and at the same time to expand his power. As he reminded his audience at the UN climate conference, 'China announced in September this year the establishment of an RMB20 billion South-South Climate Cooperation Fund. Next year, China will launch cooperation projects for developing countries, including setting up 10 pilot low-carbon industrial parks, starting 100 mitigation and adaptation programs and providing them with 1,000 training opportunities on climate change.'[29] Taking up an apprenticeship in climate protection instead of playing truant on Fridays – why not?

10

The New Silk Road

Xi's path to global power

Chinese tourists in Germany often go to see Neuschwanstein Castle or the Karl Marx statue in Trier, Marx's birthplace – a gift from the People's Republic. In 2014, when Xi Jinping visited Germany for the second time, he decided to pay a visit to the Port of Duisburg. At the port's train station, a Chinese gong sounded three times. Then, a bright-red dragon on a wooden stick danced alongside a train as it pulled into the station at a crawl. The train had run along the so-called Yuxinou railway. 'Yu' stands for Chongqing, which with a population of 32 million is by some estimates the largest city in the world; 'Xin' means 'new'; and 'Ou' is the first sign of 'Ouzhou', meaning 'Europe'. The chair of Duisburg Hafen AG, Erich Staake, took the opportunity to practise his Chinese party speak: 'The Yuxinou train is proof that any distance, no matter how long, can be mastered if connections that are useful for both ends are established.' The train transports freight from Chongqing to Duisburg, from where it is distributed across Europe via the continent's major rivers. The train journey takes two weeks – almost twice as fast as the sea route – and is half as expensive as air freight.[1] The 11,179 kilometre line runs through Kazakhstan, Russia, Belarus and Poland. Duisburg's local press was jubilant about the rail route from China, talking of 'the miracle of Duisburg'. It had made the inland harbour, in the Ruhr area, a hub of global trade, and had given it a new lease of life. Germany's minister for economic affairs, Sigmar Gabriel, was standing next to Xi Jinping. He remembers well how carefully choreographed the event had been: 'The train had stood on the tracks for several days, and was polished and made squeaky clean again for the last few metres.'

Duisburg is one of the final destinations of the new 'Silk Road' project, Xi Jinping's grandest foreign policy initiative. It was initially called 'One Belt One Road', and is now referred to as the 'Belt and Road Initiative' (BRI). Xi Jinping sees himself as working in a long tradition: 'Over 2,000 years ago, our ancestors, trekking across vast steppes and deserts, opened the transcontinental passage, connecting Asia, Europe and Africa, known today as the Silk Road', he explained at the opening ceremony of the Belt and Road Forum for International Cooperation. The most important commodity transported along the old Silk Road was Chinese silk – hence the name. 'Our ancestors, navigating rough seas, created sea routes linking the East with the West, namely the Maritime Silk Road. The ancient Silk Road, embracing both the land silk road and maritime silk route, opened windows of friendly engagement between nations, adding a splendid chapter to the history of human progress.'[2]

For Sigmar Gabriel, this focus on Eurasia only makes sense. 'That was China's sphere of influence until 600 years ago.' Back then, Portugal's Prince Henry the Navigator sent his ships to find a maritime route to India, and at about the same time the Chinese emperor scrapped his fleet. One decision led to Europe's 600-year global ascendancy, the other to China's 600-year decline. 'They now want to reverse that, which in itself is a legitimate aim', Gabriel told us.

At Duisburg, Xi invoked the Venetian trader Marco Polo and the Chinese seafarer Zheng He, and mentioned such hallowed historical cities as Baghdad, Constantinople, Samarkand and Alexandria:

> The ancient Silk Road spanned the valleys of the Nile, the Tigris and Euphrates, the Indus and Ganges, and the Yellow and Yangtze rivers. They [*sic*] connected the birthplaces of the Egyptian, Babylonian, Indian and Chinese civilizations, the lands of Buddhism, Christianity and Islam, and homes of people of different ethnic groups and races. Through the Silk Road, people of different civilizations, religions and races interacted with and embraced each other with open minds, in the

> spirit of seeking common ground while reserving differences. In the course of exchanges, they fostered a spirit of mutual respect and were engaged in a common endeavor to pursue prosperity.[3]

Given that many Muslims, Buddhists and Christians are persecuted in China today, the sentiments Xi expresses here might come as a bit of a surprise.

The new Silk Road covers the area that the old one did – that is, Asia, Africa and Europe – but in Xi Jinping's vision, it could, if necessary, be extended to Latin America. In all the places it touches, infrastructure will be developed, trade expanded and transport links boosted. In addition, China will provide finance for energy supplies to be secured and natural resources exploited. Xi Jinping intends to spend more than $1 trillion on the project over a decade.[4] The principle is comparable to that behind the Marshall Plan after World War II, but on a much larger scale: the US Congress approved only $12.4 billion for the Marshall Plan – $139 billion in today's dollars, little more than a tenth of China's intended investment.

The new Silk Road is to be Xi Jinping's personal legacy. Just as with 'Xi Jinping Thought', it has been incorporated into the Communist Party's constitution. Some sixty-four countries are involved in the undertaking in one way or another.[5] These countries are home to 4.4 billion people, or roughly 60 per cent of the world's population, and account for about 40 per cent of global GDP.[6]

The construction of the railway link between Chongqing and Duisburg is only one of many projects. A planned high-speed railway line, on which trains will travel at 320 km/h, will reduce journey times between Beijing and London from fifteen to two days.[7] Other projects include:

- freight train routes from Wuhan to Melnik and Pardubice in the Czech Republic, from Chengdu to Lodz in Poland, and from Zhengzhou to Hamburg
- nine highways connecting China with Vietnam, Laos, Cambodia, Myanmar, Thailand, Malaysia and Singapore
- airports and motorways in Pakistan
- the mining of minerals and precious stones in Kazakhstan,

Uzbekistan and Turkmenistan, and their transport across Russia, Iran and Turkey[8]

- oil refineries and terminals in Iran[9]
- cooperation between China, Mongolia and Russia in the areas of nuclear energy, wind and hydroelectric power, and solar and biomass powerplants, and linking up the Russian and Mongolian power networks with the Chinese electricity grid[10]
- hydroelectric power projects in Cambodia[11]
- telecommunication cable networks in Africa[12]
- building a high-speed train in Hungary
- expanding the Greek port of Piraeus.[13]

'We will open our arms to the people of other countries and welcome them aboard the express train of China's development', says Xi Jinping.[14] 'We have enhanced policy coordination with relevant countries for such initiatives as the Eurasian Economic Union proposed by Russia, the Master Plan on Connectivity by ASEAN, the Bright Road initiative by Kazakhstan, the Middle Corridor initiative by Turkey, the Development Road initiative by Mongolia, the Two Corridors, One Economic Circle initiative by Viet Nam, the Northern Powerhouse initiative by the UK and the Amber Road initiative by Poland.'[15]

The financial news service Bloomberg has described Xi's new Silk Road initiative as follows: 'China is building a very 21st-century empire – one where trade and debt lead the way, not armadas and boots on the ground.'[16] John Naisbitt, deputy secretary of state for education under John F. Kennedy, was a great supporter. His book *Megatrends* (1982) helped to popularize the term 'globalization'. Until his death in 2021, he lived with his wife, Doris Naisbitt, a visiting professor at Beijing's Foreign Studies University, in China and Austria, dividing his time between the two countries. 'Even though the BRI [Belt and Road Initiative], of course, pursues China's own interests, both nationally and internationally, state and private investments will invigorate markets in its wake', the couple wrote. 'These have the potential to open up the path into the 21st century for countries and regions that have so far remained outside the scope of global trade, and that so far could give their people only little hope of a better life.'[17]

There is a further similarity between the Marshall Plan and the new Silk Road initiative. The Marshall Plan produced the *Wirtschaftswunder* in West Germany and post-war economic booms around Western Europe, but of course it also served to ensure that these countries were on the side of the US in the Cold War. According to the Naisbitts, 'From the perspective of China, today's globalization equals modernization dominated by the West. The official goal of China is to use the BRI for a decentralized modernization, free of colonialism, imperialism, and hegemony.'[18] It is probably safe to say that this somewhat underestimates the strategic interests of China and its powerful ruler.

The European Union Chamber of Commerce in China is less enthusiastic about the initiative. Its study *The Road Less Travelled* accuses the Chinese authorities of a lack of transparency. Non-Chinese companies, the report says, have little chance of winning contracts that go out to tender. The chamber's president, Jörg Wuttke, is also increasingly aware of disquiet among entrepreneurs and officials inside China, whose criticisms have intensified since the outbreak of the Covid-19 pandemic: 'Why should we waste all this money in Pakistan or Venezuela? We need it here at home, in Guizhou or Gansu. And anyhow, a lot is just propaganda: the trains to Duisburg can operate only because they are 50% subsidized by the Chinese government.'

A red chili sauce is brewing. Saleswomen advertise pork offal packed in transparent plastic bags. The women behind the food counter are from Sichuan Province, and so their offering is not surprising. Spicy dishes are very popular in Sichuan. But the African boys stare in amazement at the foreign food. Amid the crowd of Chinese construction workers buying their provisions, the few locals stick out. The scene is not Asia – it is Angola.

One of the construction workers says: '300,000 Chinese people work here.' Another corrects him: 'Rubbish, we are already half a million.' The figures provided by the Chinese embassy are lower – officials do not want to create any fears about Chinese people overrunning the country. But we can say for certain that there are tens of thousands, and probably hundreds of thousands, of Chinese people in Angola, which has a population of only 30 million. The situation is the same in other regions of Africa.

At the centre of these situations are always natural resources – in Angola's case, mostly oil. The country's oil production has doubled in the past five years. The liquid gold comes out of the sea floor, and tankers carry it from the port of Luanda, the capital city, to locations around the world – 40 per cent of it to booming China.

Near the harbour, children search through rubbish, pulling wire from old radios and computers in order to sell it. In the slums, the sheets of corrugated metal that serve as roofs are held down by stones. The residents have to fetch water from public water stations. Most Angolans still live in poverty, but a growing elite benefits from the black gold rush. Posters feature models advertising SMS banking. A few kilometres from the heaps of rubbish, there are tall cranes. Before you know it, the Chinese will have built another skyscraper for Angola's nouveau riche.

China is constructing not just office blocks and villas but also apartment buildings for the middle class. The flats in these green and yellow high-rises await their new owners. The apartment blocks are situated close to the Estádio 11 de Novembro, the football stadium named for the day in 1975 when Angola became independent from Portugal. The stadium was also 'made in China' – it was built by the Shanghai Urban Construction Group.

'China operates more building sites in Angola than any other country does – even more than Brazil or Portugal, who speak the same language', the Angolan political scientist Orlando Ferraz – who studied in Bonn and Cologne – told us. 'Oil plays an important role in this, because the large loans made by China are secured with oil. This is why the Chinese have been handed so many building sites here.'

And this is how the deal works: China gives Angola cheap credit, totalling $15 billion, and Angola repays in oil. For the oil, however, the Africans get buildings instead of money. Thanks to their economic boom, the Chinese have a good deal of experience in construction work. At the feet of the new skyscrapers, Chinese workers are levelling paths and planting gardens. Some Angolans work alongside them, but they are a minority. You can see the Chinese workers bossing them around. The new world power is in charge.

'Many Chinese people work here', one of the Chinese workers tells us, introducing himself as Li. He comes from a village near Qingdao, a former German colony, and has signed a contract to work in Angola for one and a half years. 'China and Angola are business partners. The government has sent us. We have a large cooperation programme.'

China is founding provisional settlements on the African continent, including here, next to the new high-rise apartment blocks. The red flag of China flies next to the Angolan flag. The yellow five-point star is the same on both. On the Angolan flag, a machete crosses a cogwheel – the resemblance to the hammer and sickle is no coincidence.

At the workers' dormitories, counterfeit Calvin Klein briefs hang on washing lines on the balconies. Bare-chested Chinese workers squat in front of them.

The workers' living conditions are tough. Their wives and children wait for them on the other side of the globe, but they can earn twice as much here as they can at home, and can save money for their families. They also sense that their work is part of something bigger. 'It is good for China', one worker, Xue, says. Another – also called Xue, but no relation – cuts in: 'China is developing so fast. We need raw materials because our population is very big.' The first Xue adds: 'China needs oil, and this is a big oil country. We toil here, and the oil comes to us.'

The Angolan boys standing around in front of the Chinese food stand say: 'The Chinese people are arrogant; they look down on us.' The guest workers from the Far East, in turn, say: 'Chaos reigns here. We hardly ever leave our residential area. We fear for our lives in Angola.' The China Chamber of Commerce in Angola, representing forty Chinese firms there, speaks of two to three attacks per day. In Luanda, for instance, a Chinese worker had boiling water poured over him. There are rumours about several murders.

Orlando Ferraz explains the propensity towards violence with reference to the civil war, which began in 1975 and lasted almost thirty years, until 2002. It followed more or less immediately after the war of independence against the Portuguese colonial rulers, between 1961 and 1974. Ferraz is positive about Chinese involvement: 'After the civil war, when no one wanted to engage with us, China helped us quickly and unbureaucratically with loans.' But he, too, is concerned that not enough Angolans are employed in the building projects, and that the Chinese could do more to train the local population. That said, talk of a 'new colonialism' is absurd, he believes. Ferraz does not worry about the fact that most of the money from the loans flows back to Chinese companies: 'They improve our infrastructure, for example build roads. It now takes me much less time to get to the office. Bananas and other foodstuffs reach customers before they rot.'

Anyone trying to make their way through the sprawling, bustling capital Luanda quickly realizes how urgent the problem is. On weekdays, traffic grinds to a halt at 6 a.m. Nothing can move on the rugged and often single-lane roads. 'The Chinese are themselves in a period of development', says Ferraz. 'Therefore, they understand us better, find it easier to put themselves in our position, than the Europeans do.'

Europeans concede as much. The civil engineer Bernhard Streit has worked in Africa since 1972, and for the last six years in Angola for the Gauff Engineering Company, which is based in Nuremberg. He has conducted surveys, on behalf of the Angolan state, of the 1,200 kilometres of road built by the China Road & Bridge Corporation.

According to Streit, the West's policies in Africa have failed: 'We make too many demands. The Chinese, by contrast, do not behave like schoolmasters. We Europeans, whether it is Germany or the EU, and the World Bank always adopt a moralizing tone. That doesn't go down well with the Africans at all.'

Streit inspects a section of newly built road near the city of Caxito. Chinese workers drive diggers and bulldozers. Oil can also be a curse: Angola's elite sells the resource that is so plentiful here, but creates few jobs for ordinary Angolans in the process. The work goes to the Chinese. They are industrious, better trained than the Angolans and faster than the Europeans. And the Chinese government does not insist on any onerous conditions and does not complain about corruption or human rights violations.

Nevertheless, Bernhard Streit, who has a good deal of knowledge of Africa, sees Chinese involvement in a positive light: 'Apartments that are fit for human habitation and decent transport links are also part of human rights. We Europeans always want to proselytize. This may be well-meaning, but it does not achieve much. The Chinese have only their own economic interests in mind. This is why they create a good infrastructure here, which is more help to the Angolans than the West's developmental aid.'

'What we do is peanuts,' agrees Sigmar Gabriel. 'If necessary, we might throw in an important gender programme. The Chinese build a whole city. Paul Kagame, the president of Rwanda, told me: "You know, we would like to do things with you – but in the time it takes you to build a cycle path, the Chinese complete two airports."'

It all sounds great: China's Silk Road project means new infrastructure, worth billions, in countries that could never afford it themselves. But as is always the case in business, if an offer sounds too good to be true, there is usually a snag.

Take, for example, Sri Lanka, where a high-interest loan from China financed the construction of Mattala Rajapaksa International Airport. The airport was named after the country's then president, Mahinda Rajapaksa, now prime minister, who wanted an airport in his home province. China wanted to strengthen its influence in Sri Lanka. It is a modern airport, but there is one problem: there aren't really many planes taking off or landing. (We are talking, incidentally, about the time before the pandemic.) The reason is that Sri Lanka, a country the size of Bavaria, already had an international airport. The new one, built with China's support, has been described as a 'ghost airport' and the 'emptiest airport in the world.'

Only 30 kilometres from the ghost airport lies the port of Hambantota, which is also named after the prime minister: the Magampura Mahinda Rajapaksa Port. It cost $1.3 billion, which again came from China. The entrance is blocked by parked cars. The port has not been used since the opening ceremony. 'What did this bring us?,' the former government advisor Aruna Kulatunga asks. 'Nothing. Apart from the enormous debt that Sri Lanka is now saddled with.' Unable to repay its debt, the small island state was forced to lease the port to China for 99 years. The People's Republic now has an outpost on one of the most important trade routes in the world.

'The new Silk Road initiative of the Communist Party of China is nothing but a debt trap,' says H. R. McMaster, the national security advisor fired by Donald Trump. 'The governments involved end up being dependent. And they suffer not only from the burden of debt – they are also forced to adopt China's view of the world and to support the foreign policies of their credit provider.'[19]

Madeleine Albright, the former US secretary of state, also watched Xi Jinping's Silk Road initiative with concern. 'China's attempt to expand trade routes and infrastructure in Asia, Europe, and Africa – these are projects in which many countries end up heavily in debt and become economically dependent on China,' she told us. 'I once said about this that the Chinese would need to get really fat now, because the belt they are wearing is getting bigger and bigger.'

While Mao supported Maoist movements around the world, under the reformer Deng Xiaoping, China's foreign policy followed a different maxim: 'Hide your strength and wait for the right moment.' Xi Jinping thinks this moment has now arrived. Since he has been at the top, China has not held back on the world stage.

In a 2018 report on the new Silk Road, twenty-seven out of twenty-eight EU ambassadors in Beijing spoke of 'uneven power relations' in the bilateral negotiations between powerful China and its much smaller partners. The only ambassador not to sign was Hungary's – Prime Minister Orbán's dependence on China is already so great that he cannot afford to express any criticism. The other EU ambassadors warned that the tendering processes involved in the projects lacked transparency and favoured Chinese state-run companies; any firms bound by European environmental, labour and social standards had little chance of winning a contract. A year later, Greece also caved in – China owns the Port of Piraeus – and a joint EU declaration on human rights in China was scuppered by a veto from Athens.[20] China has already invested more than €7 billion in Greece, creating many jobs in the crisis-hit country. The Chinese state-owned shipping company Cosco will soon make Piraeus the largest port in the Mediterranean.[21]

The European branch of the new Silk Road initiative is the '16 + 1 group,' which China, incidentally, calls the '1 + 16 group.' This group includes China and the former socialist countries of Eastern Europe: Albania, Bosnia-Herzegovina, Bulgaria, Croatia, the Czech Republic, Estonia, Hungary, Latvia, Lithuania, Macedonia, Montenegro, Poland, Romania, Serbia, Slovakia and Slovenia. With Greece joining the group in 2019, it is now the '1 + 17 group.'

'One shouldn't blame the Chinese for having a geopolitical strategy,' is Sigmar Gabriel's retort to the critics. 'But one may well blame us for not having one. We can be part of it if the conditions are transparent, if we can establish who participates under which conditions. In addition, we should create an alternative, so that there is competition. Surely, it beggars belief that we were too dim to finance a rapid transit railway from Belgrade to Budapest – and now the Chinese finance it.'

China rightly accuses the US of interference in other countries' business. Now, however, China is using its economic power to punish countries that do not dance to its tune. When South Korea agreed to let the US station missile defence systems on its territory, China bullied South Korean companies operating in, or trading with, China, and reduced the flow of tourists to the country. When Liu Xiaobo, a Beijing-based critic of the regime, was awarded the Nobel Peace Prize, the government banned Norwegian salmon imports. And when, in 2019, there was public debate in Australia about the extent of Chinese influence over the country, China stopped buying Australian coal.[22] Sayragul Sauytbay, the whistleblower who drew the world's attention to the conditions in the re-education camps of Xinjiang, speaks of China's strategy of using 'financial deals and investments' to buy 'loyalty' from other countries, 'forcing them into dependency'.[23] She herself experienced the long arm of the Chinese state when she was temporarily imprisoned in neighbouring Kazakhstan.

Xi Jinping seeks global influence. He says: 'The CPC and the Chinese people are more than confident that we can offer the Chinese solution to the human society for people to explore for a better social system.'[24] In his first five years as president, Xi visited sixty-one countries, on every continent – from Russia to Fiji, from Saudi Arabia to Chile.[25] He travelled to twelve countries in Latin America alone – more than Obama and Trump combined.[26] Xi's aim is not world revolution, as Mao envisaged. He is happy to forge alliances, including with conservative governments of the kind in power in Poland and Hungary, for he shares their scepticism towards excessive freedom. His is a new International of nationalists, so to speak. That is an uneasy alliance: while one says 'America First', the other means 'China First'. This perhaps explains the love–hate relationship between Donald Trump and Xi Jinping.

11

Peace as Part of China's DNA?

The trade war and the troubled relationship with the US

'Hello, Grandpa Xi. Hello, Grandma Peng,' says a five-year-old American girl in perfect Mandarin. She sings a Chinese folk song: 'The jade-green river flows past sweeping rice fields. ... The quiet lake is studded with lotus flowers.' This is followed by Confucian-style pearls of wisdom, again in good Chinese: 'With no education, there'd be aberration.' The little girl performing for China's president and first lady is Arabella Kushner. It is 2017, at the Mar-a-Lago resort.[1] Arabella is the daughter of Ivanka Trump, and the granddaughter of Donald. Barack Obama's daughters, Sasha and Malia, have also learned Chinese,[2] as has the granddaughter of the current US president, Joe Biden. In 2011, Biden's granddaughter even accompanied him on a trip to China. The families of American presidents, it seems, know how to prepare for the future.

During the 2016 US presidential election campaign, Trump claimed that China was 'raping' the US.[3] This was, in his typically vulgar language, a way of saying that the trade relations between the two countries benefited China and disadvantaged the US. He was referring to the uneven balance of trade: China sells more to the US than the US sells to China. Apparently, no one had explained to him that Americans also benefit from cheap products from the Far East. This issue became something of an obsession for Trump, and overshadowed all the other important aspects of the relationship between the two most powerful countries in the world – for instance, security cooperation and issues of democratic values and human rights.

The memoirs of John Bolton, Trump's national security advisor between April 2018 and September 2019, provide a glimpse of the way Xi and Trump dealt with each other. Bolton describes a dinner that took place on 1 December 2018, at the end of the G20 summit in Buenos Aires. Xi declared that he 'wanted to work with Trump for six more years, and Trump replied that people were saying that the two-term constitutional limit on Presidents should be repealed for him.' Even Bolton, a Republican, finds it necessary to mention at this point that he had not been aware of any such 'chatter' about Trump. But the episode reveals something else: that Trump was impressed with Xi, on whose presidency there was now no such temporal limitation. Later, Xi said that the US had too many elections, and that he 'didn't want to switch away from Trump.' Trump 'nodded approvingly.'[4]

During a telephone conversation between Xi and Trump on 29 December 2018, Xi said that he hoped that 'Trump would have another term by amending the Constitution.'[5] All the while, Trump was targeting Chinese imports with large tariffs, for which, ultimately, American consumers paid in the form of higher prices. In this way, he hoped to pressure China to conclude a 'trade deal' that he could use at the next election as proof of his tough negotiating skills. This topic also featured in a telephone conversation between the presidents on 18 June 2019. Trump began by saying that he missed Xi. The trade deal with China, he said, was 'the most popular thing' he had ever done and a big political bonus for him. The conversation was in preparation for the 2019 G20 summit in Osaka. When posing for the photographer at the summit, Trump said, sweetly: 'We've become friends. My trip to Beijing with my family was one of the most incredible of my life.' Once the press had departed, Xi emphasized that the relationship between China and the US was the most important bilateral relationship in the world. Some political figures in the US wanted a new cold war, Xi said, leaving open the question of just who he was referring to – the Democratic Party or conservative Republicans such as Bolton himself, who was sitting at the same table. Trump assumed that Xi meant the Democrats, and agreed that there was a lot of hostility towards China among them. 'Stunningly,' as Bolton puts it, Trump changed the topic and began to talk about the US presidential elections. He asked Xi to help him by using China's economic capabilities, suggesting

China could buy more soybeans and wheat from American farmers, which could tip the election in Trump's favour. 'You're the greatest Chinese leader in three hundred years!' Trump flattered his Chinese counterpart. Probably because it had not been clear even to Trump why he had chosen 'three hundred years', only a few minutes later he clarified: 'the greatest leader in Chinese history'.[6]

When the thirtieth anniversary of the Tiananmen Square massacre was approaching, Trump's staff were preparing a White House statement. His secretary of the treasury, Steven Mnuchin, sought to tone down the text so as not to jeopardize the trade talks. But Trump went one better: he cancelled the statement altogether. 'That was fifteen years ago', he said – getting the date wrong. 'Who cares about it? I'm trying to make a deal. I don't want anything.' Nor was Trump interested in the fate of the pro-democracy movement in Hong Kong. In a telephone conversation of 18 June 2019, he gave Xi Jinping carte blanche for the use of violence. Hong Kong, Trump said, was a domestic issue for China, and he told his advisors not to discuss the topic in public. Xi was obviously pleased about this. On 13 August 2019, however, Trump expressed himself in public. In a statement that could have come from the Communist Party itself, he wrote on Twitter: 'I know President Xi of China very well. He is a great leader who very much has the respect of his people. He is also a good man in a "tough business". I have ZERO doubt that if President Xi wants to quickly and humanely solve the Hong Kong problem, he can do it.'[7]

Trump and Xi also agreed about the need to take a tough stance against Muslims – after all, one of the first things Trump did after becoming president was institute the 'Muslim ban', which prohibited citizens from seven countries with predominantly Muslim populations, among them war-torn Syria and its refugees, from entering the US. Bolton writes: 'At the opening dinner of the Osaka G20 meeting, with only interpreters present, Xi explained to Trump why he was basically building concentration camps in Xinjiang. According to our interpreter, Trump said that Xi should go ahead with building the camps, which he thought was exactly the right thing to do.'[8]

When the Covid-19 pandemic broke out, Trump praised Xi Jinping's handling of the crisis at least fifteen times.[9] On 24 January 2020, he wrote on Twitter: 'China has been working very hard to contain the

Coronavirus. The United States greatly appreciates their efforts and transparency. It will all work out well. In particular, on behalf of the American People, I want to thank President Xi!'[10]

As we now know, this romance would end before long. Trump began to call the coronavirus the 'Chinese virus'. He launched a frontal attack on the People's Republic, and invoked Hong Kong and Xinjiang for the purpose. But it was not that he had ceased to admire 'strong man' Xi Jinping. Rather, with high numbers of Covid-19 infections and casualties in the US, Trump simply needed a scapegoat. The broader context, however, is even more important. 'The US undoing itself under Trump is a godsend for the CP in Beijing', the sinologist Kai Strittmatter writes.[11] By calling the professional media 'fake news', Trump confirms Chinese government propaganda that says that any critical reports are always 'lies', while the US's trade war against China – and against Europe – allows Xi Jinping to present himself as the defender of global free trade.

In his opening speech at the World Economic Forum in Davos on 17 January 2017, Xi performed this role with particular aplomb. Every year, the global economic elite gathers in the snow-covered Swiss canton of Graubünden. Never before had Davos greeted a communist as it greeted Xi Jinping that day. He declaimed: 'Any attempt to cut off the flow of capital, technologies, products, industries and people between economies, and channel the waters in the ocean back into isolated lakes and creeks is simply not possible. Indeed, it runs counter to the historical trend.'[12] This statement was somewhat disingenuous: China limits foreign investment in the country – often permitting it only in the form of joint ventures with state-owned companies – and it controls the financial markets. Incidentally, there are strong arguments for these controls: they have protected China against the worst consequences of international financial crises.

Donald Trump was inaugurated as the forty-fifth president of the United States only three days after Xi's performance at Davos, but his policy of 'America First' and his plans for trade barriers were already well known. Without mentioning Trump by name, Xi effectively aimed this comment at him: 'We must remain committed to developing global free trade and investment, promote trade and investment liberalization and facilitation through opening up, and say no to protectionism. Pursuing protectionism is like locking oneself in a dark room. While wind and rain may be kept outside, the dark room also will block light and air. No one will emerge as a winner in a trade war.'[13]

By now, there is even talk of actual war between China and the US. The topic is hotly debated on Chinese social media. Hu Xijin, editor-in-chief of China's *Global Times*, warned: 'Even though most Americans may not want to go to war, their rampant populism and their displeasure at China's rapid development may be exploited by Trump to deflect blame for his failures.' He did not believe that a Democratic president would change anything about this: 'China needs to be ready for more extreme and riskier provocations from America. Hurry up and make more nuclear weapons which can serve as a deterrent to those mad Americans.' His statement garnered 100,000 likes and more than 15,000 – mostly approving – comments.[14]

Germany's former foreign minister Sigmar Gabriel does not share these fears – regardless of who governs the US. 'If there is one thing Donald Trump might actually be consistent about, it is that he does not want a war – whether that is because it is his deeply held conviction, or because his voters do not want one', he told us during our conversation at the Atlantik-Brücke headquarters in Berlin. 'Neither Republicans nor Democrats want one. There is a broad consensus about it in America, along the lines of, "Stop the endless wars, bring our boys home." The first to say this, by the way, was the left-wing candidate for the Democratic presidential nomination Bernie Sanders.' Another illustration of this development, Gabriel said, was the founding of a new think tank in Washington in 2019, the interestingly named Quincy Institute for Responsible Statecraft. John Quincy Adams was the American president between 1825 and 1829, and the first to propagate isolationism – that is, keeping the country out of international conflict. He famously said that the US 'goes not abroad in search of monsters to destroy'.[15] The institute is financed by two men who could not be more opposed to one another: the investor George Soros, who finances civil rights movements across the world and whom right-wing groups allege to be part of a 'worldwide Jewish conspiracy', and the last of the Koch brothers, the oil and chemical industry tycoons and main backers of the arch-conservative Tea Party movement.

China, too, has a reputation for not intervening in conflicts in other parts of the world, even as it actively pursues its interests. No cause for concern, then. Right?

One case that shows just how easily the two superpowers could inadvertently end up at war is the Korean War between 1950 and 1953. Similar to Germany, Korea was divided into Soviet-occupied and American-occupied zones at the end of World War II. In 1948, the two zones became the Democratic People's Republic of Korea (better known as North Korea) and the Republic of Korea (South Korea). But unlike Germany, both countries were armed. The Koreans had not lost the war. Rather, the Soviets and Americans had liberated them from the colonial rule of Japan.

On 12 January 1950, in a speech to the National Press Club, the US secretary of state Dean Acheson hinted that the Americans would not enter a war to defend South Korea.[16] This encouraged the North Korean dictator Kim Il-sung, on 25 June 1950, to send troops across the border – the 38th parallel – in an attempt to reunify Korea under his leadership. Only three days later he had taken South Korea's capital, Seoul. Then, American troops intervened after all, in action that was legitimized retrospectively by a UN mandate.

China's statements had so far been as peaceful as the US's had been before the outbreak of war: the conflict, China said, was an internal Korean dispute. A 'red line', however, would be crossed if the Americans pushed North Korea back beyond the 38th parallel and advanced towards the border with China.[17] But that was precisely what happened. Believing its own security to be under threat, China sent hundreds of thousands of 'volunteers' across the border into North Korea, joining the war against the US in October 1950.

Is this just a long-forgotten episode from a bygone world? For Xi Jinping, the answer is no. Whereas China used to mark anniversaries of the Korean War with low-key events, the seventieth anniversary, in October 2020, was quite the spectacle. To commemorate the 'war of resistance against US aggression and in aid of Korea', a celebration was held in the Great Hall of the People and Xi gave a speech to assembled political and military leaders. 'The Chinese people mean that we should speak to the invaders in a language they understand', he declared. 'The Chinese and Korean armies finally defeated the opponents and also broke the legendary US Army, who were supposed to be invincible.'[18] This is an exaggeration. The Korean War, which cost the lives of more than 4 million people,[19] ended where it began: at the 38th parallel.

'China will never seek hegemony, expansion or spheres of influence', Xi Jinping claims. His proof for this claim is rather idiosyncratic: 'For several millennia, peace has been in the blood of us Chinese and a part of our DNA.'[20] Other peoples must presumably therefore have war in their DNA. Xi's statement also contradicts the tenets of Marxism: as Mao wrote, war 'has existed ever since the emergence of private property and of classes',[21] both of which undeniably existed in China until 1949 – and in truth exist again today. From the conquests of the Zhou dynasty around 1,000 BC to the submission of the surrounding empires by Qin Shihuangdi – the name meaning 'First Supreme Divine Emperor of Qin' – and the Qing dynasty's intrusions into Tibet and Xinjiang, the history of China has been a history of war. It has this in common with most countries; at least the larger ones. The last war fought by the Chinese, incidentally, was against Vietnam – to the great horror of all die-hard leftists. China, by far the larger country, abjectly failed, just as the French and the US had before.

This brings us up to the present. There is still tension between China and Vietnam; for instance, over control of the Spratly Islands in the South China Sea, to which the Philippines, Malaysia, Brunei and Taiwan all likewise lay claim. The background is that Chinese geologists suspect there are about 900 trillion cubic metres of gas and more than 200 billion barrels of oil under the seabed around the islands, which would make it one of the largest gas and oil reserves in the world.[22] As in all such cases – another example would be the dispute between Greece and Turkey over islands in the Aegean Sea – the claims to sovereignty are contested. There is a need for negotiation and clear international rules. In 2016, the Permanent Court of Arbitration in The Hague made some rulings in favour of the Philippines, but the Chinese government has ignored the court, created artificial islands in the area, used its military to build harbours and runways, and stationed missiles there.[23] This is a superpower throwing its weight around, behaviour with which we are familiar from the US – no worse, but also no better.

The former US secretary of state Madeleine Albright feared war between her country and China. 'I am afraid that something like this could develop out of a kind of accident', she told us. 'I have in mind incidents in the South China Sea like the one in which the Chinese navy fired at Vietnamese fishing boats.'

Nowhere is the risk of war breaking out greater than in the Taiwan Strait.

12

Why Xi Jinping Fears Hong Kong and Taiwan

The other, democratic China

In 1997, the British handed Hong Kong back to China – an act that can be seen as symbolic of the end of an era of European and American dominance and the beginning of an era of Chinese dominance. Before the event, People's Liberation Army soldiers carrying rifles practised for the historical day: they ran up a barren hill, following a standard-bearer with a red flag. The same soldiers crossed the border from China to Hong Kong in the early hours of 1 July. The People's Republic was handed $69 billion in currency reserves – the 'greatest dowry since Cleopatra', as Chris Patten, the last governor of Hong Kong, had called it.[1] At the end of the ninety-nine-year lease that the United Kingdom had imposed on a weakened Chinese empire, China took charge of the area again. Seven million Hong Kong Chinese were left behind. 'The British failed to introduce democracy in Hong Kong', Emily Lau told us at the time. She was a member of the Legislative Council of Hong Kong, which in 1995 became a fully and directly elected legislature for the first – and last – time. Up until then, the British governor had ruled more or less without the population having a say. 'But their greatest betrayal is that they simply dropped us. Many people living here fled China. Now, the British surrender them to Chinese communist rule again.'

On the day that Hong Kong was handed over to China, it rained almost without interruption, as if even the sky was weeping. When we asked Chris Patten whether Hong Kong or China would change more in the coming years, he replied: 'China.'

The next two decades would prove him right. Now, however, China is tightening its grip.

Reunification Hong Kong-style was an annexation of one of the world's financial hubs by the world's most economically developed socialist country. In 1997, Hong Kong had the highest proportions of Ferrari, motorboat and mobile phone owners in the world. According to Deng Xiaoping's formula 'one country, two systems', Hong Kong was to become part of China, but for the next fifty years was to enjoy the status of a capitalist Special Administrative Region.

Hong Kong is home to a booming stock market, beautiful skyscrapers and large shopping malls. At the luxury bar Felix, situated on the twenty-eighth floor of the Peninsula Hotel, even the toilets are more extravagant than in other places: the gentlemen making use of the marble urinals are able to gaze at the skyline of the metropolis through a glass wall. Ironically, the capitalists were in favour of the communists: the handover was welcomed in particular by the city's richest. Among them was the millionaire Lam family, who own factories, hotels and real estate. Daughter Pearl showed us around her villa, which was furnished as one would have expected. She showed us one of her treasures. 'Let us take a look at the Cleopatra lamp. This is a very interesting lamp – you call it the Cleopatra light. It was created by the artist Patrice Butler. It has the form of Cleopatra's hair. All this was done together with the artist by jewellery designers. These are all lapis lazuli, semi-precious stones.' Pearl Lam thought the union with China a worthwhile venture. 'If we, the people of Hong Kong, were still afraid of communism, we wouldn't invest in China. Today, there are many Hong Kong entrepreneurs who invest in China, because we know: we are going into a third-world country. You invest in it because labour is cheap there. Here in Hong Kong, the wages are so high that we have shifted large parts of production to China, especially in the textile industry. That's all in China now.'

The state broadcaster prepared the Chinese public for the historic day through a constant drip of news and reports. Patriotic popstars looked forward to the reunion with such lyrics as: 'For how many years I could not sleep at night, and longed for the dream to come true. Now, finally, the water from ten thousand springs flows together into a long stream, and it sounds like a symphony.'

Kai Bon and Brenda Chau were chiefly known for appearing in outfits that matched their Rolls-Royce limousines – pink and gold. The couple ate with golden cutlery – even their telephone was made of gold. Like other Hong Kong millionaires, they saw the reunion as an opportunity to increase their wealth even further. 'I hope Hong Kong will continue to flourish, because it is packed with industrious and smart business people,' Kai Bon Chau told us. 'I know many Chinese manufacturers. They also make a lot of money. So why should our lifestyle not continue as before?'

At the time, cinemas were showing *Chinese Box*, a movie about the reunion of Hong Kong and China made by the Chinese-American director Wayne Wang. The film is about a British journalist who, having been diagnosed with leukaemia, does not have long to live, and spends his time shooting footage about the handover of the crown colony to China and navigating his relationships with two Chinese women. The lead roles are played by the Oscar-winning British actor Jeremy Irons and the famous Chinese actresses Gong Li and Maggie Cheung. Gong Li is mainly known from films by the Chinese director Zhang Yimou, such as *Raise the Red Lantern* and *The Curse of the Golden Flower*. She was president of the jury at the Berlinale in 2000 and at the Venice Film Festival in 2002. The day before the reunion ceremony, we met Gong Li in Hong Kong for an interview.

'I hope that the union will have a positive influence on China,' she said. 'The links are growing, economically as well as culturally. Hong Kong is economically flourishing. I hope that Beijing and Shanghai will follow the example of Hong Kong.' What she said next was remarkable, especially as she was still a member of the Chinese People's Political Consultative Conference – that is, the advisory council of China's National People's Congress: 'The union with China should not have any strong political impact on Hong Kong. For a long time, the people of Hong Kong have been used to a life without controls and restrictions, and therefore live in a very relaxed fashion. I hope that nothing will change politically.'

For some time, it seemed that at least freedom of the press and the right to protest were secure in Hong Kong. Tourists from other parts of the People's Republic stocked up on books that were prohibited elsewhere in the country. But Hong Kong never got the free, direct, general parliamentary elections promised in the constitution of Hong Kong, the Hong Kong Basic Law. The constitution was passed by China's National People's Congress ahead of the reunion and was part of the agreement between China and the UK. In reality, the people elect only a small number of representatives, and the majority are elected by business organizations that are close to Beijing.

Those who lived in Hong Kong before the reunion with China probably got the impression that the citizens of this metropolis were interested only in money – never in politics. In recent years, the people of Hong Kong have proven otherwise. In 2019, up to 2 million people took to the streets to demonstrate for their freedom – a substantial part of the population of 7 million, especially if we subtract children and the elderly. Xi Jinping was neither impressed nor pleased. 'Politicizing everything or deliberately creating differences and provoking confrontation will not resolve these problems,' he said. 'On the contrary, it will only serve to hinder Hong Kong's economic and social development.'[2]

The vast majority of the demonstrators in Hong Kong were peaceful. They composed a song that became an unofficial Hong Kong national anthem, and was sung by crowds of thousands in shopping malls and elsewhere, often accompanied by wind and string instruments:

> We pledge: No more tears on our land
> In wrath, doubts dispell'd we make our stand
> Arise! Ye who would not be slaves again
> For Hong Kong, may Freedom reign
> Though deep is the dread that lies ahead
> Yet still with our faith on we tread
> Let blood rage afield! Our voice grows evermore
> For Hong Kong, may Glory reign

Many protesters wore masks so that they could not be identified by the police. The Hong Kong government prohibited the wearing of masks by invoking a colonial-era emergency law that had not been used for more than fifty years.[3] In an ironic twist, the same government later made the wearing of masks mandatory during the Covid-19 pandemic. The police used force against the protesters, and demands for these incidents to be investigated were ignored. Some protesters did, however, throw Molotov cocktails, demolish subway stations and attack Chinese people from the mainland just for speaking Mandarin. Protesters occupied a university and the airport – something no government would tolerate. Some demonstrators demanded that Hong Kong become an independent state, which played into the hands of the Communist Party: anyone who argues that China is violating the 'one country, two systems' doctrine by failing to keep the two systems distinct, loses credibility by rejecting the other half of the formula – 'one country'. Most Chinese people recalled that it was the colonial power that had separated Hong Kong from the mainland, and the sight of some of the protesters waving British and American flags seemed to confirm to China that its enemies were behind the movement.

On 30 June 2020, one day before the anniversary of the union with Hong Kong, Xi Jinping signed the 'Law of the People's Republic of China on Safeguarding National Security in the Hong Kong Special Administrative Region'. He intentionally kept the law vague, giving the state broad scope to take action against its critics. Its provisions include the following:

- Anyone advocating the separation of Hong Kong from China or colluding with 'external elements' may be sentenced to life in prison.
- Anyone causing damage to public transport can be sentenced as a 'terrorist' – to life in prison, of course.
- Beijing will establish its own national security office in Hong Kong, which will be independent of the local authorities.
- Suspects can be tried in courts in the People's Republic.
- Trials can take place in camera.
- The power to interpret the law lies with Beijing, not the Hong Kong Legislative Council or Hong Kong courts.[4]

Shortly after the national security law came into effect, leading Hong Kong democratic activists were arrested, for example the publisher Jimmy Lai and the young activist Agnes Chow.[5] When it became clear that the democratic opposition was heading for an overwhelming victory in the elections for the Legislative Council in September 2020, the Hong Kong government delayed the elections for a year, using

Covid-19 as a pretext.[6] Donald Trump had helped the government in this by suggesting on Twitter, a day before the announcement, that the US presidential elections should be postponed because of Covid-19.[7] The chief executive of Hong Kong's government, Carrie Lam, who had been appointed by Beijing, was then given the authority to remove Legislative Council members who were suspected of being in favour of Hong Kong's independence. In November 2020, four members were removed from the Legislative Council on that basis, prompting all the other pro-democracy representatives to resign in protest.[8] Xi Jinping had thus in effect eliminated the official opposition, just as he had everywhere else in the People's Republic. His justification for such tactics comes from Ban Gu, a historian who lived at the time of the Han dynasty (202 BC–220 AD): 'Harmony brings good fortune, while discord leads to misfortune.'[9]

One of the representatives who resigned is the lawyer James To Kun-sun. He had been a member of the Legislative Council since 1991. He said: 'One might think that China today feels that it is great and powerful. But maybe this is actually not the case. Maybe the international situation worries the leadership so much that it feels vulnerable, and thus it crushes Hong Kong to shield China from its influence.'[10]

No other country follows events in Hong Kong as closely as Taiwan, officially the 'Republic of China', and considered by the People's Republic to be a breakaway province that is to be incorporated on the basis of the 'one country, two systems' formula.

More people live in China than in any other country on earth, but its history is sometimes just a family affair. 'Once upon a time, in faraway China, there were three sisters', a Chinese film begins, 'one loved money, one loved power, and one loved her country.' Not everyone may sympathize with the film's message, but the story is true. The three sisters were the daughters of the entrepreneur and revolutionary Charlie Soong. The eldest, Soong Ai-ling (born 1888), married the banker Kung Hsiang-hsi, also known as H. H. Kung and at that time China's richest man. The middle daughter, Soong Ching-ling (born 1893), married Sun Yat-sen, from 1912 the first president of the Republic of China. He is today revered in both the People's Republic of China and Taiwan. After the communist victory, Soong Ching-ling was vice-president and for some years even the honorary chairwoman of the People's Republic. She is the one who, as the film has it, 'loved her country'. The youngest daughter, Soong Mei-ling (born 1897), married Chiang Kai-shek, who became the most important figure in the Kuomintang following the death of Sun Yat-sen in 1925. Under Chiang Kai-shek's leadership, the party changed from being allies of the communists to being their enemy, leading to the civil war. During World War II, both sides fought against the Japanese, and the three Soong sisters played decisive roles in forging this alliance. In 1945, the civil war recommenced, and in 1949 Chiang Kai-shek and Soong Mei-ling fled with their followers to the island of Taiwan, where Soong remained the first lady until her husband's death.

The Soong Sisters is thus based on historical fact. It begins with an emotional scene set in Beijing in 1981. Soong Ching-ling is on her deathbed. A high-ranking government official sends a telegram to Soong Mei-ling. Another official, who happens to notice, whispers to a colleague: 'I have worked in this department for years, but I have never heard of a telegram being sent to the Chiang Kai-shek family.'

The Chiang and Soong family may be the most famous, but it is far from being the only one to have been separated by the division of China. We have already mentioned the fact that Peng Liyuan, Xi Jinping's wife, has relatives in Taiwan. In 1997, she visited the island as part of a cultural exchange. She was thirty-four, and it was the first time she had met her maternal uncle, a retired teacher. The relationship with Taiwan remains a sensitive issue. Because of her husband's position and her own role as a communist folk singer, the first lady's 'southern relatives' (geographically speaking) are rarely mentioned.[11]

A dragon winds itself around a pillar. Teenagers in sportswear wear feathers almost as big as themselves. Other youngsters are drumming. This is a ceremony at the Confucius Temple in Taipei, the capital of Taiwan. At the entrance to the temple, dozens of citizens are lighting incense. Their demeanour is grave; there is none of the touristic hullabaloo that characterizes such places in China. Unlike in China, in Taiwan the Confucian tradition stretches back unbroken into the past. And a new tradition has been added: the democratic tradition. Chiang

Kai-shek also ruled as a dictator, but after his death Taiwan became increasingly liberal, and today is a democracy. Taiwan is proof that Confucianism, 'Chinese characteristics', and constitutional democracy are compatible.

We are following the 2008 election campaign. On a pavement not far from the presidential palace, a bank director, Huang Jinchang, shouts at a pensioner, Chen Xiangmei: 'You are cheats!' She blasts back: 'Your president Chen Shui-bian is shameless!' A crowd starts to gather, with people joining one or the other side of the dispute. The bank director and his friends wear T-shirts saying 'Taiwan – my country'. They support the president, Chen Shui-bian, who is campaigning for the country to join the UN under the name 'Taiwan'.

'Our country has its own government, army and currency. We are a sovereign country and a democracy. We want our dignity', an independence supporter shouts. An opponent responds: 'Your independence is recognized by almost no one in the world, and the UN will not accept us as a member'. For us, having arrived from Beijing, the most astonishing thing about the dispute was that it took place at all. In the People's Republic of China, the police would have arrested one group or the other – possibly both.

Those on the pensioner's side of the argument fly a red flag with a blue canton bearing a white sun: the flag of all of China until the communist revolution of 1949, and the flag of the Republic of China today. Few know the country by that name, however; to most people, the island of 24 million people is Taiwan. And in 2008, its president, Chen Shui-bian, wants to officially change the country's name to 'Taiwan'.

And here he comes, running along, in white T-shirt and jogging bottoms, with a torch in hand, on his face the permanent smile that has become his trademark. No, it is not a double, or someone wearing a mask: this really is the president. He is drawing attention to the bid to join the UN with a torch relay around the country. It is a provocation to the leadership in Beijing. China's leaders had wanted the Olympic flame's journey to take in Taiwan, but on condition that the Taiwanese flag would not be flown and the Taiwanese national anthem would not be played. Taiwan's government refused.

The opposing party also donned sports gear on this day. Ma Ying-jeou, the Nationalist Party (Kuomintang) candidate, and his supporters went on a bike ride. Ma is in favour of a unified China, and for this reason is Beijing's preferred choice. Even he, however, does not want unification under communism, and for good reason – during the civil war, communists slaughtered Kuomintang forces, and the Kuomintang were forced to flee to Taiwan. This history also lies behind one of the island's contemporary rifts, namely the tension between the original residents of the island who see themselves as Taiwanese and the immigrants from mainland China who see themselves as Chinese.

'Chen Shui-bian has called us immigrant pigs,' Chen Xiangmei claims. She holds her flag, and begins to cry. An eighty-five-year-old man, Liu Shanbin, rolls up his sleeves to reveal his wounds from the Sino-Japanese war. He depends on welfare benefits, and sleeps on a straw matt inside the train station because he cannot afford a flat. He complains: 'Chen Shui-bian takes the money we made with our blood and sweat and gives it to small countries so that they will support Taiwan's independence.' Only fifteen states still recognize Taiwan, with Haiti and Vatican City among the better known of them.

Supporters of the Kuomintang are not just older people and those stuck in the past. As in Hong Kong, it is the capitalists who seek friendly relations with a China governed by communists. Taiwanese companies locate their factories in the People's Republic – more than $200 billion has been invested there – and almost half of Taiwan's exports go to mainland China. It is not just entrepreneurs who benefit – the employees of the companies do too. The People's Republic is also a key market for Taiwanese popstars and singers, who mainly tour in the vast Chinese-speaking mainland.

Ximending is the flashy part of Taipei. Here, young women wear hotpants and high heels. The restaurants offer sushi and Japanese grilled meat. The shops sell sweets in the shape of condoms, and pens that emit the groans of a female orgasm. Bolivian musicians play in the street. On the mainland, the busking alone would be enough for the police to intervene. The freedom-loving young people here are, however, not much interested in politics. Ahead of the 2008 election, many have not yet decided who they will vote for. Some tell us that Ma, China's preferred candidate, is a 'gentleman,' and Chen Shui-bian a 'peasant.' Heidi Wu, a twenty-four-year-old office employee, who also speaks German, is sauntering around with a female friend. She says:

'I don't care about the elections – or about independence. The main thing is: get the economy booming again!'

Ma Ying-jeou would go on to win the 2008 election with 58 per cent of the vote. His predecessor, Chen Shui-bian, was later imprisoned for corruption and money-laundering, accusations that had been levelled against him even by many on his own side. He resigned from the party before it could expel him. Nowhere else in the Chinese-speaking regions is the rule of law as strong as in Taiwan.

In 2005, the Chinese National People's Congress passed an 'anti-secession law', which threatens Taiwan with war should it officially declare its independence. But the victory of the Kuomintang in 2008 improved relations. Travellers could finally take direct flights between Beijing and Taipei, and there was a ceremony with drums and dragon dances to celebrate. Previously, people had had to travel via Hong Kong or Japan. China still aims missiles at its 'brothers and sisters' to warn them against disobedience. Any conflict could set the whole world alight. The US provides Taiwan with missile defence systems and military helicopters, and the US's 1979 Taiwan Relations Act commits the country to standing by Taiwan if it is attacked. Trump's former national security advisor John Bolton is not so sure: 'When Trump abandoned the Kurds in Syria, there was speculation about who he might abandon next. Taiwan was right near the top of the list.'[12]

Is it possible to find a two-state solution, so that other countries can have diplomatic relations with both the People's Republic of China and the Republic of China, as eventually happened with the Federal Republic of Germany and the German Democratic Republic? 'You can take that position', Sigmar Gabriel told us, 'but you have to be aware that it would really be you yourself who was comfortable with it. Down there, you may trigger a military conflict. We Germans are very good at this: we always feel good when we take the righteous side. But German and European politics needs to be careful not to bite off more than it can chew, given that we are not able to intervene even in our immediate vicinity, for instance in Catalonia. Don't forget, we are the last vegetarians in a world of meat eaters.'

In November 2015, Xi Jinping met with Taiwan's president, Ma Ying-jeou. Official reports of the meeting made sure to describe it as a 'talk with Taiwan leader Ma Ying-jeou', lest any impression be given that Taiwan was a state rather than a Chinese province. But, whatever the description, it was a historic meeting: the first time that a president of the People's Republic of China had met with the foremost Taiwanese politician. 'Over the past 60 years the two sides across the Straits have followed different paths of development, and practiced different social systems,' Xi said at the meeting. 'The judgment on the path and system will be made by history and the people. Both sides should respect each other's choice of development path and social system.'[13] Those remarkably reconciliatory words sounded like a formula for successful cooperation – if only Xi Jinping had not frightened the citizens of Taiwan with the aggressive measures he was imposing in Hong Kong. At the election that took place two months after the meeting, the crackdown in Hong Kong helped the Democratic Progressive Party, which is critical of Beijing, to win. The party's candidate, Tsai Ing-wen, became president.

Tsai Ing-wen supports the continuing democratization of Taiwan. When it comes to LGBTQ rights, Taiwan is one of the most liberal countries in Asia: Taiwan was the first Asian country to legalize same-sex marriage. Tsai Ing-wen's opponents used this as the basis for personal attacks, alluding to the fact that she is unmarried and childless – something that is out of step with traditional Chinese notions of womanhood. They called on her to reveal her sexual orientation, which she refused to do.

It is a credit to Taiwan that those attacks did not harm her public image – quite the contrary. Far more problematic for her was the sluggish growth of the Taiwanese economy. In January 2020, she was nevertheless re-elected with a clear majority. In Taiwan, the people elect the president directly, and she received 57 per cent of the popular vote. Her rival, Han Kuo-yu, of the pro-Chinese Kuomintang, received 39 per cent of the vote. In her victory speech, Tsai Ing-wen thanked everyone who took part in the election, regardless of which candidate they voted for. 'With every election we show the world how much we cherish our free and democratic way of life,' she said. She appealed to the international community for more recognition for the republican island that China seeks to isolate. 'All countries should see Taiwan as a partner, not as a problem.'[14] Taiwan is a truly democratic country. It has the rule of law, and there have been several changes of government in recent decades. At the same time, Taiwan has developed very well overall. The country stands as a refutation of the claim that parliamentary democracy and Chinese values cannot go together.

'Forces and activities for "Taiwan independence" remain a real threat to the peace of the Taiwan Straits',[15] Xi Jinping claims. He openly warns of war, as if the small Taiwanese population of 24 million represented a threat to the 1.4 billion mainland Chinese. 'We will enhance our combat readiness through full-scale combat simulation exercises, and reinforce the belief that as soldiers our mission is to fight, and as officers our mission is to lead our men to victory.'[16]

Taiwan's digital minister, Audrey Tang, is a transgender former hacker. She is partly responsible for Taiwan's exceptional response to the Covid-19 crisis, which was better even than China's: by March 2021, Taiwan had had only 955 cases and nine deaths. When the supply of face masks was running low early in the pandemic, Audrey Tang made information on supplies available to everyone, so that people knew where they could still get masks. She developed an online platform, 'Join', for citizens to discuss proposed legislation. She sums up the difference between digitalization in the People's Republic and digitalization in Taiwan as follows: 'In China, the citizens are meant to be transparent for the state. We want to make the state transparent for the citizens.'[17]

This could pose a threat to Xi Jinping, and he intends to counter it. According to Ai Weiwei's contacts in Beijing, the main reason that Xi removed the limitation on his time in office was his desire to 'liberate' Taiwan. Ai remembered: 'Every year Premier Zhou Enlai in the last sentence of his congressional speech said: "For sure we have to liberate Taiwan."' Xi intends to make good on that promise. Zhou's statement recalls the Roman statesman Cato the Elder, who ended his senate speeches, regardless of the topic, by declaring: 'Ceterum censeo Carthaginem esse delendam.' ('Furthermore, I consider that Carthage must be destroyed.')

13

Will the Whole World Benefit from the Chinese Dream?

This of all places was where they wanted to land their small spaceship: on the other side of the moon, the 'dark side'. The dark side of the moon is, of course, not dark at all, but you cannot see it from earth, not even with the best of telescopes, because, well, it is the side that faces away from the earth. There probably was a reason, though, why early in 2019 the China National Space Administration decided to set down the lunar rover 'Yutu-2' in an area where no one had landed before. Fifty years earlier, the three Americans aboard Apollo 8 had been able only to glance briefly at the dark side of the earth's satellite when they orbited the moon at Christmas time. On Christmas Eve, they read aloud from the Book of Genesis.

The Chinese spoke not of divine blessing but of a 'historical moment' that they themselves had created. Their electric vehicle drove around the moon's surface powered by clean, environmentally friendly energy that was produced by a solar sail. Whether or not the project was a 'giant leap for mankind' to rival the Americans' moon landing, it was an indication that the Chinese are now top players not only on earth but also in space. As in the 'space race' between the US and the Soviet Union, the Chinese mission to the moon was not a purely scientific affair; it was also a demonstration of military power. Whoever can launch a rocket that reaches the moon is able to launch rockets aimed at anywhere on earth. It makes sense that the Chinese space programme is part of the military.

Under Xi Jinping, China has become a great power once again. China achieved this by means of a system of government that no one ever thought could be as productive as capitalist liberal democracy. What lifted China to the top was a one-party state that combines communism and Confucianism.

China's position today is not unprecedented. In antiquity and in medieval times, the country was a leading world power. That said, China's rise is still the greatest comeback in world history. Today, there is no discussion of economic topics that does not mention China's successful resurgence, illustrating it with impressive figures relating to the trade war with the US or the takeover of innovative enterprises and vast areas of land in Africa.

The US ambassador in Berlin was probably glad that his president, Donald Trump, needed to speak to one person only, Xi Jinping, when negotiating a trade deal. At home, Trump could not even reach agreement with the Democratic Party in Congress. He would have loved to have been able to go level with the Chinese by building a Great Wall of America to deter refugees crossing the border from Mexico. Such was the contrast between China's resolve and US dithering even before the US descended into chaos over disputed election results.

It seems that democratic principles and the proper functioning of states are increasingly standing in an antagonistic relation to each other, and not just in the US. The British have Brexited themselves into crisis. The EU failed to procure sufficient supplies of Covid-19 vaccines. In Germany, a stable democracy and still economically successful country, unachievable emissions regulations led car manufacturers to lie to the world, and the car makers were then pursued by an environmental protection organization financed with taxpayers' money. Germany's rushed energy transition might produce all sorts of outcomes, but clean energy is not one of them. Changing regulations and design indecisions meant that the Berlin Brandenburg airport took fourteen years to complete – just in time for the emergence of the pandemic, when most planes were grounded. In comparison, Beijing's significantly larger Daxing mega-airport was completed in four years. Over the next fifteen years, China plans to build 216 new airports.[1]

Meanwhile, many Europeans are busy navel-gazing, contemplating the impending climate apocalypse. The Fridays for Future demonstrations increasingly call for a radical departure from industrial society.

We do not wish to paint too gloomy a picture, but Europeans need to act now if they want to remain internationally competitive. Of the 3.3 million patents that were registered in 2018, almost half came from China – about three times as many as came from the US.

The average Chinese person works 8.5 hours more per week than an average German – adding, in effect, an extra working day to the Chinese week.[2] Ephraim Kishon puts the point succinctly: 'The Asians have conquered the world market using unfair methods – they actually work during working hours.'[3]

After the two world wars, the world's economic centre of gravity – and thus its political centre of gravity – moved from Europe to the US. Now, it is undeniably shifting towards Asia. As our colleague Gabor Steingart comments in his *Morning Briefing* newsletter: 'The time of Western dominance is coming to an end. We should look to the East with goodwill and respect, but without naivety.'[4]

Before the disintegration of the Soviet Union, the advanced age of its leaders was seen as a sign of its moribund condition. Leonid Brezhnev ruled until his death at the age of seventy-five, his successor, Yuri Andropov, until the age of sixty-nine and, following him, Konstantin Chernenko, until the age of seventy-three. Yet they were still younger than Joe Biden, who was seventy-eight when he took office. And at that point in time, his antagonist Donald Trump was seventy-four; the Speaker of the House of Representatives Nancy Pelosi was eighty; and the Republican Senate minority leader Mitch McConnell was seventy-eight. Of course, older people can be very fit, thanks not least to modern medicine, and politicians always rely on ministers and advisors who are often younger than they are. And yet there is a certain symbolic dimension to this: the US is a superpower in decline.

Today, the American president is no longer the most powerful man in the world. The Chinese president is. One reason for this is that the country Xi leads is essentially united – and united not just because of his dictatorial powers. The Chinese people accept Xi Jinping far more wholeheartedly than the deeply divided American public accepts Joe Biden or accepted Trump. By not accepting his defeat and speaking, without evidence or proof, of a rigged election, Trump dealt a severe blow to trust in American democracy. And, while US presidents have to compromise with the bicameral legislature, and courts can overrule their decisions, the Chinese constitution guarantees the leading role of the Communist Party: the party is above the National People's Congress and the courts.

Is dictatorship therefore superior to a free society? At the beginning of the Covid-19 pandemic, the illness was able to spread in China because openly talking about it was prohibited. Perhaps, then, the answer should be no. Then again, the People's Republic was later able to contain the virus. So, should the answer be yes? Are dictatorships better able than free societies to reduce poverty, develop and digitalize the economy, and fight crime?

In the first chapter, we talked about Ai Weiwei's film *CoroNation*. The documentary illustrates that, such are the successes of Xi's dictatorship, even a dissident may inadvertently turn into a propagandist, and even be praised by the intelligence services that are tasked with keeping tabs on him. We asked Ai how the West might arrest its decline. He gave a wry smile: 'this really is the Western way of thinking: we find a problem, we see a problem, then we treat a problem. That is an understanding as if any problem is solvable. But in Eastern philosophy it is very much: There is no solution, because there is no problem. I mean, why you always have to be a winner. No tree is always green. In the autumn the leaves come down. You already had your boom time. Now some other grass may have its turn.'

Democracy is imperilled not because of the 'Chinese threat' but because it no longer fulfils its promises. A system persuades through the power of its example. Most people are not ideologues or activists; they do not categorically support this or that political system. Rather, they are interested in a system's consequences for their own lives. If you need a doctor or a tradesman, it is much easier to find one in a Chinese city than in Germany. Some members of the political elite might think this a trivial problem – in fact, that elite attitude is the problem. People know whether they are better off today than they used to be – as they are in China – or whether conditions are stagnating or even regressing. In many countries, the gap between those at the top and those at the bottom is widening. Again, the pandemic provides a good illustration: while the salaries and expenses of politicians remained untouched, the laws they passed destroyed the livelihoods of millions of people.

A pandemic is an infectious disease that spreads globally, and it can therefore be successfully combated only if all countries coordinate their efforts. In the case of Covid-19, however, each country did its own thing. In the US, President Trump closed the borders first to the Chinese, then to Europeans. Europe protested vehemently, but just days later the EU's external borders, and even its internal ones, were also closed. China, too, sealed itself off from the rest of the world. International travel came to an almost complete standstill.

From a medical perspective, these border closures made no sense. Once a virus has spread globally, long-distance travel contributes no more to its further spread than a journey on the subway does. And for the most part, travel restrictions did not apply universally but only to the citizens of other countries – as if the level of infectiousness depended on nationality. This is reminiscent of the Middle Ages, when Jews were accused of being responsible for the Black Death.

Nationalism is a far more dangerous contagion than a coronavirus. It was rampant even before the pandemic, but Covid-19 acted as a catalyst. Countries sealed themselves off from each other in a way that was unprecedented in the post-war era. For a ruler, nationalism is a powerful tool. This is especially true for Xi Jinping. His slogans about Chinese greatness always go down better with his audience than his Marxist-Leninist boilerplate does. On the international stage, by contrast, he presents himself as a champion of cooperation and an opponent of US hegemony and the new American protectionism. The future of China, and of the whole world, will be shaped by which of these sides of his persona becomes more dominant in the years to come.

For his part, Xi sees no contradiction between the two sides. 'We will bring benefits to both the Chinese people and the people of the rest of the world. The realization of the Chinese dream will bring the world peace, not turmoil, opportunities, not threats.'[5] In terms of the economy, this sounds plausible. Millions of people the world over can afford mobile phones and laptops because they are produced cheaply in China.

But what about politics? How should we approach this new, powerful China? 'We', in this context, refers to all the democratic countries of the world, sometimes loosely referred to as 'the West', a term that should in this context not be confused with a geographical region. Democracies such as South Korea, Japan, Australia and New Zealand lie to the east of China, and former military dictatorships like Chile, Brazil and Argentina – the rulers of which, incidentally, like Xi, justified their rule with reference to the need to prevent chaos – were situated far in the west.

Further, talk of 'Western values' implies that these values apply only to certain parts of the world and are inappropriate for certain peoples and cultures – a thesis that the Communist Party of China also likes to invoke. Ultimately, this is a form of racism; its implication is that some peoples are not yet 'mature' enough for democracy.

Every people, however, has to find its own way towards democracy. We must actively defend our ideas of freedom and human rights. We must not opportunistically adapt, but we also should not be arrogant – and of course should not compel. The countries of the Middle East have shown what happens when the US or others try to 'export' their values: war, suffering and waves of refugees. Donald Trump's 'America First' strategy was a reaction against this. Many mistakenly believed that Trump's strategy was an attempt to defend and expand the US's global leadership. That, in fact, was rather the aim of his rival, Hillary Clinton. Trump thought that the US should scale back its international commitments and concentrate more on its own domestic problems. For this reason, he did not stand up for human rights in China; rather, he thought that the US should 'decouple' from China, weaken its economic competitor and reduce its dependence on Chinese products and supply chains.

Economic sanctions became the new weapon. They are a questionable tool: in the past, the imposition of sanctions on Russia, for instance, boosted Putin's popularity at home. Whether the recent tougher sanctions following Russia's full invasion of Ukraine will change this remains to be seen. At least in the initial stages of the full-blown war, polls still showed wide support for Putin at home. China is no different in this respect. When their country is under pressure from abroad, especially from former colonial powers, the Chinese rally around their leadership. And what is more, the Chinese economy is so closely intertwined with our own that any sanctions would do at least as much damage to us as they would to them. China is also economically more powerful than Russia and therefore less vulnerable as far as possible sanctions are concerned.

Trump weakened democratic alliances. Now, there is a lot of talk about the need for Europe, the US, Japan, South Korea, New Zealand and Australia to form a common strategy on China. But Xi Jinping was quicker. On 15 November 2020, even before Joe Biden took office as the forty-sixth president of the United States, China and fourteen other states in the Asia-Pacific region signed the world's largest free trade agreement: the Regional Comprehensive Economic Partnership (RCEP). Its member states are home to 2.2 billion people and account for about a third of global GDP.[6] China's erstwhile arch-enemy Japan is among the members, as is South Korea, which was at war with China between 1950 and 1953. Among the other members are Indonesia – home to more Muslims than any other country – and the two old democracies of Australia and New Zealand, which were the first to introduce suffrage for women. The other member states are Singapore and Brunei, two of the world's richest countries, and Malaysia, Thailand, the Philippines, Myanmar, Laos, Cambodia and Vietnam. In a strongly symbolic gesture, the virtual summit at which the RCEP was signed was hosted from Vietnam's capital Hanoi, which the US had bombed during the Vietnam War. After Trump, who once said that 'the EU is worse than China, only smaller', the US will now have to rely more on Europe's support again.[7]

According to *Der Spiegel*, 'China's industrial base, the size of its market and the ambitions of its leadership are greater than those of any rival who has ever challenged the US before.'[8] While the success of the new superpower makes some people nervous, others are inspired. 'China's achievements are remarkable', said the former prime minister of Pakistan and erstwhile cricket world champion, Imran Khan. 'I admire the way in which China's leadership has led 700 million people out of poverty within the short time span of forty years. That is the model I want to emulate in Pakistan. Even without elections, they know how to develop the best people in their country. The system is based on performance. I have seen how the Communist Party sieves through all the talents and lifts the best of them to the top.'[9]

China and its allies do not form a solid bloc in the way that the Soviet Union and its allies did. Take, for example, the Shanghai Cooperation Organization, which comprises, apart from China itself, Russia, India, Pakistan, Kazakhstan, Kyrgyzstan, Tajikistan and Uzbekistan. There is only one common denominator between them: they are all opposed to Western hegemony. Besides that, they are arch-enemies. Listen, for instance, to what Imran Khan has to say about his neighbour India: 'India has the most extreme, racist government on the continent and is a threat to its neighbours, that is, to Bangladesh, Sri Lanka, even China. It is a fascist state, inspired by the Nazis of the 1920s and 1930s.'[10] Not exactly a declaration of love.

Putin's attack on the entire Ukraine, which began on 24 February 2022, also drew the world's attention to Xi and to China's relation with Russia. Instead of the frequent talk about a 'sudden' change in the global order, we should follow the Chinese example and look to the larger historical context. Exactly fifty years before the attack, between 21 and 28 February 1972, US President Richard Nixon visited Beijing, Hangzhou and Shanghai. Nixon was anything but a do-gooder and was later removed from office in the course of the Watergate scandal. But he had realized that the US would find it hard to confront an alliance between the Soviet Union and China. Thus, he put aside ideological differences and established good relations with China, at a time when it had merely a fraction of the economic and military power it possesses today. China's subsequent rise also owed much to Nixon's visit.

When the Soviet Union collapsed two decades later, it would have been possible to help the successor states in becoming worthy members of the democratic camp. Instead, the US and Western Europe indulged in complacency and arrogance. In terms of the profits to be gained by doing business with China, the sky seemed the limit – yet it was precisely this business that helped China to grow and become the West's most powerful opponent. At the same time, the US and Europe did not mind that the peoples of Russia and other countries of the former Soviet Union were plundered by oligarchs and corrupt politicians. Russia is no more than a regional power, Barack Obama rejoiced at the time, while the attacks on Iraq and Libya and the persecution of critics such as Edward Snowden and Julian Assange were blatant violations of the West's own moral standards.

It is understandable that countries of the former Eastern bloc wanted to join NATO. But the fact that Russia's reservations about such NATO expansion were ignored drove Putin into the arms of Xi Jinping. Despite the pictures from the Russian invasion of Ukraine, which may seem to suggest otherwise, the main problem in the long term is not Russia's actions, representing the death throes of a declining superpower. The real problem is that China is on its way to becoming the world's leading superpower – and a much stronger one than Russia or the Soviet Union ever were.

On 4 February 2022, Xi Jinping opened the Beijing Winter Olympics, making China's capital the first city to have hosted both the summer and winter games. On this same day of great personal triumph for Xi, he welcomed Vladimir Putin as an Olympic guest. The purpose of their meeting was not limited to an exchange of niceties, as is common for such encounters on the margins of large sporting events. Instead, the two men signed a 'Joint Statement of the Russian Federation and the People's Republic of China on the International Relations Entering a New Era and the Global Sustainable Development.'[11] The statement is fourteen pages long, but the title alone sounds sarcastic given that just twenty days later Russia started its general war against all of Ukraine. The fourteen pages contain sentences of Orwellian proportions: 'The sides note that Russia and China as world powers with rich cultural and historical heritage have long-standing traditions of democracy.' The rich cultural and historical heritage part is unquestionable, but up to that point many Chinese and Russians, especially those who are pro-government, would have argued that their countries lack a democratic tradition and therefore need an authoritarian form of rule. What the authors of the document really want to signal is that, as international relations enter a 'new era,' China and Russia want to decide not only what happens in the world but also what it is called, for instance whether the bombing of a children's hospital or a theatre packed with civilians is part of a 'war' or a 'special military operation.'

With the 'Joint Statement,' Xi Jinping gave Putin carte blanche to attack Ukraine. The document explicitly adopts Putin's arguments: 'The sides oppose further enlargement of NATO and call on the North Atlantic Alliance to abandon its ideologized cold war approaches.' And as Xi scratches Putin's back, so Putin scratches Xi's: 'The Russian side reaffirms its support for the One-China principle, confirms that Taiwan is an inalienable part of China, and opposes any forms of independence of Taiwan.'

Fifty years after the meeting between Nixon and Mao, China and Russia are brothers again – and both are enemies of the US. But whereas after 1949, Mao was Stalin's little brother, the relation is now reversed: Xi Jinping is the big brother and Putin the little one. While their alliance offers opportunities to both parties, it also carries risks. China's state media repeats claims made by Russian propaganda about Ukraine; at the UN Security Council, however, China abstained in the vote concerning the war. Xi was probably equally unhappy about Russia's botched military advance and the consequences for the global economy. Putin's war has also united NATO and the European Union, at least for the time being, while the intention behind the Chinese-Russian alliance had been to weaken their unity.

Does Xi Jinping aspire to rule the world? Or is his goal only – as he himself declares – to ensure that, with the 100th birthday of the Communist Party, all of China enjoys a moderate level of prosperity, and that, on the 100th anniversary of the foundation of the People's Republic, in 2049, China will have been transformed into a wealthy and modern country that lives in harmony with everyone else?

The question may be put differently. Is Xi's role model the ideologue Mao, who once wrote: 'The communist ideological and social system alone is full of youth and vitality, sweeping the world with the momentum of an avalanche and the force of a thunderbolt'?[12] Or is it the pragmatist Deng Xiaoping, who in 1978 visited Singapore – the 'running dogs of American imperialism', according to the Chinese party press at the time – and declared that China should follow its example?[13]

The founding father of Singapore, the late Lee Kuan Yew, explained to us his Confucian model of education and social responsibility. He was blunt: 'It is very difficult to educate people to become citizens of the "first world". We didn't find it easy to change traditionally engrained habits. It took many years; we had to re-educate the people. How should one behave when living in a high-rise building? People had to stop spitting on the floor, throwing rubbish into the street and urinating everywhere. When they lived in the slums, they simply went over to the next tree to answer nature's call. And so when they found themselves on an escalator, they would answer the call there. Breaking down these habits was a long process. It took decades of education.'

Its well-thought-out rules and regulations mean that Singapore is indeed a model to follow in many respects. People of different nationalities and religions live peacefully together – partly because quotas ensure that they are distributed evenly across social housing developments, preventing the formation of ghettos. The allocation of school places follows the same principle. And because smoking, drinking and eating in the streets is forbidden, the city is kept clean. Chinese officials were sent to Singapore to learn from this approach. In recent years, however, Xi Jinping has scaled down this programme.[14]

Xi Jinping is no longer interested in following examples set by others. He wants to put his own mark on China – and on the world.

Xi's 2021 New Year's speech – available not only on Chinese websites and social media networks but also on YouTube, which is prohibited in China – sounds like the acceptance speech of a world president.[15] He greets his audience inclusively: 'Comrades, friends, ladies and gentlemen.' As we are shown images of care staff in protective suits, Xi presents himself as the foremost fighter against the pandemic. The video is far more professional, modern and emotive than a typical head of state's bland New Year greetings tend to be. One nurse has bruises and cuts to her face from wearing a mask for so long. Doctors save a patient by cardiac massage.

'China is the first major economy worldwide to achieve positive growth,' following the pandemic, Xi says in his speech. We are shown a video of him visiting villages where poverty has been eradicated. The high-rise buildings of Shanghai and Shenzhen rise into the blue sky; later they are shown illuminated at night. 'We are not alone on the great way,' Xi says. 'The whole world is one family.' Then there is a sudden cut to a video conference where Macron, Merkel and von der Leyen are waving at him – almost as extras – before Xi turns to the most important event of 2021: the 100th birthday of the Communist Party of China. 'The centenary only ushers in the prime of life,' he enthuses. 'We have crossed ten thousand rivers and thousands of mountains. We will continue to strive, march ahead with courage, and create brighter glory!'

Notes

1 Who Cares If a Sack of Rice Falls over in China?

1 发哨子的人, 人物 [The Whistleblower], 10 March 2020. Translated from Chinese by Adrian Geiges.

2 World Health Organization, 'Summary of Probable SARS Cases with Onset of Illness from 1 November 2002 to 31 July 2003', 24 July 2015.

3 发哨子的人, 人物 [The Whistleblower], 10 March 2020. Translated from Chinese by Adrian Geiges.

4 Georg Fahrion, 'Das Vermächtnis des Whistleblowers', *Der Spiegel*, 7 February 2020.

5 Martin Scholz, 'Es gibt hier keine wirkliche Meinungsfreiheit', *Die Welt*, 12 February 2020.

6 Fang Fang, *Wuhan Diary*, New York: Harper Collins, 2020, p. 14.

7 Ibid., p. 34 and p. 241.

8 Ibid., p. viii.

9 Veronika Hackenbroch, Bernhard Zand, and Wu Dandan, 'Was geschah in Wuhan und wer hat Schuld an der Pandemie?', *Der Spiegel*, 8 May 2020.

10 全党的核心 [Core of the whole Party], see e.g. here: 坚决维护党的核心和党中央权威（学习贯彻党的十九届六中全会精神), 人民日报 [Firmly maintain the Party's core strength and central authority of the Party (Study and implement the spirit of the Sixth Plenary Session of the 19th Central Committee of the Communist Party of China), *People's Daily*], 25 November 2021.

11 'China verdrängt USA als weltgrößte Volkswirtschaft', *Spiegel Wirtschaft*, 30 April 2014.

12 See https://www.noz.de/deutschland-welt/panorama/artikel/china-streicht-hunde-und-fledermaeuse-aus-liste-essbarer-tiere-20336284.

13 Interview in *Inside Wuhan*, a film by Gebrüder Beetz Filmproduktion produced for *SWR*, 2020.

14 David Cyranoski, 'Inside the Chinese Lab Poised to Study the World's Most Dangerous Pathogens', *Nature*, 542, 23 February 2017.

15 Ibid.

16 Ibid.

17 See https://twitter.com/zlj517/status/1238111898828066823.

18 See https://www.defense.gov/Explore/Spotlight/CISM-Military-World-Games.

19 See https://www.aerzteblatt.de/nachrichten/112050/Wuhan-korrigiert-seine-Zahlen-1–290-Tote-mehr-als-bisher-gemeldet.

20 'China Identifies 14 Hubei Frontline Workers, Including Li Wenliang, as Martyrs', *Global Times*, 2 April 2020.

21 Fahrion, 'Das Vermächtnis des Whistleblowers'.

22 'Coronavirus: Wuhan Doctor Ai Fen Speaks Out against Authorities', *Guardian*, 11 March 2020.

23 Fang Fang, *Wuhan Diary*, p. xi.

24 Ibid., p. 3. Transl. note: The German and English editions differ; the passage has been amended in light of the German version. See Fang Fang, *Wuhan Diary: Tagebuch aus einer gesperrten Stadt*, Hamburg: Hoffmann und Campe, 2020, p. 17.

25 See https://www.youtube.com/watch?v=sUvBNpkxrJo&t=9s.

26 See https://www.aiweiwei.com/coronation.

27 Fang Fang, *Wuhan Diary*, pp. 7f.

28 *Corona – Peking atmet auf*, a film by Sébastien Le Belzic shown on *arte*, 30 June 2020.

29 Shi Jiangtao, 'Chinese Authorities Say Coronavirus Control at Heart of Clampdown on 10 Broad Categories of Crime', *South China Morning Post*, 12 February 2020.

30 See https://coronalevel.com/de/Italy/Toscana/Prato/ and https://coronalevel.com/de/Italy/Lombardia/Bergamo.

31 Ibid.

32 See https://www.nzz.ch/podcast/diskriminierung-vonchinesen-in-italien-wegen-corona-nzz-akzentld.1562430.

33 See http://www.xinhuanet.com/english/2020–03/10/c_138863498.htm.

34 Fang Fang, *Wuhan Diary*, p. xiv.
35 Interview in *Inside Wuhan*.
36 See https://www.wiwo.de/my/politik/ausland/ungarns-china-connection-wie-weit-wuerde-orban-gehen-wenn-der-entzug-von-eu-toepfen-droht/27463528.html.
37 Matthias Kamp and Michael Settelen, 'Pekings Covid-19-Diplomatie läuft auf Hochtouren', *Neue Zürcher Zeitung*, 24 March 2020.
38 See https://beta.blickpunktfilm.de/details/468880.
39 See https://www.kas.de/documents/252038/11055681/Corona-Impfstart+in+Lateinamerika+-+Zwischen+Pandemiebek%C3%A4mpfung+und+Geopolitik.pdf/58dd0055-5129-0346-84bc-2b830840e4de?version=1.0&t=1613508773305.

2 Xi Jinping's Family Background: The Formative Years

1 Kerry Brown, *The World According to Xi: Everything You Need to Know About the New China*, London: I. B. Tauris, 2018, p. 10.
2 Victor Erofeyev, *Good Stalin*, London: Glagoslav Publications, 2014, p. 89.
3 'Man of the People: Profile of Xi Jinping, General Secretary of the CPC', appendix in Xi Jinping, *The Governance of China I*, Beijing: Foreign Language Press, 2014, p. 479. References are to the English edition. However, all quotations have been checked against the Chinese original: 习近平, 谈治国理政, 第一卷, 北京, 2014.
4 Martin Macmillan, *Together They Hold Up The Sky*, Campbell, CA: FastPencil, 2012, p. 6.
5 Interview in *Die Welt des Xi Jinping*, a film by Sophie Lepault and Romain Franklin, *arte*, 18 December 2018.
6 Jung Chang and Jon Halliday, *Mao: The Unknown Story*, New York: Alfred A. Knopf, 2005, p. 517.
7 Macmillan, *Together They Hold Up The Sky*, p. 24.
8 Ibid., pp. 27f.
9 Ibid., p. 25.
10 Quoted from *Die Welt des Xi Jinping*.
11 Macmillan, *Together They Hold Up The Sky*, pp. 33f.
12 'Man of the People: Profile of Xi Jinping', in *The Governance of China I*, pp. 479f.
13 See https://i.ntdtv.com/assets/uploads/2017/05/p8198781a698761967.jpg.

14 Macmillan, *Together They Hold Up The Sky*, p. 35.
15 'Man of the People: Profile of Xi Jinping', in *The Governance of China I*, pp. 480ff.
16 Ibid., p. 481.
17 'Xi Jinping, Generalsekretär des Zentralkomitees der KP Chinas im Porträt', appendix in Xi Jinping, *China regieren*, Beijing: Foreign Language Press, 2014, p. 535. Transl. note: This sentence is not part of the English edition.
18 Macmillan, *Together They Hold Up The Sky*, pp. 50f.
19 Interview in *Die Welt des Xi Jinping*.
20 Quoted after Andreas Lorenz, 'Redder than Red: An American Portrait of China's Next Leader', *Spiegel International*, 5 December 2010.
21 Brown, *The World According to Xi*, p. 15.
22 Macmillan, *Together They Hold Up The Sky*, p. 62.
23 'Man of the People: Profile of Xi Jinping', in *The Governance of China I*, p. 480. Transl. note: The German edition differs significantly and runs: 'In order to expand the area of arable land, the villagers built a dyke under his leadership to stem erosion. They did this during the frosty winter when there was no agricultural work to be done. Xi always stood barefooted on the snow and ice and broke open the ice so that a foundation for the dyke could be laid.' 'Xi Jinping, Generalsekretär des Zentralkomitees der KP Chinas im Porträt', *China regieren*, pp. 533f.
24 Quoted after *Die Welt des Xi Jinping*.
25 'Man of the People: Profile of Xi Jinping', in *The Governance of China I*, p. 480.
26 Xi Jinping, 'The Chinese Dream is the People's Dream', in Xi Jinping, *The Governance of China II*, Beijing: Foreign Language Press, 2017, p. 29. References are to the English edition. However, all quotations have been checked against the Chinese original: 习近平, 谈治国理政, 第二卷, 北京, 2017.
27 Ibid.
28 Xi Jinping, 'What is the New Normal in China's Economic Development?', speech of 18 January 2016, in *The Governance of China II*, p. 270.
29 See https://www.worldbank.org/en/country/china/overview.
30 See https://www.reisevor9.de/inside/reisestopp-fuer-chinesen-kostet-touristik-weltweit-milliarden.
31 Xi Jinping, 'Accelerate the Development of Housing Security and Supply', in *The Governance of China I*, p. 213.

32 See https://www.handelsblatt.com/finanzen/immobilien/immobilien-chinas-regierung-will-gegen-spekulation-am-immobilienmarkt-vorgehen/27882712.html.

33 Xi Jinping, 'How to Resolve Major Difficulties in Realizing the First Centenary Goal,' in *The Governance of China II*, p. 83.

34 Xi Jinping, 'Take Targeted Measures Against Poverty,' in *The Governance of China II*, p. 88.

35 Xi Jinping, 'Address the People's Most Immediate Concerns,' passage from a speech during a visit to Beijing Bayi School, 9 September 2016, in *The Governance of China II*, p. 394.

36 Xi Jinping, 'Achieving Rejuvenation is the Dream of the Chinese People,' speech made when visiting the exhibition 'The Road to Rejuvenation,' 29 November 2012, in *The Governance of China I*, p. 38.

37 Xi Jinping, 'What is the New Normal in China's Economic Development?,' in *The Governance of China II*, p. 269.

38 Xi Jinping, 'A Deeper Understanding of the New Development Concepts,' speech of 18 January 2016, in *The Governance of China II*, p. 223.

39 Xi Jinping, 'Join Hands to Consolidate Peace and Development in Cross-Straits Relations,' speech of 7 November 2015, in *The Governance of China II*, p. 469.

40 Letter by Victor Hugo to Captain Butler, dated 25 November 1861. The French original is available at https://chine.in/mandarin/vocabulaire/index.php?id=1618. English version: https://thinkglobalheritage.wordpress.com/2017/11/11/dark-heritage-an-old-palace-with-a-miserable-history.

41 Quoted after the German History in Documents and Images webpage at https://ghdi.ghi-dc.org/sub_document.cfm?document_id=755.

42 On this part of colonial history, see Stefan Aust and Adrian Geiges, *Mit Konfuzius zur Weltmacht*, Berlin: Quadriga, 2012, pp. 29 ff.

43 See Frank Dikötter, *Maos großer Hunger: Massenmord und Menschenexperiment in China*, Stuttgart: Klett-Cotta, 2014.

44 John Bolton, *The Room where It Happened*, New York: Simon & Schuster, 2020, p. 302.

45 Xi Jinping, 'Stay True to Our Original Aspiration and Continue Marching Forwards,' speech of 1 July 2016, in *The Governance of China II*, p. 37.

46 Quoted after http://en.people.cn/dengxp/vol2/text/b1260.html.

47 See Aust and Geiges, *Mit Konfuzius zur Weltmacht*, p. 43.

48 Macmillan, *Together They Hold Up The Sky*, pp. 91 ff.

49 习仲勋：我要看着深圳发展 [Xi Zhongxun: I want to watch the development of Shenzhen], at http://news.sina.com.cn/c/2010-08-25/181020974306.shtml. Translated from the Chinese by Adrian Geiges.
50 See http://dimsums.blogspot.com/2012/02/xi-jinpings-doctoral-thesis.html.
51 Xi Jinping, 'Study, Disseminate and Implement the Guiding Principles of the 18th CPC National Congress', speech at the first group study session of the Political Bureau of the 18th CPC Central Committee, 17 November 2012, in *The Governance of China I*, p. 8.
52 Brown, *The World According to Xi*, p. 130.
53 Ibid., p. 33.

3 A Colourful Character in a Uniform Crowd

1 See Macmillan, *Together They Hold Up the Sky*, pp. 94f.
2 See ibid., pp. 103ff.
3 'Man of the People: Profile of Xi Jinping', in *The Governance of China I*, p. 481.
4 Macmillan, *Together They Hold Up the Sky*, p. 149.
5 See ibid., p. 150–2.
6 See ibid., pp. 168ff.; quotation: p. 170.
7 See ibid., pp. 3f.
8 See ibid., pp. 29ff.; quotation: p. 30.
9 Mao Zedong, *Quotations from Chairman Mao Tse-Tung*, Beijing: Foreign Language Press, 1966, p. 61. Chinese original: 毛主席语录, 北京, 1966.
10 A detailed account of Peng Liyuan's life can be found in Martin Macmillan's *Together They Hold Up the Sky*.
11 See ibid., pp. 193–200.
12 'Man of the People: Profile of Xi Jinping', in *The Governance of China I*, p. 482.
13 Ibid., p. 483.
14 See https://thehill.com/opinion/civil-rights/445934-chinas-lament-could-xi-jinping-repeat-tiananmen.
15 See https://nsarchive2.gwu.edu/NSAEBB/NSAEBB16/documents/32-01.htm.
16 See Macmillan, *Together They Hold Up the Sky*, p. 217.
17 Ibid., p. 260.
18 See ibid., p. 215.

19 See ibid., pp. 210f.
20 See ibid., pp. 228–30.
21 See ibid., pp. 237f.
22 See ibid., pp. 262f.
23 Ibid., pp. 265f.
24 'UN Health Agency Appoints Chinese Singer as Goodwill Ambassador', *UN News*, 3 June 2011.
25 'US Embassy Cables: China's Next Leader Reveals Taste for Hollywood Movies', *Guardian*, 4 December 2010.
26 See Adrian Geiges, *Gebrauchsanweisung für Peking und Shanghai*, Munich: Piper, 2009, pp. 162f.
27 See Macmillan, *Together They Hold Up The Sky*, p. 291.
28 These impressions from China's preparations for the Olympic Games are based on Adrian Geiges, 'Ein Land lernt das Lächeln', *Stern*, no. 3, 2008.
29 Aust and Geiges, *Mit Konfuzius zur Weltmacht*, pp. 196f.
30 'Den Bauch voll und auf China zeigen', *Süddeutschen Zeitung*, 17 May 2010.

4 The Fight against Corruption

1 John Pomfret, 'Xi Jinping's Quest to Revive Stalin's Communist Ideology', *Washington Post*, 16 October 2017.
2 *Geschichte der Kommunistischen Partei der Sowjetunion*, Berlin (GDR): Dietz, 1971, p. 702.
3 Dimitriĭ Volkogonov, *Stalin: Triumph and Tragedy*, New York: Grove Weidenfeld, 1991.
4 See Adrian Geiges, *Revolution ohne Schüsse: meine Erlebnisse mit der Perestroika – am Fliessband und im Klassenzimmer*, Cologne: Weltkreis, 1988, p. 86.
5 Ibid.
6 Bernhard Zand, 'Harte Strafe für den gefallenen Star', *Der Spiegel*, 22 September 2013.
7 See https://www.manager-magazin.de/politik/artikel/a-855300.html.
8 Xi Jinping, 'Power Must Be "Caged" by the System', main points of the speech at the Second Plenary Session of the 18th CPC Central Commission for Discipline Inspection, 22 January 2013, in *The Governance of China I*, p. 426.

9 Xi Jinping, 'The Mass Line: Fundamental to the CPC', part of the speech at the Conference of the Program of Mass Line Education and Practice held by the CPC Central Committee, 18 June 2013, in *The Governance of China I*, pp. 406f.

10 Kai Strittmatter, *Die Neuerfindung der Diktatur: Wie China den digitalen Überwachungsstaat aufbaut und uns damit herausfordert*, revised paperback edition, Munich: Piper, 2020, pp. 39f.

11 Xi Jinping, 'Observe Discipline and Rules', part of the speech at the Fifth Plenary Session of the 18th CPC Central Commission for Discipline Inspection, 13 January 2015, in *The Governance of China II*, p. 165.

12 跳楼上吊撞火车 官员为何这么极端? [Jump off the building, hang themselves, jump in front of a train, why are officials so extreme?], *Beijing News*, 7 April 2017. Translated from the Chinese by Adrian Geiges.

13 Richard McGregor, *Xi Jinping: The Backlash*, Sydney: Penguin/The Lowy Institute, 2019, p. 34.

14 Interview with Björn Ahl, professor for Chinese legal culture at Cologne University and president of the European-China Law Studies Association (ECLS), at https://www.dw.com/de/justiz-auf-parteilinie-in-china/a-37179929.

15 Strittmatter, *Die Neuerfindung der Diktatur*, p. 41.

16 Xi Jinping, 'Power Must Be "Caged" by the System', p. 429. Xi Jinping uses the same formulation in his speech at the welcome reception for Chinese expatriates in Seattle on 23 September 2015, and in his speech at the celebration of the ninety-fifth anniversary of the foundation of the Communist Party.

17 Xi Jinping, *The Governance of China I*, p. 431.

18 Xi Jinping, 'Observe Discipline and Rules', in *The Governance of China II*, p. 168.

19 Ibid., p. 165.

20 Ibid.

21 Ibid., p. 166.

22 See https://www.welt.de/geschichte/article167845373/Als-Stalin-die-Quoten-fuer-Todesurteile-erhoehte.html.

23 McGregor, *Xi Jinping: The Backlash*, p. 48.

24 Evan Osnos, 'What Did China's First Daughter Find in America', *The New Yorker*, 6 April 2015.

25 Ibid.

26 Michael Forsythe, 'As China's Leader Fights Graft, His Relatives Shed Assets', *New York Times*, 17 June 2014.

27 'Man of the People: Profile of Xi Jinping', in *The Governance of China I*, p. 494.

28 McGregor, *Xi Jinping: The Backlash*, p. 43.

5 Persecuted by Mao – Revered Like Mao

1 See https://www.ndtv.com/world-news/mao-fans-bow-before-gold-image-of-communist-chinas-founder-545710.

2 Chang and Halliday, *Mao: The Unknown Story*, list of interviewees, pp. 637–50.

3 Ibid., p. 204.

4 Ibid., p. 316.

5 See Dikötter, *Maos großer Hunger*.

6 Chang and Halliday, *Mao: The Unknown Story*, p. 438.

7 Ibid., p. 439.

8 Jean-Paul Sartre, 'Les Maos en France', in *Situations X*, Paris: Gallimard, 1964, p. 45.

9 Quoted after Chang and Halliday, *Mao: The Unknown Story*, p. 587. Chang and Halliday give as the original source: 'Kissinger briefing to White House Staff, 19 July 1971 (Nixon Project, President's Office Files, Memoranda for the President, Box 88, File Beginning 27 Feb. 1972, p IO; Box 85, File Beginning 18 July 1971, p 4)', ibid., p. 733.

10 John Pomfret, 'Chairman Monster', *Washington Post*, 11 December 2005.

11 'Späte Reue einer Rotgardistin', *Frankfurter Allgemeine Zeitung*, 15 January 2014.

12 Strittmatter, *Die Neuerfindung der Diktatur*, p. 108.

13 Transl. note: The transcript of the interview with Ai Weiwei has been edited.

14 See https://www.wsj.com/video/china-rap-song-features-president-xi-jinping/28941DB1-FA43-4301-AFD2-36882477E553.html.

15 Brown, *The World According to Xi*, p. 117.

16 'Want to Escape Poverty? Replace Pictures of Jesus with Xi Jinping, Christian Villagers Urged', *South China Morning Post*, 14 November 2017.

17 'China to Add "Xi Jinping Thought" to National Curriculum', *Reuters*, 25 August 2021.

18 Strittmatter, *Die Neuerfindung der Diktatur*, pp. 127f.

19 国家的掌舵者 人民的领路人，人民日报 2018年03月17日 [The leader of the country, the leader of the people], *People's Daily*, 17 March 2018, at http://opinion.people.com.cn/n1/2018/0317/c1003-29873350.html. Translated from the Chinese by Adrian Geiges.

20 Xi Jinping, 'Confidence in the Political System of Chinese Socialism', part of the speech at the meeting marking the sixtieth anniversary of the National People's Congress, 5 September 2014, in *The Governance of China II*, p. 313.

21 McGregor, *Xi Jinping: The Backlash*, p. 10.

22 All quotations are taken from the resolution's official English translation published by Xinhua, 16 November 2021, at http://www.news.cn/english/2021-11/16/c_1310314611.htm.

6 Confucianism and Communism

1 Peter Dittmar, 'Seit 2500 Jahren belehrt der Philosoph Konfuzius die Chinesen, *Die Welt*, 5 May 2006.

2 Xi Jinping, 'Promote Socialist Rule of Law', part of the speech at the second full assembly of the Fourth Plenary Session of the 18th CPC Central Committee, 23 October 2014, in *The Governance of China II*, pp. 130f.

3 This translation at http://classics.mit.edu/Confucius/analects.3.3.html. Confucius, *Lunyu: Understanding the Analects of Confucius*, New York: SUNY, 2017, p. 372 (*Lunyu*, 15.39) has: 'In offering instruction, there is no classification.' The German translation renders this more explicitly as: 'Education should be available to everyone. There should be no differences based on social status.'

4 Confucius, *Lunyu*, p. 194 (7.7).

5 Ibid., p. 364 (15.24).

6 Immanuel Kant, *Critique of Practical Reason*, Cambridge: Cambridge University Press, 2015, p. 28.

7 Confucius, *Lunyu*, p. 132 (4.2).

8 Ibid., p. 340 (14.27)

9 Ibid., p. 360 (15.15).

10 Confucius, *Lunyu*, p. 289 (12.11); transl. amended.

11 'Das Comeback des Konfuzius', *Welt*, 12 July 2017.

12 Xi Jinping, 'Promote Socialist Rule of Law', part of the speech at the second full assembly of the Fourth Plenary Session of the 18th CPC

Central Committee, 23 October 2014, in *The Governance of China II*, p. 125.

13 Xi Jinping, 'Be a Good County Party Secretary,' speech at the meeting with a class of County Party secretaries at the Central Party School, 12 January 2015, in *The Governance of China II*, pp. 162f.

14 Xi Jinping, 'The Rule of Law and the Rule of Virtue,' 9 December 2016, in *The Governance of China II*, p. 147.

15 Mencius (ca. 372–289 BC) was most important successor of Confucius and developer of Confucian thought.

16 The *Book of Rites* is a classic text of Confucianism.

17 Xi Jinping, 'A Deeper Understanding of the New Development Concepts,' speech on 18 January 2016, in *The Governance of China II*, pp. 236f.

18 Vladimir Ilyich Lenin, 'The Tax in Kind,' in *Collected Works*, vol. 32, Moscow: Progress Publishers, 1973, pp. 329–65; here: p. 354.

19 Ibid., p. 350.

20 Egon Krenz, *China: Wie ich es sehe*, Berlin: edition ost, 2018, p. 49.

21 Ibid., p. 55.

22 Ibid., pp. 132f.

23 McGregor, *Xi Jinping: The Backlash*, p. 52.

24 Alexandra Stevenson, 'China's Communists Rewrite the Rules for Foreign Businesses,' *New York Times*, 13 April 2018.

25 Xi Jinping, 'Speech at the National Conference on Party Schools, December 11, 2015,' in *The Governance of China II*, p. 355.

26 Ibid., p. 356.

27 Strittmatter, *Die Neuerfindung der Diktatur*, pp. 139f.

28 Ibid., p. 83.

29 See e.g. Xi Jinping, 'Stay True to Our Original Aspiration and Continue Marching Forward,' part of the speech at the ceremony marking the 95th anniversary of the founding of the CPC, 1 July 2016, in *The Governance of China II*, p. 37 and p. 47.

30 Rosa Luxemburg, 'The Russian Revolution,' in *The Russian Revolution* and *Leninism or Marxism?*, Ann Arbor: University of Michigan Press, 1961, pp. 25–80; here: pp. 71f.

31 Xi Jinping, 'Develop and Popularize Marxism in the Modern Chinese Context,' main points of the speech at the 43rd group study session of the Political Bureau of the 18th CPC Central Committee, 29 September 2017, in *The Governance of China II*, pp. 68f.

32 Xi Jinping, 'Today We Must Succeed in a New Long March', part of the speech at the ceremony commemorating the 80th anniversary of the victory of the Long March, 21 October 2016, in *The Governance of China II*, p. 54.
33 The scene is part of Ai Weiwei's documentary *CoroNation*, at www.aiweiwei.com/coronation.
34 Xi Jinping, 'Promote Socialist Rule of Law', part of the speech at the second full assembly of the Fourth Plenary Session of the 18th CPC Central Committee, 23 October 2014, in *The Governance of China II*, pp. 119f.
35 Fang Fang, *Wuhan Diary*, p. 179.

7 From 5G to TikTok

1 'Apple's New China Partner', *Week in China*, 31 July 2020.
2 Xi Jinping, 'A Deeper Understanding of the New Development Concepts', speech of 18 January 2016, in *The Governance of China II*, p. 222.
3 See http://german.beijingreview.com.cn/China/201810/t20181026_800145375.html.
4 See https://de.statista.com/infografik/3553/anteil-von-glasfaseranschluessen-in-ausgewaehlten-laendern/#:~:text=3%2C6%20Prozent%20aller%20station%C3%A4ren,mehr%20als%20im%20Juni%202015.
5 Carsten Senz, 'Kontrolliert der chinesische Staat das Unternehmen Huawei?', *Journalist*, July/August 2020.
6 McGregor, *Xi Jinping: The Backlash*, p. 55.
7 See https://www.bmwi.de/Redaktion/DE/Artikel/Aussenwirtschaft/laendervermerk-china.html.
8 See https://www.dw.com/de/china-nicht-mehr-unter-top-investoren-in-deutschland/a-53508855.
9 See https://www.nzz.ch/technologie/china-investiert-milliarden-in-seine-chip-industrie-trotzdem-bleibt-es-von-den-usa-abhaengig-ld.1576153.
10 See https://www.dw.com/de/peking-stellt-weichen-f%C3%BCr-politik-der-zwei-kreisl%C3%A4ufe/a-54930330.
11 Xi, 'We Need to Walk Down the Path of Independent Innovation', at https://www.youtube.com/watch?v=jUufVBCjGZk; English subtitles amended.
12 See https://www.nzz.ch/wirtschaft/shenzhen-chinas-hauptstadt-der-hardware-ld.1448786.

13 Jürgen Trittin and Friedbert Pflüger, 'Europa, wehr dich!', *Der Spiegel*, 18 August 2020.

14 See https://www.handelsblatt.com/technik/it-internet/videoplattform-tiktok-das-chinesische-unternehmen-das-keines-sein-will/26028444.html?ticket=ST-14494659-DLkiUUxQmqus6eg6ZlKu-ap1.

15 Xifan Yang, 'Winnie Puuh, der gefährliche Bär', *Zeit Magazin*, no. 11, 2019.

16 See https://www.faz.net/aktuell/politik/ausland/asien/china-onkel-xi-und-seine-blogger-13316080.html.

17 Strittmatter, *Die Neuerfindung der Diktatur*, pp. 69f.

18 'Das chinesische Fintech Ant plant den größten Börsengang aller Zeiten', *Der Spiegel*, No. 45, 2020.

19 '网络达人'习近平 ['Internet expert': Xi Jinping], at http://xinhuanet.com/politics/2016-11/17/c_1119932744.htm. Translated from the Chinese by Adrian Geiges.

20 *Überwacht: Sieben Milliarden im Visier*, film by Sylvain Louvet, *arte*, 21 April 2020.

21 Ibid.

22 'China Experiments with a New Kind of Megalopolis', *Spiegel International*, 6 September 2019.

23 Ephesians 4:22–24 (KJV).

24 Heinrich Heine, *Deutschland: A Winter's Tale*, London: Angel Books, 1986, p. 30.

25 *Überwacht: Sieben Milliarden im Visier*.

26 See http://www.chinahirn.de/2020/10/22/gesellschaft-i-auch-chinesen-haben-eine-privatsphaere.

27 'Beijing Metro to Begin Security "Sorting" Based on Facial Recognition', *Radio Free Asia*, 30 October 2019.

28 *Überwacht: Sieben Milliarden im Visier*.

29 Ibid.

30 Ibid.

8 The Dalai Lama and the Uyghurs

1 See http://german.tibet.cn/themen/thema2015/1433406000947.shtml.

2 'Does China's Next Leader Have a Soft Spot for Tibet?', *Reuters*, 1 September 2012.

3 Ibid.

4 See https://www.scmp.com/article/635686/tung-praises-tibets-gains.
5 Xi Jinping, 'Speech at the second full assembly of the Sixth Plenary Session of the 18th CPC Central Committee, October 27, 2016', in *The Governance of China II*, p. 395.
6 'Does China's Next Leader Have a Soft Spot for Tibet?'
7 See https://www.sueddeutsche.de/politik/china-cables-uiguren-terror-faktencheck-1.4691481.
8 See https://www.dw.com/de/emp%C3%B6rung-in-china-nach-anschlag-in-xinjiang/a-17609001.
9 See https://www.sueddeutsche.de/politik/us-studie-500-000-iraker-starben-im-irak-krieg-1.1795930.
10 Sayragul Sauytbay and Alexandra Cavelius, *The Chief Witness: Escape from China's Modern-Day Concentration Camps*, Victoria: Scribe, 2021, p. 173.
11 Ibid., pp. 176–7.
12 Ibid., p. 181.
13 Ibid., p. 185.
14 *China: A New World Order*, Part 1, documentary by Richard Cookson and John O'Kane, BBC Two, 29 August 2019.
15 Sauytbay and Cavelius, *The Chief Witness*, p. 4.
16 Harald Maass, 'Die Welt, von der niemand wissen soll', *Süddeutsche Zeitung Magazin*, 14 March 2019.
17 'Searching for Truth in China's Uighur "Re-education" Camps', BBC News, 21 June 2019.
18 Ibid.
19 Xi Jinping, 'Speech at the National Conference on Religion, April 22, 2016', in *The Governance of China II*, pp. 329f.
20 Ibid.
21 'Searching for Truth in China's Uighur "Re-education" Camps'.
22 Ibid.
23 Ibid.
24 Sauytbay and Cavelius, *The Chief Witness*, p. 207.
25 Ibid., p. 216.
26 Ibid., p. 140, p. 189, and pp. 153–4.
27 Maass, 'Die Welt, von der niemand wissen soll'.
28 *Panorama*, BBC 1, 25 November 2019, at https://www.youtube.com/watch?v=NGDr38eU62U &feature=youtu.be.

29 'Singapore Founding Father Lee Kuan Yew Says Xi Jinping is in Mandela's Class', *South China Morning Post*, 7 August 2013.
30 Maass, 'Die Welt, von der niemand wissen soll'.
31 Sauytbay and Cavelius, *The Chief Witness*, p. 118.
32 Maass, 'Die Welt, von der niemand wissen soll'.
33 'Searching for Truth in China's Uighur "Re-education" Camps'.
34 Quoted after Maass, 'Die Welt, von der niemand wissen soll'.
35 'Schweigen oder reden', *Spiegel Sport*, 13 June 2018.

9 Xi for Future

1 Johnny Erling, 'Greta auf Chinesisch', *Die Welt*, 14 June 2019.
2 See https://www.co2online.de/klima-schuetzen/klimawandel/co2-ausstoss-der-laender.
3 Xi Jinping, 'A Deeper Understanding of the New Development Concepts', speech of 18 January 2016, in *The Governance of China II*, pp. 230f.
4 See Adrian Geiges, 'Dreckschleuder der Welt', *Stern*, no. 51, 2005.
5 Xi Jinping, 'Usher in a New Era of Ecological Progress', main points of the speech at the sixth group study session of the Political Bureau of the 18th CPC Central Committee, 24 May 2013, in *The Governance of China I*, p. 232.
6 Xi Jinping, 'Promote Ecological Progress and Reform Environmental Management', speech at the Fifth Plenary Session of the 18th CPC Central Committee, 26 October 2015, in *The Governance of China II*, p. 423.
7 Barbara Finamore, *Will China Save The Planet?*, Cambridge: Polity, 2018, pp. 53 ff.
8 Ibid., p. 34.
9 北京：加强地铁防控 防止疫情蔓延 [Beijing: Strengthen subway precautions and control to prevent the spread of the pandemic], at http://www.gov.cn/xinwen/2020-02/04/content_5474539.htm. Translated from the Chinese by Adrian Geiges.
10 5号线南延伸和13号线二、三期12月30日起试运营 [The southern extension of Line 5 and the second and third phases of Line 13 will start trial operation on December 30], at http://www.shmetro.com/node49/201812/con115165.htm. Translated from the Chinese by Adrian Geiges.
11 '1.300 Kilometer in viereinhalb Stunden', *Zeit Online*, 2 October 2019.
12 See https://www.berliner-zeitung.de/politik-gesellschaft/hochgesch

windigkeitsnetz-in-japan-und-china-sind-zuege-puenktlich-auf-die-sekunde-li.66916.

13 Xi Jinping, 'Transition to Innovation-Driven Growth', part of the speech at the 17th General Assembly of the Members of the Chinese Academy of Sciences and the 12th General Assembly of the Members of the Chinese Academy of Engineering, 9 June 2014, in *The Governance of China I*, pp. 132f.

14 See https://www.elektroauto-news.net/2020/china-neue-quoten-fuer-elektrofahrzeuge.

15 See https://de.statista.com/statistik/daten/studie/243993/umfrage/bestand-elektrofahrzeuge-nach-laendern.

16 'China im Jahr 2019: Wie gestaltete sich das Energiesystem?', *Energy BrainBlog*, 10 March 2020.

17 'Dirty Coal, Clean Future', *The Atlantic*, December 2010.

18 'Ohne Volldampf in die Verkehrsrevolution', *Spiegel Wirtschaft*, 25 June 2018.

19 Xi Jinping, 'Guide Development with New Concepts', part of the speech at the second full assembly of the Fifth Plenary Session of the 18th CPC Central Committee, 29 October 2015, in *The Governance of China II*, p. 218.

20 See https://pubs.usgs.gov/periodicals/mcs2021/mcs2021-rare-earths.pdf.

21 Xi Jinping, 'Leave to Our Future Generations Blue Skies, Green Fields and Clean Water', letter of congratulations to the Eco Forum Annual Global Conference Guiyang 2013, 18 July 2013, in *The Governance of China I*, p. 232.

22 'China stapelt oft tief und übertrifft sich dann selbst', *Spiegel Ausland*, 20 September 2019.

23 See Finamore, *Will China Save The Planet?*, p. 70.

24 Ibid., p. 24.

25 Johnny Erling, 'Chinas KP-Chef verdonnert Parteispitze zur Selbstkritik', *Die Welt*, 29 December 2017.

26 Finamore, *Will China Save The Planet?*, p. 24.

27 Xi Jinping, 'Build a Win-Win, Equitable and Balanced Governance Mechanism on Climate Change', speech at the opening ceremony of the Paris Conference on Climate Change, 30 November 2015, in *The Governance of China II*, p. 578.

28 Xi Jinping, 'A New Partnership of Mutual Benefit and a Community

of Shared Future', speech at the General Debate of the 70th Session of the UN General Assembly at the UN headquarters in New York, 28 September 2015, in *The Governance of China II*, pp. 573f.

29 Xi Jinping, 'Build a Win-Win, Equitable and Balanced Governance Mechanism on Climate Change', in *The Governance of China II*, p. 580.

10 The New Silk Road

1 See https://rp-online.de/nrw/staedte/duisburg/duisburg-china-praesident-xi-besucht-hafen_bid-9578889#1.

2 Xi Jinping, 'Work Together to Build the Belt and Road', speech at the opening ceremony of the Belt and Road Forum for International Cooperation, 14 May 2017, in *The Governance of China II*, p. 553.

3 Ibid., p. 554.

4 Doris Naisbitt, John Naisbitt and Laurence Brahm, *Im Sog der Seidenstraße*, Stuttgart: Langen-Müller, 2019, p. 20.

5 Ibid., p. 197.

6 Ibid., p. 25.

7 Ibid., p. 59.

8 Ibid., pp. 77ff.

9 Ibid., pp. 101f.

10 Ibid., p. 114.

11 Ibid., p. 116.

12 Ibid., p. 121.

13 Strittmatter, *Die Neuerfindung der Diktatur*, p. 300.

14 Xi Jinping, 'Shoulder the Responsibilities of Our Time and Promote Global Growth Together', keynote speech at the opening ceremony of the World Economic Forum in Davos, Switzerland, 17 January 2017, in *The Governance of China II*, p. 528.

15 Xi Jinping, 'Work Together to Build the Belt and Road', in *The Governance of China II*, pp. 556f.

16 'China's Empire of Money Is Reshaping Global Trade', *Bloomberg/Quint*, 2 August 2018.

17 Naisbitt, Naisbitt and Brahm, *Im Sog der Seidenstraße*, pp. 18f.

18 Ibid., p. 26.

19 *China: A New World Order*, Part 2, documentary by Richard Cookson and John O'Kane, BBC Two, 5 September 2019.

20 Strittmatter, *Die Neuerfindung der Diktatur*, pp. 298–300.

21 See https://www.focus.de/finanzen/boerse/konjunktur/vorbei-an-bremerhaven-der-kopf-des-drachen-waechst-china-macht-piraeus-zum-einfallstor-nach-europa_id_12028052.html.
22 McGregor, *Xi Jinping: The Backlash*, p. 106.
23 Sauytbay and Cavelius, *The Chief Witness*, p. 295.
24 Xi Jinping, 'Stay True to Our Original Aspiration and Continue Marching Forward', part of the speech at the ceremony marking the 95th anniversary of the founding of the CPC, 1 July 2016, in *The Governance of China II*, p. 37.
25 Naisbitt, Naisbitt and Brahm, *Im Sog der Seidenstraße*, p. 186.
26 See https://www.kas.de/documents/252038/7938566/Lateinamerikas+Parteien+im+Fokus+Chinas.pdf/bbbafd51-853b-7ed7-efbd-5fe725acda8e?version=1.0&t=1600847740801.

11 Peace as Part of China's DNA?

1 'Watch: Trump's Granddaughter Is Entertainment at Chinese Dinner', *The Mercury News*, 9 November 2017.
2 'Sasha Obama Speaks Chinese with President Hu Jintao', CBS News, 21 January 2012; 'More Americans See Benefits of Learning Chinese', *China Daily*, 18 July 2017.
3 'Trump wirft China "Vergewaltigung" der USA vor', *Spiegel Ausland*, 2 May 2016.
4 Bolton, *The Room Where It Happened*, p. 297.
5 Ibid., pp. 297f.
6 Ibid., pp. 301f.
7 Ibid., pp. 310f.
8 Ibid., p. 312.
9 '15 Times Trump Praised China as Coronavirus Was Spreading across the Globe', *Politico*, 15 April 2020.
10 Ibid.
11 Strittmatter, *Die Neuerfindung der Diktatur*, p. 14
12 Xi Jinping, 'Shoulder the Responsibilities of Our Time and Promote Global Growth Together', in *The Governance of China II*, p. 521.
13 Ibid., p. 525.
14 'Talk of War Gets Louder on WeChat', *Week in China*, 31 July 2020.
15 'Can a New Think Tank Put a Stop to Endless War', *The Nation*, 29 July 2019.
16 See https://journals.lib.unb.ca/index.php/jcs/article/view/366/578.

17 A video from the China Global Television Network (CGTN), the foreign branch of the Chinese state television, presents a summary of the run up to the war from a Chinese perspective: https://www.youtube.com/watch?v=v4PX8vxzqc8. Part 2 at https://www.youtube.com/watch?v=nENRByc50zg.

18 'China's Xi Jinping Delivers Thinly-veiled Swipe at US During Korean War Anniversary Speech', CNN, 23 October 2020.

19 See https://www.faz.net/aktuell/feuilleton/politik/stalins-unerklaerter-krieg-1359099.html?printPagedArticle= true#pageIndex_2.

20 Xi Jinping, 'Towards a Community of Shared Future for Mankind', speech at the United Nations Office in Geneva, 18 January 2017, in *The Governance of China II*, p. 597.

21 Mao Zedong, *Quotations from Chairman Mao Tse-Tung*, p. 58.

22 See https://www.dw.com/de/kampfumeinflusssph%C3%A4ren/a-18491793.

23 'Insel oder Felsen? Worum es beim Streit im Südchinesischen Meer geht', *Spiegel Ausland*, 12 July 2016.

12 Why Xi Jinping Fears Hong Kong and Taiwan

1 'First Beijing Visit for Hong Kong's Governor', *New York Times*, 21 October 1992.

2 Xi Jinping, '"One Country, Two Systems": Long-Term Prosperity and Stability for Hong Kong', part of the speech at the Meeting Celebrating the 20th Anniversary of Hong Kong's Return to China and the Inaugural Ceremony of the Fifth-term Government of the Hong Kong Special Administrative Region, 1 July 2017 in *The Governance of China II*, p. 475.

3 See https://www.sueddeutsche.de/politik/hongkong-vermummungsverbot-1.4626785.

4 'Hong Kong Security Law: What Is It and Is It Worrying?, BBC News, 30 June 2020.

5 See https://www.dw.com/de/verleger-jimmy-lai-und-andere-aktivisten-in-hongkong-festgenommen/a-54511718.

6 See https://www.sueddeutsche.de/politik/hongkong-wahl-verschoben-1.4984900.

7 See https://www.handelsblatt.com/politik/international/beunruhigender trump-tweet-kann-ein-us-praesident-eine-wahl-canceln/26052282.html?ticket=ST-12112520-Upd0wXMTn9T3zVe0IMxJ-ap5.

8 'Hong Kong Pro-Democracy Lawmakers Resign En Masse After Beijing Moves to Quash Dissent', CNN, 12 November 2020.
9 Xi Jinping, '"One Country, Two Systems": Long-Term Prosperity and Stability for Hong Kong'. The reference to Ban Gu as the author of the quotation can be found in a footnote to the authorized German translation of the speech: Xi Jinping, *China regieren II*, Beijing: Foreign Language Press, 2018, p. 536.
10 '"Hongkong wird erdrückt"', *Spiegel Ausland*, 12 November 2020.
11 Macmillan, *Together They Hold Up The Sky*, pp. 243f.
12 Bolton, *The Room Where It Happened*, p. 314.
13 Xi Jinping, 'Join Hands to Consolidate Peace and Development in Cross-Straits Relations', p. 467.
14 '2020 Elections: Tsai Wins by a Landslide', *Taipei Times*, 12 January 2020.
15 Xi Jinping, 'Handle Cross-Strait Relations in the Overall Interests of the Chinese Nation', main points of the talk with Wu Poh-hsiung, honorary chairman of the Kuomintang of China, and his delegation, 13 June 2013, in *The Governance of China I*, p. 258.
16 Xi Jinping, 'Building Strong National Defense and Powerful Military Forces', main points of the speech during his inspection visit to the Guangzhou Military Command, 8 and 10 December 2012, in *The Governance of China I*, p. 241.
17 Klaus Bardenhagen, 'Made in Taiwan', *Focus*, no. 27, 2020.

13 Will the Whole World Benefit from the Chinese Dream?

1 See https://www.derstandard.at/story/2000103037393/chinasmegaprojekte216neueflughaefenin15jahren.
2 See https://www.handelsblatt.com/politik/international/arbeitszeit-china-die-nord-sued-schere/9006188-6.html?ticket=ST-7798182-jd62Zgrsxp3dccsrse4k-ap2, and https://www.destatis.de/DE/Themen/Arbeit/Arbeitsmarkt/Qualitaet-Arbeit/Dimension-3/woechentliche-arbeitszeitl.html#:~:text=34%2C8%20Stunden%20betrug%20die,jedoch%20getrennt%20voneinander%20betrachtet%20werden.
3 'Das Zitat ... und Ihr Gewinn', *Zeit Online*, 6 October 2011.
4 See https://www.thepioneer.de/originals/thepioneer-briefing-economy-edition/briefings/asien-die-heimliche-machtverschiebung.
5 Xi Jinping, 'The Chinese Dream Will Benefit Not Only the People of China, But Also of Other Countries', part of the answers in a written

interview with reporters from Trinidad and Tobago, Costa Rica and Mexico, May 2013, in *The Governance of China I*, pp. 61f.

6 'China schmiedet weltgrößte Freihandelszone', *Spiegel Wirtschaft*, 15 November 2020.

7 Bolton, *The Room Where it Happened*, p. 304.

8 'Die Teilung der Welt', *Der Spiegel*, no. 45, 2020.

9 'Ich bewundere Chinas Führung', *Der Spiegel*, no. 45, 2020.

10 Ibid.

11 See http://en.kremlin.ru/supplement/5770, and http://www.lawinfochina.com/display.aspx?id=8215&lib=tax&SearchKeyword=&SearchCKeyword=.

12 Mao Zedong, *Quotations from Chairman Mao Tse-Tung*, pp. 23f.

13 Mark R. Thompson, 'How Deng and his Heirs Misunderstood Singapore', *New Mandala*, 1 February 2019.

14 'Does China Still Have Anything to Learn from Singapore?', *South China Morning Post*, 16 December 2019.

15 Chinese President Xi Jinping gives 2021 New Year address, at https://www.youtube.com/watch?v=ZUevNynvlkw.

Sources

Where no references are given, quotations are from interviews conducted by ourselves (see list below). Descriptions of scenes and situations are based on personal witness, unless a source is given. The authors have made regular visits to China since 1986. Adrian Geiges studied Chinese in Beijing and lived in the country for ten years. Stefan Aust frequently travelled to China in his role as the editor-in-chief of *Der Spiegel*. Adrian worked there as a foreign correspondent for *Stern* and as the CEO of the Chinese subsidiary of the German publishing house Gruner + Jahr.

This is our second co-authored book on China. Adrian has previously published four books on China.

List of Interviewees

The following individuals were interviewed especially for this book:

Ai Weiwei: The world-famous Chinese artist belongs to the same generation as Xi Jinping and the two had similar experiences during the Cultural Revolution. Their fathers, Ai Qing and Xi Zhongxun, were friends and both lived at the same time in Yan'an, the communists' final destination on their Long March.

Jörg Wuttke: As the president of the European Chamber of Commerce in China, Wuttke has lived in the country for thirty years, and has had frequent opportunities to meet Xi Jinping. Wuttke studied Chinese in Shanghai and Taipei. Since 1997, he has been Head of Office and Chief Representative of BASF in China.

Sigmar Gabriel: As Germany's federal minister for economic affairs and energy, and then federal minister for foreign affairs and vice-chancellor, Gabriel met Xi Jinping on numerous occasions. He also met him in his role as party chair of the Social Democratic Party, which entertains inter-party relations with the Communist Party of China. Together with Xi, he opened an important terminal station of the 'new Silk Road', at the Port of Duisburg, where trains from Chongqing make their final stop.

Madeleine Albright: The late Madeleine Albright was US Secretary of State between 1997 and 2001, the first woman to hold this office. She continued to be active on the international stage as a political advisor. Albright met Xi Jinping several times.

Christopher Jahns: Jahns is an economics professor and CEO of the Berlin-based XU Group. He taught at the renowned Tongji University in Shanghai and maintains close relations with Chinese tech companies. He is an expert on the digitalization process driven forward by Xi Jinping.

We also led interviews with Chinese academics and journalists whose names, in the interest of their safety, are not given. They provided valuable background information for the writing of this book.

We also drew on a large range of interviews we had conducted before embarking on this project:

Li Keqiang: the current premier of the People's Republic of China

Jiang Zemin: president of the People's Republic of China and general secretary of the Chinese Communist Party. He was succeeded by Hu Jintao and then Xi Jinping

Zhang Qingli: vice chairperson of the Chinese People's Political Consultative Conference (CPPCC) and former head of the Chinese Communist Party in Tibet

Jung Chang: Chinese writer and co-author of a biography of Mao Zedong

Yu Dan: professor at Beijing Normal University

Gong Li: famous Chinese actress

Chris Patten: the last British governor of Hong Kong

Orlando Ferraz: political scientist in Angola working on the Chinese influence in Africa

Numerous citizens of China from all walks of life

Bibliography

John Bolton, *The Room Where It Happened: A White House Memoir*, New York: Simon & Schuster, 2020.

Kerry Brown, *CEO, China: The Rise of Xi Jinping*, London: I. B. Tauris, 2016.

Kerry Brown, *The World According to Xi: Everything You Need to Know About the New China*, London: I. B. Tauris, 2018.

Jung Chang and Jon Halliday, *Mao: The Unknown Story*, New York: Alfred A. Knopf, 2005.

Fang Fang, *Wuhan Diary: Dispatches from a Quarantined City*, New York: HarperCollins, 2020.

Barbara Finamore, *Will China Save The Planet?*, Cambridge: Polity, 2018.

贾巨川，《习仲勋传》上，北京: 中央文献出版社, 2008; Jia Juchuan, *Biography of Xi Zhongxun, I*, Beijing: Central Archives Press, 2008.

金波，习近平在浙江考察纪实，《浙江日报》2008年11月3日; Jin Bo, 'Report of Xi Jinping's Inspection in Zhejiang Province', *Zhejiang Daily*, 3 November 2008.

Nicholas D. Kristof and Sheryl WuDunn, *China Wakes: The Struggle for the Soul of a Rising Power*, New York: Vintage, 1994.

陆树群，习近平在正定,《石家庄日报》2007年5月18日; Lu Shuqun, 'Xi Jinping in Zhengding', *Shijiazhuang Daily*, 18 May 2007.

Richard McGregor, *The Party: The Secret World of China's Communist Rulers*, London: Penguin, 2010.

Richard McGregor, *Xi Jinping: The Backlash*, Sydney: Penguin/The Loewy Institute, 2019.

Martin Macmillan, *Together They Hold Up The Sky*, Campbell, CA: FastPencil, 2012.

《毛主席语录》, 北京: 人民出版社, 1966; *Quotations from Chairman Mao Zedong*, Beijing: People's Press, 1966.

Doris Naisbitt, John Naisbitt, and Long Anzhi, *Creating Megatrends: The Belt and Road*, Beijing: China Federation of Industry & Commerce Press, 2017.

齐心，<我与习仲勋风雨相伴的55年>，《大往事》，北京: 中国文史出版社, 2008; Qi Xin, 'My 55 Years through the Wind and Rain with Xi Zhongxun', *Da Wang Shi*, Beijing: Chinese Communist Party History Press, 2008.

Sayragul Sauytbay and Alexandra Cavelius, *The Chief Witness: Escape From China's Modern-day Concentration Camps*, London: Scribe, 2021.

David Shambaugh, *China's Leaders: From Mao to Now*, Cambridge: Polity, 2021.

Kai Strittmatter, *We Have Been Harmonised: Life in China's Surveillance State*, New York: Old Street Publishing, 2020.

王音旋，《我和彭丽媛-山东文坛纪事》，济南: 山东文艺出版社, 1989; Wang Yinxuan, *Peng Liyuan and I: Stories from Shandong Cultural Arena*, Jinan: Shandong Wenyi Press, 1989.

王幼辉，《我与习近平在正定的交往》，文史博览，2011，第11期; Wang Youhui, 'My Encounters with Xi Jinping in Zhengding', *Wen Shi Bo Lan*, Issue 11, 2011.

习近平，我如何进入政界的，《中华儿女》，2000年第7期; Xi Jinping, 'How I Got Into Politics', *Zhonghua Ernü*, Issue 7, 2000.

习近平，《关于社会主义市场经济的理论思考》，福州: 福建人民出版社, 2003; Xi Jinping, *Thoughts About Socialist Market Economy Theory*, Fuzhou: Fujian People's Press, 2003.

习近平，我是一个能够提醒自己，约束自己的人，《人民文摘》2004第三期; Xi Jinping, 'I Am a Man Who Is Self-Reflective and Able to Restrain Myself', *People's Digest*, Issue 3, 2004.

习近平，采访习近平，《国际金融报》，2006年02月09日; Xi Jinping, 'Interview with Xi Jinping', *International Finance*, 9 February 2006.

习近平，《之江新语》，杭州: 浙江人民出版社, 2007; Xi Jinping, *Zhijiang New Sayings*, Hangzhou: Zhejiang People's Press, 2007.

习近平，2009中央党校开学典礼讲话，中央党校《学习时报》12期; Xi Jinping, 'Speech at the Opening Ceremony of the Central Party School', *Xuexi Shibao*, Issue 12, 2009.

习近平,《谈治国理政》, 第一卷, 北京, 2014; Xi Jinping, *The Governance of China*, vol. I, Beijing: Foreign Languages Press, 2014.

习近平,《谈治国理政》, 第二卷, 北京, 2017; Xi Jinping, *The Governance of China*, vol. II, Beijing: Foreign Languages Press, 2017.

习近平,《谈治国理政》, 第三卷, 北京, 2020; Xi Jinping, *The Governance of China*, vol. III, Beijing: Foreign Languages Press, 2020.

Zheng Yongnian, *The Chinese Communist Party as Organizational Emperor: Culture, Reproduction, and Transformation*, London: Routledge, 2010.

Index